GIVE ME A FAST SHIP

GIVE ME A FAST SHIP

THE HEROIC ACTIONS OF ERNEST EVANS AND THE CREW OF USS *JOHNSTON*

THOMAS J. CUTLER

Naval Institute Press
Annapolis, Maryland

Naval Institute Press
291 Wood Road
Annapolis, MD 21402

Library of Congress Cataloging-in-Publication Data
Names: Cutler, Thomas J., author
Title: Give me a fast ship : the heroic actions of Ernest Evans and the crew of USS Johnston / Thomas J. Cutler.
Description: Annapolis, Maryland : Naval Institute Press, [2025] | Includes bibliographical references and index.
Identifiers: LCCN 2025023108 (print) | LCCN 2025023109 (ebook) | ISBN 9781682477991 hardcover | ISBN 9781557500670 ebook
Subjects: LCSH: Evans, Ernest Edwin, 1908–1944 | United States. Navy—Officers—Biography | Johnston (Destroyer : DD 557) | Sailors—United States | Leyte Gulf, Battle of, Philippines, 1944 | World War, 1939–1945—Naval operations, American
Classification: LCC D774.L48 C88 2025 (print) | LCC D774.L48 (ebook) | DDC 940.54/2599092 [B]—dcundefined
LC record available at https://lccn.loc.gov/2025023108
LC ebook record available at https://lccn.loc.gov/2025023109

♾ Print editions meet the requirements of ANSI/NISO z39.48-1992 (Permanence of Paper).
Printed in the United States of America

33 32 31 30 29 28 27 26 25 9 8 7 6 5 4 3 2 1
First printing

Maps created by Chris Robinson.
Unless otherwise indicated, photos are from the U.S. Naval Institute photo archive.

For Francesca
Words cannot begin to convey . . .

CONTENTS

MAPS AND IMAGES

MAPS

IMAGES

FOREWORD

The USS *Johnston* literally changed my life. I have either dived on or have been part of the expedition team for some very historically important shipwrecks but none—not even the fabled *Titanic*—have affected me as deeply as did the scrappy destroyer commanded by Commander Ernest Evans. The sight of the remains of USS *Johnston* sitting upright on the deep ocean floor, buried into the sediment up to her waterline, guns and director trained to starboard . . . she looked on the occasion of her discovery in 2021 to still be fierce and ready for action despite having been battered, sunk, and torn in half almost eighty years previous. Having come to rest in the deepest region of the ocean, where hydrographic and biologic activity is minimal, the ship was frozen in time. Even the scars the wreck dug into the ocean floor hadn't changed perceptively since 1944.

The condition of the wreck was such that I could easily visualize the events of the crew's last fight aboard. The area underneath Mount 44 where a Japanese shell exploded among a group of sailors seeking shelter looked strangely dark to my eye. Try as I might, I could not see either into or through the gloom. I experienced the same around the officer's Wardroom hatch through which a Japanese shell entered and exploded, killing the ship's doctor and the wounded inside whom he was trying to help evacuate. But that perceived darkness evidently was just in my mind, as it does not show in the digital imagery captured by the submersible's cameras. I understood . . . the wreck, by then one of the last surviving witnesses to the battle, was telling me her stories in a way that I would feel emotionally. I have never before experienced that feeling on any other wreck. I was so moved by the experience that I abandoned my professional career as an aerospace engineer and became the executive director of the nonprofit entity that cares for

Johnston's sister ship—and one of the last surviving *Fletcher*-class destroyers—USS *Kidd* (DD 661), in Baton Rouge, Louisiana.

The caretakers of our nation's current fleet of museum ships share a running joke: "How do you eat an elephant? One bite at a time." This dark humor represents the challenge that all museum ships face . . . how to stay ahead of the elements threatening to destroy our ships with the insufficient funding that all nonprofit museums face. As I consider Evans' actions off Samar, I see him likewise working through that metaphorical elephant one bite at a time. How else can a small destroyer go head-to-head with the most powerful battleship of all time (just one of *Yamato*'s main gun turrets weighted more than *Johnston* herself) and prevail? Evans figured it out . . . he couldn't out-gun the enemy, so he instead out-thought the enemy. He made sure that *Johnston* was everywhere the Japanese wanted to be, distracting them, complicating their intentions, and ultimately causing them to burn fuel and expend ammunition to the point where logistically, Admiral Kurita would be unable to carry out his mission to disrupt General MacArthur's invasion plans. Evans might not have been considering that last bit of strategy during the heat of battle, but his actions nevertheless made it so. His success gives me heart that I too can succeed in figuring out how to properly maintain *Kidd* so that she can continue to educate the American public about the virtues of service and sacrifice.

Tom Cutler has done a masterful job of illuminating how Ernest Evans and *Johnston* came together to determine the outcome of this pivotal moment in naval history. He traces Evans' upbringing in rural Oklahoma, his development as a critical thinker, and the factors that led him to the surface Navy. Tom gives particular emphasis on Evans' experience in the Asiatic Fleet at the outbreak of the war, where Evans experienced the pain and humiliation of retreat and defeat and how from this grew a deep conviction that if and when he ever commanded a fighting ship, Evans would take that ship into harm's way and never retreat. Evans said as much during *Johnston*'s commissioning ceremony, which in my experience must stand as one of the few naval ceremonies ever held where the featured speaker sincerely meant every word.

Concurrently, Tom also walks the reader through the evolution of the destroyer from a counter to a new technological threat during the late

1800s—the self-propelled torpedo—to the multipurpose workhorse of the Fleet that exists to this day. One can see from the story that Tom has weaved how a finely developed ship like *Johnston*, matched with a determined and experienced commander like Evans and a crew that trusted in their commander, could achieve the impossible.

The story of the Battle off Samar was termed "The Last Stand of the Tin Can Sailors" by the late Pacific War historian James Hornfischer. In his book of the same name, Hornfischer quoted Herman Wouk's *War and Remembrance* where Wouk wrote, "The vision of Sprague's three destroyers—the *Johnston*, the *Hoel*, and *Heermann* [Author's note: I would also include the destroyer escort USS *Samuel B. Roberts*]—charging out of the smoke and the rain straight toward the main batteries of Kurita's battleships and cruisers, can endure as a picture of the way Americans fight when they don't have superiority. Our schoolchildren should know about that incident, and our enemies should ponder it." Please read on and let Tom fill you in on the details of this important and amazing story.

Parks Stephenson, LCDR, USN (Ret.)
Executive Director, USS KIDD Veterans Museum

PREFACE

While working on my book *The Battle of Leyte Gulf* in the early 1990s, I had the honor and privilege to interview many veterans of that great battle. I attended numerous reunions and was able to meet many of them in person. Others I was able to interview over the phone. Because I was covering the largest naval battle in history, I could not use all I learned from these men and reluctantly left a sizable portion "on the cutting room floor." In this, my third book on the subject, I have made extensive use of that material to tell a somewhat different story.

This is unquestionably a biography. But it is an unusual one in that it is a biography of both a man—Ernest E. Evans—and his ship, USS *Johnston* (DD 557). And, by extrapolation, it is also a kind of biography of the crew who made the deeds of both that man and his ship possible.

There have been many books about the Battle of Leyte Gulf—including my own, published at the time of the fiftieth anniversary of that momentous clash, followed by a retrospective for the seventy-fifth anniversary. I have decided not to wait for the hundredth anniversary to write this book! This one differs from my own previous works and the many others because it is about more than that battle. It covers Evans' entire career—including his earlier participation in the 1942 Battle of the Java Sea. But in another sense, this is different in that it is about less than the others because it focuses on that one year of USS *Johnston*'s short existence—from her commissioning to her final battle off Samar in the Philippines.

While the narrative of course includes some contextual explanation, I have tried to portray that year almost entirely from the point of view of that single ship's crew and their commanding officer. While they were certainly aware of the major events of the wider war, their view of the operations they participated in was rather myopic. To them it mattered little whether they were in the Third Fleet under Admiral William F. "Bull" Halsey or the Seventh Fleet under Vice Admiral Thomas C. Kinkaid. They had little understanding of grand strategy and virtually no idea what the enemy was up to. Their view of the war consisted of an assortment of islands that needed shelling, various groups of ships that needed escorting, a few atolls that offered a temporary respite from the tedium and the tension of operations, and a whole lot of ocean!

Among the many reviews of my first book on Leyte, I am particularly pleased by one published in the *Chicago Tribune* that was written by famed naval biographer Thomas Buell (*Master of Sea Power: A Biography of Fleet Admiral Ernest J. King* and *The Quiet Warrior: A Biography of Admiral Raymond A. Spruance*), who wrote, "This book sparkles with authority and authenticity, for Thomas J. Cutler is one of the few authors of naval works who (1) as a mariner has gone down to the sea in ships and (2) as a naval historian understands why ships go to sea." I especially treasure the follow-on line: "The reader vicariously shares the salt spray in the face." For this book, I have tried to do the same, to lean on my personal experiences as a surface warrior in conveying to the reader the truly unique experiences of sailors at sea. While I did not serve in a *Fletcher*-class destroyer, I did serve in a *Sumner*-class that was built during the war and was the follow-on class to the *Fletcher*s. I did indeed feel the sting of salt spray while serving in her and two other destroyers, among several other ships. My Navy career included service as both an officer and an enlisted man, giving me an appreciation for life before and after the mast.

A word about conventions. Today there are some who prefer the gender-neutral "it" when referring to ships. Because it was standard to use "she" and "her" in the time period covered in this book, I have chosen to use those terms. Likewise, it has become more common to refer to ships using the definite article "the" before the ship's name (as in "the *Johnston*"), but I have used the more traditional form of simply using the ship's name without "the"; this is also more appropriate for a "biography" of a ship, as discussed earlier. And I hope that it goes without saying that any use of the derogatory term "Jap" is included only as it was used conventionally during the war.

Although this is a nonfiction book, it is not a conventional academic treatise. I have not included formal citations, which would be awkward when relying so heavily on personal interviews. Readers will also note that I include some information that is nonverifiable, such as in chapter 3, when I write, "As Coley, Evans, and their British guest sat at the dining table in the wardroom over cups of steaming tea and coffee . . . " I of course have no way of knowing whether there was tea and coffee on that table at that moment. But in the interest of "color" I took the liberty of assuming that with both British and American officers present, those beverages were likely to be there. Such assumptions were never made over matters of substance or consequence, only when I felt they would enhance the reader's vicarious experience, their sense of being there in the moment I describe.

Similarly, I have conveyed some information by converting documentary records into dialogue among the participants to make it more understandable and experiential for the reader. This is an accepted technique first used by Thucydides in his *History of the Peloponnesian War,* where he quotes long speeches made by Pericles and other participants. Given that no recording equipment was available in ancient Greece, and the writing instruments of the time make it unlikely that the words he recorded are verbatim records of those ancient utterances, we must trust that he has nonetheless captured the meaning of such speeches without using the speakers' exact words. Although I have resorted to this technique, I have used it sparingly, and most of the words and thoughts of the participants are derived from oral histories, memoirs, and (most especially) the interviews I conducted with the men of USS *Johnston*.

Because it is my hope that this book will appeal to an audience wider than mere Navy veterans, I have attempted to make nautical and military terms clear in the context presented. But when unable to accomplish that, I have resorted to parenthetical insertions that I hope are informative without being overly distracting.

One of the tasks of a biographer is to avoid hagiography by being open to both the dimples and warts of those being written about. On this count, I may have failed because I am admittedly in awe of Ernest Evans and the men who crewed this ship. I have experienced some of the things they endured, so I have a true appreciation of their stories. But in many cases, their experiences go beyond my own and are much magnified in degree and importance, so my appreciation is likewise magnified. Today we overuse the term "hero," and by doing so we dilute its meaning. But this is unquestionably a story of true heroism, and if that shows through in my treatment, I suspect I may be forgiven.

The men of the destroyer *Johnston* have been my frequent companions for several years while writing this book. They have vicariously taken me back to sea and reminded me of the importance of the Navy we served in our own ways. And I will miss them . . .

CHAPTER 1

GENESIS

It was a wedding of sorts. But in this case the "bride" was dressed not in white but in wartime blue, and the "groom" wore the uniform of a Navy lieutenant commander. There was the usual gathering of participants and witnesses, including a man of the cloth, but they were assembled not in a chapel or other religious structure but on the deck of a U.S. Navy destroyer. There was the solemnity and celebration of a wedding, but it was the marriage not of a man and a woman but of a man and his ship. Ernest E. Evans was assuming command of USS *Johnston*, a union that would ultimately personify the traditional marriage vow "till death do us part."

The 27th of October 1943 was a bright day, the sun's late-fall warmth enhanced by the dark blue of the sailor's dress uniforms. Rain was a frequent companion at the Seattle division of Todd Pacific Shipyard, and Lieutenant (jg) Edward M. Digardi was not alone in his gratitude for this day's hospitable weather. Standing "at ease" in formation with his new shipmates, the young lieutenant looked around with a sense of awe. Selected members of the crew and a small contingent of VIP visitors took up nearly every inch of the destroyer's fantail, already crowded with depth charge tracks and antiaircraft guns. The angled barrel of the ship's aftermost 5-inch/38 gun loomed above the assembly, casting an ominous black shadow that seemed to bisect the gathering.

IMAGE 1 • Crew of the *Fletcher*-class destroyer USS *Johnston* (DD 577) assembled on the fantail for the ship's commissioning ceremony on 27 October 1943. Lieutenant Commander Ernest E. Evans, USN, her commanding officer, is speaking from just below the gun barrel of her Mount 55. *Naval History and Heritage Command*

Chaplain Maurice W. Smith stepped forward and offered the invocation as the ship's crew bowed their heads. The staccato of a chipping hammer from somewhere off to starboard made it difficult to hear the chaplain's words and reminded the young officer that this was wartime, and not even the sanctity of talking with God took priority over the construction and repairs feverishly underway in the bustling shipyard. Digardi did manage to make out the words "Preserve us from the dangers of the sea and the violence of the enemy that we may return in safety to enjoy the blessings of the land." Amen to that, he thought.

Digardi watched in fascination as the ceremony proceeded—the reading of orders, a lot of saluting, and the breaking of the commissioning pennant—all reminders of the often-ritualistic nature of the Navy that he was getting used to since his enlistment just five months after the Japanese attack on Pearl Harbor on 7 December 1941. Because he had been a second-year student at Hastings College of Law at the time of his enlistment, the Navy decided that he was officer material and sent him to the wartime Midshipmen's School at Columbia University, where he earned his commission as an ensign in February 1943. Assigned to the precommissioning crew, Digardi had arrived in Seattle on 25 August and was slated to be the assistant communications officer.

As though responding to some cue, the cacophonous shipyard hammering ceased as a short, barrel-chested man stepped forward to the microphone that had been rigged for the occasion. Three gold stripes on his lower sleeve glinted in the sunshine as he glanced down at a small paper in his right hand.

Some of the fledgling crew did not yet even realize that this was their commanding officer, or "Captain" in Navy parlance—the man who would have their fates, their very lives, in his hands from this moment forward. In the ancient but ongoing traditions of the sea, they would have no choice but to go where he would go; they would trust in his judgment, with no other choices, and they would follow his orders whether they agreed with them or not. Fate and the U.S. Navy had brought these men together to function in an autocracy while defending a democracy. Short of desertion, death, or official transfer, these men were inextricably linked to their captain and to the ship he now commanded.

That ship, christened USS *Johnston* with the hull number DD 577, was the latest in a long line of *Fletcher*-class destroyers, and her captain was Lieutenant Commander Ernest Edwin Evans, USN. He was a handsome man—some likened him to the movie star Clark Gable, but that was most likely because of his thin, tightly trimmed mustache, somewhat unusual for an officer. Digardi had heard the captain was part Cherokee but saw nothing to indicate that, other than what might have passed for a mild suntan and very black hair.

When the Japanese had attacked Pearl Harbor, Evans was serving as executive officer of USS *Alden* (DD 211), a World War I–vintage destroyer, as part of the so-called Asiatic Fleet operating in Western Pacific waters. That far-flung fleet was no match for the Imperial Japanese Navy (IJN) in the early months of the war, and after suffering defeat in the Battle of the

IMAGE 2 • Ernest Evans' official Navy Department photo. Some of his contemporaries described him as looking like the movie star Clark Gable. *Naval History and Heritage Command*

Java Sea, *Alden* and the other surviving ships had been forced to flee the oncoming Japanese juggernaut. Memories of that ignominious rout were clearly on Evans' mind as he looked up from his paper and began to speak.

His voice was sonorous, and his words impressed Digardi as he briefly recounted the circumstances of *Alden*'s retreat. Pausing for a brief moment, Evans looked about at the bunting-draped ship, the hint of an inscrutable smile briefly emerging. Glancing upward at the gun barrel a few feet over his head, he said, "This is going to be a fighting ship," and the smile was displaced by a look of fierce determination as he quoted Navy hero John Paul Jones: "I intend to go in harm's way."

Some of the crew dismissed the captain's words as the kind of thing officers typically said on such occasions, but Digardi had no doubt that Evans' declaration was sincere and irrevocable. He was particularly impressed when the captain said, "I will never again retreat from an enemy force," and then, gesturing toward the gangway, offered those who did not wish to accompany him a last chance to leave the ship. No one took him up on that.

Evans' evoking of John Paul Jones, regarded by most as the father of the U.S. Navy, was certainly not unique. Jones' heroic exploits during the

American Revolution provided much-needed inspiration during those trying years when the fledgling nation was fighting for its very existence, and those actions have continued to serve as an iconic symbol of indomitable courage to sailors ever since. But there may have been more than the obvious at work in Evans' reliance on those stirring words. He had graduated with the Naval Academy class of 1931, and the front cover of the class yearbook—the *Lucky Bag*—was embossed with a gold image of Jones in profile. The book's inside front cover was elaborately decorated with images of Jones and his most famous battle scene. Prominently covering both pages were the words "I do not wish to have command of any ship that does not sail fast, for I intend to go in harm's way." The inside back cover is similarly configured but features the words chosen by the first-class midshipmen on the *Lucky Bag* editorial committee: "This is our pledge: Give us fast ships and we, too, shall follow swiftly by land and sea."

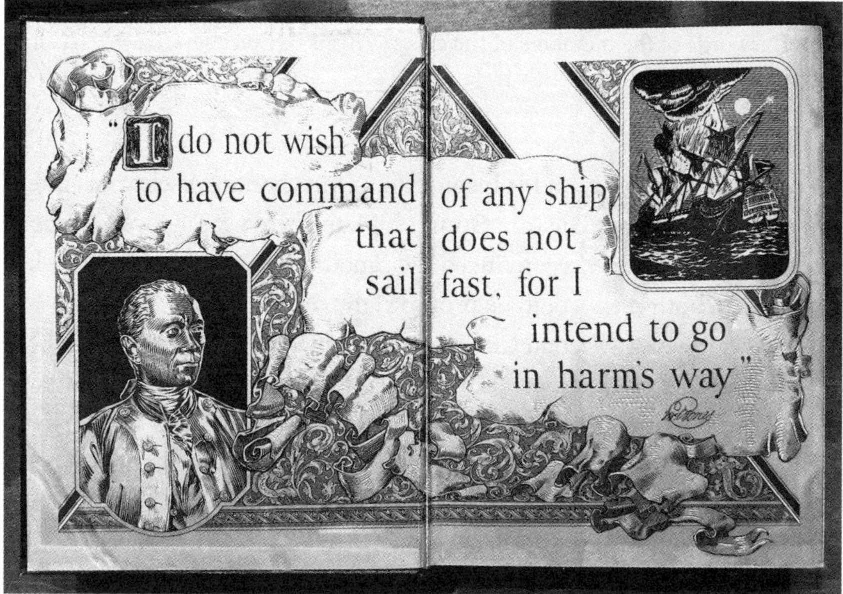

IMAGE 3 • The inside front cover of the 1931 Naval Academy yearbook, *Lucky Bag*, with John Paul Jones' famous quote, "I do not wish to have command of any ship that does not sail fast, for I intend to go in harm's way." *Author*

IMAGE 4 • The inside back cover of the 1931 Naval Academy yearbook, *Lucky Bag*, with the words of the members of the class: "This is our pledge: Give us fast ships and we, too, shall follow swiftly by land and sea." *Author*

Whatever the source of his inspiration, Evans had made clear his intentions. Like Lieutenant Digardi, Gunner's Mate Third Class Lloyd Campbell later recalled that he was convinced the captain meant what he said. In less than a year, both men would be proved right.

Boatswain's Mate Second Class Bob Hollenbaugh had been one of those sailors who had not been much impressed by the captain's words. He was a rather pragmatic individual who had enlisted in the Navy primarily to avoid being drafted into the Army and had no intention to stay in the Navy any longer than was necessary. But that did not mean he would not do his best to serve well while in. He had a sharp mind and was a born leader who was assigned as lead boatswain's mate of Second Division, whose responsibilities included operation and maintenance of all of the ship's armament and ammunition stowage except for the torpedoes and antisubmarine depth charges.

When the ceremony had ended and the guests were gradually departing, Hollenbaugh took advantage of the lull and strolled up forward to the forecastle (that part of the ship extending forward from the bridge—roughly a third of the total length), climbing the gentle rise of the deck until he was standing just below the Union Jack that now fluttered in the light breeze from atop the jackstaff at the ship's prow. Turning to look aft, he assessed his new home. Clad mostly in the Navy's ubiquitous color—blue—the ship nonetheless was a handsome girl. All the clutter that had been so abundant during the final days of construction was now gone, and her freshly applied paint glistened slightly in the late-morning sun. From this angle, he was aware of how narrow in the beam she was, only about 40 feet, as he recalled from the shipyard briefing he had attended a few weeks back.

Her slim figure and her fresh paint could not conceal the latent ferocity that defined her, first and foremost, as a warship. The two 5-inch gun mounts in front of him were motionless, and the tampions in the ends of their barrels signaled their current impotence, but Hollenbaugh knew that below those mounts were ammunition handling rooms and magazines that soon would be filled with powder cases and projectiles that could be hurled in explosive anger at surface and air targets. And there were three more 5-inch mounts aft of the ship's smokestacks as well as an array of seven 20-mm and ten 40-mm antiaircraft guns, ten torpedo tubes, six depth charge projectors, and two tracks of depth charges that could be rolled off the fantail as the ship passed over an enemy submarine. Pound for pound, this little lady could put up a hell of a fight.

Johnston stood in sharp contrast to Hollenbaugh's prior ships. After being transformed from citizen to sailor in boot camp, his first assignment was to a special unit in San Diego whose primary task was to resurrect World War I–vintage destroyers that had been mothballed after the Great War and were being readied for transfer to the Royal Navy prior to America's entry into the war. Much of the South Bay was covered by these relics, and the area was known locally as Red Lead Row, a reference to the preservative paint extensively used to combat corrosion on naval ships.

Shortly after the Japanese attack on Pearl Harbor, Hollenbaugh's commanding officer gathered his men together and announced, "Boys, let's keep our gear packed. There's a couple of destroyers we might be working on at Pearl." Those destroyers proved to be *Cassin* and *Downes*, both of which had been in drydock at the time of the attack. When Hollenbaugh arrived at Pearl Harbor they were still there, both grievously damaged, with *Cassin* knocked off her keel blocks and leaning against *Downes*. The ships were covered in oil and soot, and Hollenbaugh found it frighteningly difficult to make his way over the hulks while attempting to salvage what little had survived the attack. His supervisor, a first-class boatswain's mate, took pity on him and sent him to wash the coveralls that the salvage crew were going through at the rate of three or four pairs a day. Little wonder that he was happy to be assigned to a glistening new ship whose topsides were unadorned with either red lead or fuel oil.

Stepping over the anchor chains that lay taut across the forecastle deck, he walked down the starboard side of the sloping forecastle, past the gun mounts and through the breakwater that would shield the after two-thirds of the ship from the crashing waves that would inevitably envelop the forecastle in heavy weather. Shortly after he had reported on board, a heavily tattooed petty officer first class who had been in the Navy more years than Hollenbaugh had been on the earth had told him that the Pacific Ocean had been misnamed and that he could expect some "wet roller-coaster rides" as "this here tin can fights her way to Tokyo." Hollenbaugh knew the old-timer was having some fun with the new guy, but he played along by responding with a wide-eyed look of fear.

The old-timer's use of the term "tin can" was common in the Navy when referring to destroyers. It was derogatory in the sense that it referred to those ships' thin skins and lack of armor, but it was also used with swashbuckling pride by those serving in them. The crews of the old sailing Navy had been described as "iron men in wooden ships," and this "tin can" reference was a nod toward the same kind of tough individuals who faced the challenges of sea and combat with ruggedness and fortitude.

Growing up in Goshen, Indiana, Hollenbaugh had never seen a body of water larger than a lake. But his father had served in the Navy during World War I and had prepared him for some of what to expect.

Although *Johnston* was bigger than the older destroyers he had encountered in San Diego and Hawaii, she was still quite diminutive compared to the cruisers he had seen sortieing from Pearl. He knew that petty officer first class had spoken truth when he described frequent "white water" waves breaking over the bow and the occasional immersion in "green water" as the ship plowed into swells too large to ride over and her forecastle was momentarily submerged beneath a mountain of seawater.

But even though she was considered small by Navy ship standards, Hollenbaugh marveled that *Johnston*'s 376-foot length was longer than the football field he had traversed many times back in high school, end zones included.

As he headed aft along the starboard side, he saw stretchers made of chicken wire and life rafts secured to the sides of the superstructure and hoped he would never have need of either.

Along the way he saw an escape hatch from one of the engineering spaces below and recalled his father's words when his draft notice had arrived: "Volunteer for the Navy but stay topside." Having served in the so-called black gang in a coal-driven ship, the elder Hollenbaugh had spent most of his time belowdecks in the engineering spaces, rarely seeing the light of day as he labored in a Stygian world of piping, valves, roaring forced-draft blowers, and huge boilers that swallowed prodigious amounts of coal and water to make the steam that would turn the ship's screws and propel her through the water. *Johnston*'s boilers consumed oil instead of coal, which was a marked improvement, but Hollenbaugh was glad he had heeded his father's advice and had become a boatswain's mate—one of the occupational specialties that the Navy called "ratings" that involved working with lines, anchors, weapons, and other topside gear—ensuring that he would stay out of those firerooms and engine rooms. Besides the terrible heat and noise those spaces offered, it was difficult to imagine what it would be like going into battle when you were already below the ship's waterline.

Hollenbaugh dodged a cluster of officers still lingering on the fantail and quickly descended the angled ladder below the open hatch leading from the main deck to his berthing compartment below, one of seven (three forward, four aft). Hollenbaugh's berthing compartment was the farthest one aft, just forward of the after steering machinery room.

Hollenbaugh shared the sleeping quarters with men of different ratings. Before the war, sailors had berthed with their shipmates of the same rating, but now they were dispersed among the berthing compartments to ensure that a fatal hit to one area of the ship did not eliminate the personnel of an entire division.

Rows of bunks three tiers high filled most of the space. Perhaps in reference to the ancient torture device of the same name, sailors often referred to their bunks as "racks" (and sometimes more sardonically as "coffin lockers"). As a petty officer, Hollenbaugh was privileged to occupy the bottom rack, not only easier to get into and out of but also farther away from the overhead, which was just inches above the man in the top rack—not a serious consideration here in the Pacific Northwest, but once the ship began operating in the South Pacific, the dark blue steel of the main deck would absorb the heat of the blazing sun during the day and only gradually relinquish it at night. For the hapless sailors in the top racks, it would be like having a radiator in one's face while trying to sleep.

When not being used, the three racks were triced up to allow access to the low metal lockers underneath, where the men stowed their belongings. Another privilege of being a petty officer granted Hollenbaugh an additional upright locker nearby, but the nonrated men would have to make do with only the lower lockers for their gear.

Knowing the ship would be getting underway once all the visitors were ashore, he changed out of his dress-blue uniform into the working uniform—a blue chambray shirt and dungaree-like trousers. Carefully stowing his spit-polished dress shoes, he then pulled on a pair of boot-like "boondockers" and laced them up, still using the right-over-left configuration that had been mandated in boot camp.

Making his way forward, he climbed up one ladder to the after head, which was located inside the after deckhouse between the ammunition-handling rooms for two of the 5-inch mounts (53 and 54) that were perched on top of the deckhouse (51 and 52 were on the forecastle and 55 was on the fantail). He stepped over the coaming at the base of the doorway that prevented water from sloshing into the compartment and entered the head, where a remnant of steam lingered from the morning showers mixed with the faint aroma of Aqua Velva aftershave. The deck was painted red because the head served as an emergency first-aid station to care for casualties, and legend had it that the red served as a camouflage to obscure the blood that might accumulate there.

Before the arrival of his draft notice and his subsequent enlistment in the Navy, Hollenbaugh had been attending college at Western Michigan University, where he had been less than pleased at having to share rather spartan bathroom facilities in his dorm. But that now seemed luxurious compared to this head that he shared with over 150 shipmates. Privacy was completely absent: Strange-looking toilet seats were mounted close together atop three water troughs that had faucets on one end and drains on the other with a continuous flow of saltwater flowing fore to aft to carry away the deposits. The seats were all black save one that was painted red, reserved for those whose adventures ashore had left them with medical conditions that no one wanted to share.

As he was relieving himself at one of the metal urinals, Hollenbaugh heard the boatswain's pipe over the 1MC general announcing system. The voice of the Boatswain's Mate of the Watch followed the shrill whistle, announcing, "Now set the special sea and anchor detail."

The newly commissioned USS *Johnston*, Petty Officer Second Class Bob Hollenbaugh, and the other 350-plus crewmembers were about to get underway for the first time, beginning a journey that would last just two days less than a year and would end thousands of miles away in a deep trench on the bottom of the Western Pacific Ocean.

World War II began with the "gun club versus flyboys" debate still unresolved. Even though the Japanese had pulled off a stunning attack at Pearl Harbor—carried out by a massive use of aircraft—their main target had been the battleships gathered there, and their theory of victory continued to rely significantly on bringing their battleships and cruisers to bear on their American counterparts in a great gun duel that they expected to win.

Many of the senior officers in the U.S. Navy continued to think in myopic terms of big guns, with aircraft carriers viewed as supplements to that effort, helpful in terms of reconnaissance and targeting but not as the main striking power of the fleet.

But even the most steadfast gun advocates on both sides accepted that a potential Achilles' heel of those formidable ships was their vulnerability to torpedo attacks. Invented in 1866 by the British engineer Robert Whitehead, the torpedo could strike below the waterline of a targeted vessel, delivering enough high explosive to disable or sink even the most powerful battleship.

Eventually torpedoes would be delivered by submarines and aircraft, but the earliest employment was via surface craft—small, fast torpedo boats that could be produced inexpensively and in quantity. The idea that expensive leviathans could be countered by a torpedo boat was a real game changer.

To counter this new and potentially dire threat, ships added armor below their waterlines. The added weight of course slowed them down, requiring them to include more powerful engines to counter the loss of speed. Another antidote was the "torpedo boat destroyer," a newly designed vessel that was larger than torpedo boats and had a greater range and better seakeeping ability. Their large, powerful engines and rapid-firing guns could effectively counter the torpedo boats. As the name was abbreviated to "destroyer," and with the addition of torpedoes—the daunting weapon they were primarily designed to counter—and other weapons and emerging technologies, this new type of combatant rapidly grew in numbers and potency. Over time, oil replaced coal, turbines superseded reciprocating engines, and destroyers' missions expanded to include antisubmarine and antiair warfare, along with their ability to combat one another, as naval warfare itself evolved.

The United States was slower than other nations to develop and produce destroyers in quantity, but when they did build them, they were bigger than most of their counterparts from other nations because America's geographic position was so far from potential hostile waters that additional fuel capacity was required to extend their range. Several classes emerged, as the earlier ones designed with a raised forecastle to improve seakeeping were eventually replaced by the so-called flush-deck destroyers, whose main deck extended from the forecastle to the fantail at the same level. The flush-deck design became standard and included the *Clemson* class.

Submarines had proven to be a formidable threat in the Great War, but there were no major changes in the destroyers' antisubmarine capabilities until the 1940s; sonar and depth charges made up the standard equipment. One significant improvement was in the shape of the depth charges themselves. Early versions, called "ash cans," were cylindrical. When rolled off the fantail, they would descend at a rate of nine feet per second. Later designs incorporated a teardrop shape, which increased their speed of descent to twenty-three feet per second, giving the submarine target less time to make defensive maneuvers.

The ongoing guns-versus-aviation debate manifested itself in destroyer design in the 1930s. While the Royal Navy's destroyers reflected the continued expectation that surface actions would be the determinant of victory at sea, U.S. planners were already beginning to think in terms of the aviation threat in the 1930s. Because British designers assumed that their destroyers would be fighting other destroyers, they designed their guns to maximize the impact of their shells by assuming a relatively flat trajectory of fire. But U.S. designers were thinking in terms of antiaircraft defense more than surface engagement, so they designed their guns to be able to fire effectively at high elevations, which required a deeper pit beneath the gun and a taller mount that would allow room for the gun's recoil when it was fired while pointing upward at high angles.

These and other considerations influenced destroyer design during the 1930s, a period characterized by many different classes and modifications in an attempt to design the perfect destroyer. They came close eventually, when the *Fletcher* class was born.

Construction started before the war, but the first of the *Fletcher*s did not debut until late 1942, too late to participate in the struggle for Guadalcanal, where destroyers played a large role. But by war's end they had earned the reputation of *the* destroyer class of World War II, particularly in the Pacific.

In a postwar interview, Ed Digardi remembered his ship as "a thing of absolute beauty," adding, "DDs [destroyers] are often called 'tin cans' and 'greyhounds.' To me, greyhound made more sense—especially the *Fletchers*. They just looked like they wanted to run. And fast!" Speaking wistfully, he added, "When she revved up to flank speed, you could feel her engines throbbing, and you just knew she wanted to fight."

That "thing of absolute beauty" had been christened USS *Johnston* in March 1942 with the hull number DD 557. (Hull numbers are the system the Navy uses to identify individual ships. They begin with two or more letters to designate the type of ship—DD for destroyer, BB for battleship, CA for heavy cruiser, CL for light cruiser, CVE for escort carrier, and so on—and the numbers following the letters, which identify each individual vessel within that type, are generally assigned sequentially in the order that each hull was authorized in the budget. Ships built from the same design are considered to be of a particular class, and collectively they take on the name of the first ship built. USS *Fletcher*'s hull number was DD 445, and ultimately there would be 175 of this class built in eleven different shipyards all over the United States.) On that sunny day of 27 October, she became the forty-ninth *Fletcher*-class destroyer to be commissioned. Almost exactly a year later, she would meet her fate as one of the twenty-five *Fletchers* lost in World War II.

Overall, the Navy had given Ernest Evans a good crew. Many of them were new to the Navy, coming to the ship fresh out of boot camp or from follow-on specialized training schools. Their motivations for joining the Navy ranged from a strong sense of patriotism to a fear of being drafted into the Army. Their neophyte status was offset by the eagerness to do well that often characterizes young men embarking on a new challenge, driven as much by the desire to not embarrass themselves among their peers as by the oaths of enlistment they had taken just months before.

Another important factor countering the inexperience of so many of the crew was the assignment of enough men—like Bob Hollenbaugh—with enough prior experience to effectively serve as mentors and leaders. It was the way of the military to grant authority and responsibility based on rank, but it was the nature of the men themselves that determined how well the system would work. Some were born leaders, wielding charisma or the fear they evoked in ways that could not be taught. Others took their Navy training to heart, carefully practicing such axioms as "Set the proper example" or "Praise in public, reprimand in private." Some were content to be followers—avoiding roles and opportunities that required leadership—and a few would fail as leaders, more often than not weeding themselves out before doing serious damage but occasionally managing to put themselves and their shipmates in danger.

And it was that danger that largely formed them all. Life at sea is inherently dangerous under normal circumstances, but these men—and thousands of others like them—were going to sea while their nation was engaged in the greatest sea war in history. Young men often seem oblivious to their own mortality, and here in Seattle, Washington, in 1943, many of these young men retained that ignorance. But by this time in the war, long casualty lists and, for some, knowing someone who had been killed or wounded tempered that youthful ignorance with a persistent awareness that the specter of death might be lurking just over the next horizon. Here in Seattle, that phantom remained distant enough, but their preparations and training kept them aware of where they were headed, and even the most stoic or naive among them could not dismiss that lingering apprehension.

A few of the original commissioning crew would depart the ship in the next year, and more would be added, but those who had been present when Evans promised he would take them in harm's way would see that promise fulfilled almost exactly one year to the day later.

USS *Johnston* had shed her ceremonial bunting and was now cloaked in wartime blue and black as befitting a warship. Only the Jack at her bow, the national ensign at her stern, and her commissioning pennant at the gaff amidships offered a colorful contrast. Barely visible wisps of gray smoke emanated from her stacks as her boilers built up steam pressure down in the firerooms.

It had not taken long for the guests to depart the ship once the commissioning ceremony was complete. With only the crew remaining on board, the ship was pulsing with activity as her neophyte crew went about their newly appointed duties, many of them carrying out important tasks, while some of the nonrated men merely struggled to look busy rather than suffer the wrath of a petty officer accusing them of skylarking.

At 1115, Lieutenant Commander (now "Captain" by virtue of his assuming command) Ernest Evans ordered his second-in-command, executive officer (XO) and navigator Lieutenant Commander Howard Baker, "to set the watch and prepare to get underway." The XO ordered the word passed to "man the sea and anchor detail," and sailors began to move smartly to their assigned stations, many of them eager to leave the clamor and clutter of the shipyard that had been their habitat for many months.

Once all stations had reported "manned and ready," Evans—now on the open bridge—leaned over the starboard rail and ordered all mooring lines except the bow line taken in. Using the brass speaking tube that carried his voice from the open bridge to the helmsman and lee-helmsman stationed in the pilot house, he ordered "left standard rudder; port engine ahead one-third; starboard engine back one-third." The helmsman responded with "left standard rudder aye," immediately moving the heavy brass wheel until the pointer indicated 15 degrees. The lee helm responded similarly to the engine orders and moved the levers on the engine order telegraph (EOT) appropriately. Down in the engine rooms the EOT receiver duplicated the order, and firemen moved their pointers accordingly to acknowledge the order while several men began turning the valves that would admit steam to the turbines in the appropriate quantities to carry out the captain's instructions.

With the ship's screws turning in opposite directions—"twisting," in conning parlance—*Johnston*'s stern began to swing gently away from the pier. Evans then barked, "All engines stop," followed by "Take in the bow line." Now disconnected from the pier, the ship was officially underway, and the boatswain's mate of the watch announced over the 1MC, "Underway. Shift colors," cueing sailors at the jackstaff forward and the flagstaff aft to yank down the Union Jack and National Ensign respectively as another sailor smartly hoisted the underway ensign to the gaff just aft of the after stack. A throaty, prolonged blast erupted from the ship's whistle, alerting other vessels in the vicinity that *Johnston* was now underway.

Evans next ordered "rudder amidships; all engines back one-third," and as the ship's whistle now sounded three short blasts, the 2,000-ton destroyer began to move slowly backward away from the pier, the screws churning up clouds of tan-colored mud from the bottom just a few feet below the hull.

Once clear, Evans ordered "all engines stop," then "all engines ahead two-thirds," and *Johnston* began moving down the channel toward the more open waters of Puget Sound. Just a few feet from Evans, Lieutenant (jg) Ed Digardi had previously noted that the captain often appeared to be half smiling, but at this moment it was more obvious. With *Johnston* now underway for the first time, he surmised that Evans was probably enjoying this moment as only a ship's captain could.

As the ship emerged into Puget Sound, Digardi noted that only one tug and her tow was headed north, and another pushing a large barge filled with scrap iron plodded along in the opposite direction. Wartime fuel rationing had reduced the amount of traffic in the sound, which Digardi figured was a good thing for a brand-new crew operating a brand-new ship for the first time. Not much to collide with, he concluded.

Less than two hours later, *Johnston* fell in astern of a ferry heading into Bremerton and soon the Puget Sound Navy Yard loomed into sight, readily

IMAGE 5 • The newly commissioned USS *Johnston* (DD 557) off Seattle, Washington *Official U.S. Navy photograph*

identifiable by the gigantic 2,400-ton "Hammerhead" crane towering at Pier 6, so massive that it had been given a building number (28) painted in bright yellow on its olive-green house-like structure that sat at the back end of the crane.

As *Johnston* made her way to her berth at five knots, USS *California*, one of the battleships that had been severely damaged at Pearl Harbor, loomed into view, a cocoon of scaffolding obscuring her once-majestic lines. She and four others (*Tennessee*, *Maryland*, *Nevada*, and *West Virginia*) had all been resurrected in the aftermath of the infamous attack and moved to Bremerton for repairs and modernization. Locally known as the "Pearl Harbor Ghosts," *Maryland* and *Tennessee* had since departed, but the more seriously damaged *California* and *West Virginia* were still there, healing their wounds and biding their time until they could return to the fight.

Johnston, too, would have to wait before she would be ready to sail in harm's way. The ship remained dockside for the next two weeks, fitting out and receiving the remainder of her crew before getting underway again for local operations in Puget Sound. During this period, captain, crew, and ship got used to one another, building the symbiosis that would make them into a smoothly functioning organism that could handle both tedium and terror in the months ahead.

Their bonding had begun during the commissioning ball held at a local hotel that first night they spent together as a crew. It was an opportunity for them to begin getting to know one another. But as the evening wore on, the mix of alcohol and testosterone led to several brawls that eventually led to the arrival of the shore patrol, and a number of the newly formed crew continued to get to know each other as they shared the rest of the night and next morning in a cell in the local brig. Lieutenant (jg) Ellsworth Welch arrived late to the party with an attractive and rather demure young lady on his arm and was mortified to find some of his shipmates throwing punches and furniture at one another. He quickly escorted the sorority sister out of the room and to a nearby diner, where the loudest noise was a jukebox with the Andrews Sisters singing "Don't Sit under the Apple Tree (with Anyone Else but Me)." Over a shared piece of apple pie and two cups of coffee, he explained that his preferred nickname was "Els."

Back at the party, Lieutenant Robert Hagen—as of that morning officially the ship's Gunnery Officer—failed to duck at the appropriate moment and nearly had his jaw broken when the wife of a petty officer hit him squarely in the face with her purse. Once he had recovered from the blow, Hagen made sure that Captain Evans—who had himself imbibed—was able to find his room in the hotel.

The next morning, the first thing Evans said to Hagen when they met in the ship's wardroom was "Great party!" He was smiling broadly, but Hagen watched the smile soon disappear when the ship's supply officer handed Evans a ten-thousand-dollar invoice for damages that the hotel had sent by courier very early that morning.

Bonding brawls aside, the men assigned to this brand-new destroyer began making the transition from mere sailors to shipmates. Seasoned petty officers took fledgling sailors under their wings and helped them adjust to the new routines, where drills and watch standing and swabbing and sweeping took precedence over all else save eating and sleeping. They taught the neophytes how to speak the language of the sea, where floors were always "decks," walls were "bulkheads," ceilings were "overheads," stairwells were "ladders," upstairs was "topside," and downstairs was "below." Customs and courtesies were strictly practiced: Enlisted sailors steered clear of "officer's country," where the ensigns and lieutenants resided; covers (caps) were never worn in the mess decks during meals; and salutes were exchanged when watches were relieved. Time was expressed in twenty-four-hour format (where 1 p.m. became 1300), dates took on the Navy format of day-month-year, letters were always spoken phonetically ("A" now "Able," "B" now "Baker," and so on), and prurient substitutes were often used in training (for example, a round being inserted into a chamber was expressed in more colorful metaphors).

Military regulations and peer pressure did most of the work in turning once-rebellious teenagers into obedient sailors, but occasionally more stringent methods were needed. Sometimes a boatswain's boondocker to the back pockets of a helmsman who strayed off course by more than a degree kept the ship on her navigational track. To ensure that sailors stowed their personal belongings in their lockers when not in use, "gear adrift" was confiscated and placed in the "lucky bag"; it would be later auctioned off to the highest bidder and the money placed in the welfare and recreation fund. Serious offenses could result in the offender being subjected to a court martial, or to what was formally known as "nonjudicial punishment" but more often called "captain's mast."

Captain Evans held his first mast on 11 November just before the ship got underway for operations in Puget Sound. The characteristic half-smile that Ed Digardi had noted was absent as the first of three offenders was brought before Evans, accompanied by the B Division leading chief. The young fireman third class was visibly trembling as he stood at attention before the captain. He had returned from leave one day, five hours, and fifteen minutes late. Evans explained to him that he was fortunate that the ship had been in port at the time—that "missing ship's movement" was an even more serious offense. He added that his shipmates in the fireroom depended on him to be there when needed. After the young sailor assured the captain that it would never happen again, Evans awarded him thirty days restriction to the ship, and he was dismissed, still trembling. A seaman second class who had been shirking his duties was next up and was given twenty-five hours of extra duty. Finally, a seaman first class who had been caught with two ID cards in his possession was sentenced to three days confinement with only bread and water to eat and drink. (This punishment had been adopted from the early days of the Royal Navy. The latter stopped using it in 1891, but it remained in effect in the U.S. Navy until it was finally removed from the Uniform Code of Military Justice in 2019. The offender was allowed as much bread and water as he wanted, and the maximum duration of the punishment was three days.)

Concluding her local operations in Puget Sound, *Johnston* tied up at Pier 41 in Seattle for one final night in Washington before departing for San Diego the next day. Ed Digardi had drawn the midwatch. The evening watch (also called the "first watch") begins at 2000 (8 p.m.) and ends four hours later, at midnight. The midwatch follows, ending at 0400 (4 a.m.). The forenoon watch runs from 0800 to 1200 and is followed by the afternoon watch from 1200 to 1600 (noon to 4 p.m.). The four-hour pattern is "dogged" (broken into two-hour segments) in order to accommodate the evening meal: The first dog watch lasts from 1600 to 1800 (4 to 6 p.m.), and the second dog watch completes the cycle at 1800–2000 (6–8 p.m.). The men with the first dog watch eat the evening meal after standing their watch, and those with the second dog watch eat before assuming the watch.

As in-port officer of the deck that night and, since the wind had picked up a bit, Digardi had gone down the brow to the pier to check the mooring lines. As he moved from one set of bitts to the next, observing that the doubled-up lines showed no sign of strain and that the rat guards remained in place, he reflected on how world events had so changed his life. Not that long ago, he had been a college kid, worrying about grades and getting to class on time. Now he was an officer on a warship destined for battle. It was both a sobering and exciting thought. The war had been raging in the Pacific for nearly two years, and all indications were that it would go on for several more. There had been much to lament and much to celebrate. There had been terrible losses of men and matériel at Pearl Harbor, and, in the Solomon Islands (a place he had never heard of before the war), Savo Sound had earned the sobriquet "Iron Bottom Sound" because of the many ships that had been sunk there. But there had been a great U.S. victory in the battle over Midway, a small island northwest of Hawaii; and the struggle for Guadalcanal had nearly been a disaster, but the Japanese had ultimately lost the island and adjacent waters after a long struggle of attrition that had apparently cost them dearly. Digardi recalled seeing a map in a past issue of *Time* magazine that made it clear that the Pacific Ocean they would be entering tomorrow was vast, and much of it was still controlled by the Japanese.

As he climbed the sloping brow and returned to *Johnston*'s quarterdeck, the messenger of the watch, a kid who looked barely old enough to attend high school, offered him a steaming cup of black coffee and a shy smile, causing Digardi to suddenly feel reassured. The men who had come from all over America with all manner of backgrounds were but small cogs in a very large machine, yet it was an important machine, one that would determine the future of the world. God willing, they would all come home together and then scatter back to their former places, having done their part in this cataclysmic struggle that to him and many others was one of good versus evil. Perhaps he and this young man holding a cup of coffee would not survive the war, but in that moment he felt strongly that they were on the side of good and that their sacrifice—should it come to that—would be worthwhile and would help ensure the victory that he was sure would come.

The next day—15 November—*Johnston* emerged from Puget Sound via the Strait of Juan de Fuca and was immersed in ocean salt water for the first time. Almost immediately it became clear that there was a big difference between a sound and an ocean. A brisk wind caused a humming sound in the ship's rigging and carried showers of spray across her decks as the destroyer began riding the swells in a relentless rising and falling motion. The first time the ship dipped into a trough and shuddered violently as her bow slammed into the next wave, Seaman Second Class Harley Chronister thought they had run aground. At first he thought it was fun—kind of like riding a roller coaster—but then he began to feel woozy and soon joined several of his shipmates at the lee rail, where they contributed their lunches to the foaming water as it rapidly swept past the bucking destroyer.

Chronister later recounted, "I didn't realize one could be so sick and still live, nor did I know a ship could survive such rough water and still float." Some of the more seasoned sailors who were immune to the mal de mer seemed to enjoy the suffering of their shipmates, one deliberately reminiscing in a loud voice about those "greasy pork chops we had for lunch." But Chronister gratefully remembered Chief Boatswain's Mate Clyde Burnett, who took pity on the novices and offered them helpful advice like "Eat a stack of soda crackers after lunch to settle your stomach" and "Keep your eye on the horizon when you are on deck." It helped, and Chronister never forgot that act of kindness.

Burnett had not been part of the ship's company when she was commissioned and was still getting to know the crew. He had come aboard after *Johnston*'s first chief boatswain had proven to be a problem. The latter was loathed by the crew, and Lieutenant Bob Hagen, the gunnery officer and third officer in seniority, harbored similar feelings. Telling Captain Evans, "I don't like the son of a bitch," Hagen added, "He has a bad attitude and goes around with his cap on backwards and his jacket unbuttoned." Evans had urged some tolerance, but when the chief went AWOL, Hagen had been vindicated and the problem had been solved. But it created a new one by leaving *Johnston* without a key member of her crew. The captain then earned much gratitude from the crew when he went ashore to the personnel receiving station in San Diego and came back with Clyde Burnett.

An orphan reared by four different families in South Texas, Burnett served in the Civilian Conservation Corps before joining the Navy in 1939 just after his eighteenth birthday. Initially assigned to a destroyer, he had been at Pearl Harbor when the Japanese had attacked. Shortly after that infamous day, the Navy issued a plea for volunteers for submarine duty. "I was just mad enough at the Japs that I volunteered," Burnett later recounted. "My thinking was that being aboard a submarine was probably the quickest way to get back at the Japs."

Burnett became a submariner and proved himself a capable sailor. After passing the exam for chief petty officer, he was promoted in minimal time. Impressive as that was, he had promoted himself out of a job because the submarine he was serving in did not have a billet for a chief boatswain. Sent ashore, he was not happy with his new assignment as chief master at arms in charge of maintaining good order and discipline among sailors who, in many cases, were hell-bent on blowing off steam upon returning from arduous war patrols. So he asked to be sent back to surface ships, and his request was granted.

He had been at the receiving station in San Diego for only two days when he was summoned to the personnel office. There he was introduced to Evans, who wasted no time telling him that he had a new ship with a new, mostly inexperienced crew that needed a chief boatswain to get them ready for sea duty and combat. Evans made it clear that he intended to get his ship into the war zone as soon as possible, which for Burnett was not a strong selling point based on his previous experience. Burnett candidly told Evans that he had been hoping for some stateside time after having been overseas for the last five years. His reluctance was compounded when Evans told him that the last chief boatswain had gone "over the hill." Burnett wondered if the man had deserted for good reason.

But there was something about Lieutenant Commander Evans that impressed Burnett. He seemed "very sharp," and Burnett sensed that this was not your typical officer. More than the stripes on his shoulder boards, there was something in his manner—a "controlled intensity"—that compelled "followership."

Captain Evans returned to *Johnston* with Clyde Burnett in tow. Thanks to his experience and quiet manner, he would prove to be the perfect fit. Though he was only twenty-four, he was comparatively old to many of the green crew, and they looked up to him as a kind of father figure. Bob Hollenbaugh thought highly of him, and the respect was mutual. Evans would grow to rely on Burnett as a liaison to the enlisted men, and Hagen would later describe him as "the captain's right-hand man."

During the transit to Southern California, in calmer seas, Evans tested the ship's depth charges, dropping one from each rolling track on the fantail. When the charges exploded, a white mushroom boiled up out of the green water, bursting into the air and then cascading back into the frothing sea. Next, he ordered one each fired from the K-guns, projectors mounted on the port and starboard sides of the ship. These were more exciting to watch, as the cans of explosive were hurled into the air and arced away from the ship before plunging into the depths and exploding. As Bob Hollenbaugh watched the K-guns firing, he thought they made more sense; having to run directly over an enemy submarine to deliver the rolling depth charges did not much appeal to him.

At 1300 on 18 November, *Johnston* passed Main Channel Buoy "Able" and proceeded into San Diego Harbor, where she moored to Buoy No. 20, a tricky maneuver that she did well. The next day she would begin her "shakedown"—a series of training exercises and drills designed to hone the skills that could make the difference between victory and defeat, life and death.

For the men of the *Johnston*, San Diego was a welcome change from the rainy Northwest. It was much sunnier and warmer, and to those who had never seen them, the proliferation of palm trees gave the Southern California city an exotic feel. On liberty, the sailors soon discovered Balboa Park and the beaches. Downtown they found cafes that never closed, and long lines of servicemen waiting to be served were a reliable indicator of which ones were the best. The Chicken Pie Shop was one of those, and at a lunch counter christened Overleaf, a sailor could find tuna sandwiches for twenty-five cents, Spam or turkey for twenty cents, peanut butter and jelly for fifteen cents, and Coca-Colas for a nickel. The Bomber Café on Fourth Avenue was another popular destination for the hungry, but because its theme was the Army's B-24 bomber that was being built at the Consolidated Vultee Aircraft plant outside the city, sailors tended to pass it by.

Most pleasing of all the sights were those of the feminine variety. Whether referred to as "ladies," "girls," "dames," "broads," or sobriquets of the more prurient type, women were often the subjects of conversations, fantasies, and interactions. Pompadours and curled bangs were popular hairstyles, and hats were not infrequent. Skirts were hemmed below the knee, and the visible parts of the legs were frequently covered by stockings—many of them made of wartime-necessitated rayon, which tended to stretch out of shape ("stretches and stays stretched" was a frequent lament). Bobby socks were a substitute among younger women, and least popular among the girl-watching servicemen were the work pants worn by those women who were employed at the factories that were working around the clock producing war matériel.

There were USO centers, dancehalls, bars, and dark streets where servicemen could find varying forms of interaction among the distaff populace. For those men who had given up trying to make such acquaintances or were too shy to try, the Hollywood Theatre offered a "Big Girl Revue"—something the midwestern farm boys had never encountered back home—and amusement centers offered coin-operated peep shows along with mechanical peanut vendors and other coin-swallowing machines that tested the striking power of a fist or provided target shooting that used light beams rather than bullets.

Bootblacks proliferated for those who were weary of shining their shoes, and photographers were available to those who wanted pictures of themselves in uniform to send back home. "Sam the Tailor" at 825 Fourth Avenue offered clean-and-press-while-you-wait services, as well as tailor-made uniforms, or alterations to regulation uniforms that often made them less regulation by taking them in so effectively that a sailor might need a shipmate's help in pulling his jumper off over his head.

All in all, it was possible to find many distractions to help these men in uniform temporarily forget why they were so attired. But the ubiquitous posters reminding them that "loose lips sink ships," and newsstands with headlines that included the words "Nazi" and "Jap," were jarring reminders of what lay ahead. Bob Hollenbaugh, strolling down Broadway with some of his *Johnston* shipmates, looked up to see barrage balloons hanging motionless over the city, placed there right after Pearl Harbor to protect against a similar surprise attack that many San Diegans remained convinced was still coming. He figured that such a thing was doubtful but then reasoned that Hawaiians had probably had similar thoughts two years before.

One week into their San Diego stay, several of *Johnston*'s crew got into a drunken brawl with the shore patrol. Lieutenant Commander Baker, the XO, wanted to throw the book at them. Ed Digardi was pleased when Evans suggested that he defend the offenders. When Digardi (who would become a highly successful trial lawyer after the war) succeeded in getting the offenders off, Evans gave him an approving smile that he did not share with Baker.

According to some, Baker often seemed condescending and dismissive of others and was quick to pass judgment. He was an Annapolis graduate who seemed to look down on those officers who had earned their commissions through other means. It was common in the fleet for this difference between the "regulars" (who had graduated from the Academy and whose names and ranks were always followed by "USN") and the reservists (who had earned their commissions through officer candidate schools and were designated "USNR") to manifest itself in fleet wardrooms, often good-naturedly but sometimes with unpleasant rancor. It was usually more obvious in ships that had seen little or no combat—that great equalizer that often removed or subdued the prejudices that had seemed important in less arduous circumstances.

Lieutenant Bob Hagen was one of those with "USNR" appended to his name. He had wanted to attend the Naval Academy—his father was a 1911 graduate—and in fact he had done so, but only for one day. After having received an appointment over sixty other applicants in 1938, he failed a routine eye exam the day he reported to Annapolis and was immediately sent home. Fate sometimes compensates for disappointments. Hagen returned to Brownsville, Texas, where his father was currently stationed, and attended junior college there, completing his studies in little over a year. Subsequently completing reserve officer training at Northwestern University, he earned a commission as an ensign in 1941, three months before his would-have-been classmates at the Naval Academy, something he was not shy about pointing out whenever he crossed paths with any of them.

His first assignment was as assistant service school selection officer at Great Lakes, Illinois, where he tested new enlistees to determine which, if any, of the specialty schools they would attend after boot camp. Testing revealed individual aptitude and helped in deciding who would go to specialties like electronics training or marine engineering. Men might be assigned and even promoted if they had prior relevant experience, so that a journeyman carpenter with ten years' experience might be promoted to chief petty officer and assigned to one of the Navy's construction battalions (popularly known as "SeaBees") that would play a vital role in building airfields and port facilities across the Pacific as the war moved westward. Those who had no experience and did not stand out in testing were sent straight to the fleet, where they would receive hands-on training and likely spend considerable time painting and swabbing before proving themselves worthy of promotion to petty officer with a rating like gunner's mate or signalman.

While sorting through the growing numbers of sailors in this fashion, Hagen had a fateful encounter with five young men from Waterloo, Iowa—all brothers named Sullivan. They had been promised by their recruiter that they could stay together by all serving in the same ship. By this time the war had begun, and Hagen thought that was a very bad idea. "What if that ship got sunk?" he argued to his commanding officer. "Can you imagine being the chaplain who would have to deliver the news to that mother?" His protest fell on deaf ears, and all five Sullivans were sent to a light cruiser.

Anxious to leave the stultifying world of desk duty, where logic seemed to Hagen to be in short supply, he appealed to his father for help in getting him a sea assignment. The elder Hagen, then serving in the Bureau of Ordnance, apparently succeeded, and orders arrived for his son to report to the destroyer USS *Aaron Ward*. Assigned triple duty as assistant communications officer (apparently because he could type twenty-three words per minute), assistant supply officer, and radar officer, Hagen would soon see the action he thought he craved.

On 13 November 1942, during what has become known as the "Naval Battle of Guadalcanal" (somewhat of a misnomer because there were multiple naval engagements related to the struggle over that island in the Solomons), *Aaron Ward* led the rear section of destroyers in a column that included five cruisers and seven other destroyers as it made its way westward through Sealark Channel into Savo Sound. At 0140, USS *Cushing*—leading the column in the ebony darkness—encountered at close range an approaching Japanese force of two battleships and twelve screening cruisers and destroyers. A general melee erupted that would prove to be one of the bloodiest surface battles of the war. The Japanese lost a battleship and two destroyers, while the Americans lost two cruisers and four destroyers. When the battle began, USS *Juneau* was just ahead of *Aaron Ward* in the column. She was one of the cruisers sent to the bottom of "Iron Bottom Sound" . . . *taking with her all five of the Sullivan brothers*. Fate can be a harsh arbiter at times.

Ensign Hagen was *Aaron Ward*'s officer of the deck (OOD) when the battle began, and he had been on the starboard bridge wing when a Japanese shell exploded in the wardroom below, and was hit by shrapnel in several places. The most serious damage was to his left bicep, which was torn open and likely would have cost him his life from arterial bleeding had a pharmacist's mate not stopped the profuse flow with a tourniquet. He later recalled, "I didn't consider myself lucky at the time the doctors were cutting a useless artery from my arm and removing shell fragments from my leg, but those wounds kept me off the *Aaron Ward* when she went down later off Tulagi." Hagen was awarded a Purple Heart for his injuries and a Silver Star for his actions that night.

Among the lessons Hagen learned from this early experience was that he was not fond of communications and had decided that he was better suited for weapons duty. "The gun boss could fire a hundred shots and only hit once and he was a hero," he opined during his convalescence. "In communications, if you screw up in transcribing one letter, all hell breaks loose, and you've committed a mortal sin. I'd rather be hero." When he was again fit for duty, Hagen happily landed a seat in the gunnery and fire control school in Washington, DC, before reporting to *Johnston* as her gunnery officer, a job that involved much more than *Johnston*'s many guns and the men who maintained and operated them. He would also be responsible for the operation of torpedoes, depth charges, fire control directors, and sonar.

When Hagen, now a senior lieutenant, joined the crew of USS *Johnston*, he was one of the few men with combat experience, which Evans recognized (and might have even envied a bit). The captain relied on Hagen to help him forge a combat-ready crew out of the sailors assigned to the fledgling destroyer, most of whom had never even been to sea before reporting for duty.

By most accounts, Hagen was an intense individual who took his job very seriously, so much so that when he had become overwrought over a sailor's slovenly appearance, Evans had counseled him, "Relax, Hagen. There's a war on."

During *Johnston*'s shakedown in San Diego, Hagen was, in his own words, a nervous wreck, and chain-smoking was just one of the outward symptoms. Patience was not in his sea bag, and he too often dressed down an errant sailor in the presence of his shipmates. To his credit, he knew his shortcomings and tried—sometimes without success—to correct such flaws. And he was quick to give credit to others where due, often citing the proficiency of Bob Hollenbaugh, who had been assigned as gun captain for Mount 54, and praising Julian Owen, a gunner's mate who was at home with machinery, often making repairs when others had given up. He also thought highly of his torpedo officer, Lieutenant Jack Bechdell.

Hagen's intensity paid off in terms of results, if not always crew morale. In six weeks, he was able to turn the gunnery department into a competent working team. The crews in the five main gun mounts—51, 52, 53, 54, and 55, from fore to aft—were competing to see which gun crew could deliver the most rounds in the shortest time. Mount 55 was able to fire eighty-four rounds during one four-minute firing drill, an average of twenty-one per minute—six more than the established average of fifteen. In a moment of self-congratulatory repose, Hagen wrote to a friend, "You may now bring on the Japanese fleet!" This was in sharp contrast to an earlier letter—written at the beginning of shakedown—to the same friend in which he had confided, "My gun crews don't know what they are doing and I'm not sure I do either," adding, "Stay out of our gun range; anything can happen!"

Captain Evans had given Hagen much latitude as the latter struggled to turn neophytes into competent warfighters. Hagen was grateful, having served under a micromanaging "screamer" in his previous ship, and it helped that he admired and respected Evans and wanted to measure up to the captain's apparent trust. He also was certain that Evans meant what he said at the commissioning about taking his ship into harm's way. Consequently, the two men shared a reverence for repeated practice, and Evans not only allowed but encouraged Hagen to initiate drills whenever he saw fit. On his last ship, drills were always scheduled in advance, which made no sense to Hagen. "The enemy isn't likely to announce when he is going to attack," he wrote to that same friend, "so why should we indulge ourselves in that luxury?" Consequently, the crew found themselves responding to the general quarters (battle stations) alarm at all hours of the day and night and so often that they began to refer to the ship as "GQ Johnny," a sure sign—however sardonic—that the bonds between the crew, the captain, and the ship were solidifying.

After the shakedown, *Johnston* returned to Puget Sound for a maintenance availability to make repairs and final installations of new equipment. Some of the crew were happy to renew previous "friendships" with some of the local girls, but most considered it a burden to go back to the often depressing weather and the cacophony of the clamorous shipyard.

Underway for San Diego again on New Year's Day 1944, the ship again resounded with the summoning claxon and the age-old words "All hands, man your battle stations!" Damage-control and abandon-ship drills anticipated the undesirable or unthinkable, and both equipment and personnel casualty drills were designed to transform the crew's reactions from chaotic to routine. In his official war diary report for that second day of the new year, Evans wrote, "The crew seems slow in becoming war conscious." Aware that few of his crew had any combat experience, he knew that the antidote was simulation and repeated practice. It was all about preparing the men for the worst that war might bring their way, ensuring that they could function effectively in the face of fear or horror when thinking would be difficult or impossible as hearts pounded and adrenaline flooded their systems.

Again and again, they practiced fighting fires, dewatering spaces, patching holes, and shoring up damaged bulkheads. They mastered the art of passing occupied stretchers through the ship's confined passageways, up ladders, and through scuttles. Applying bandages, tourniquets, and splints became as familiar as dressing for watches. Knowing the redundancies of communication circuits, piping systems, and ventilating shafts became second nature, and it was not unusual to see a man making his way through the ship with his eyes closed in preparation for the possibility of power failures or the blinding effects of smoke.

The pace was demanding, and gripe sessions would occasionally emerge. The most frequent antidote was sardonic humor. "I don't see how we're going to win this war if we use up all the ammo in drills" or "I never knew USS stood for 'Underway Saturday and Sunday' until now" were typical utterances heard on the mess decks and in the berthing compartments. On one occasion, Ed Digardi was sipping a lukewarm cup of coffee and enjoying a moment's peace on the 01 level with the sun setting into a tranquil sea off the starboard quarter when he overheard a group of sailors grousing about the next day's ammunition-handling drills. Chief Clyde Burnett was among them, sitting quietly on an ammunition box, and he let the younger sailors go on for several minutes with their complaints. Then he slowly got up and quietly said, "Gentlemen (and I use that term loosely), it is far better to sweat over here than to *bleed* over there." He motioned over his shoulder toward the sun as it was just touching the horizon in the west. The sailors all fell silent as he headed aft.

In her final week of workups, *Johnston* left San Diego early on Sunday morning, 9 January, to join up with other destroyers of Squadron 55 for more gunnery practice. After shooting down a drone that was simulating a dive-bombing run on the ship, the crew conducted more antiaircraft firing drills for the rest of the day and did not secure until just before the evening watch.

Johnston spent the night steaming independently in the waters near San Clemente Island. Evans retired to his sea cabin a little after midnight. Ed Digardi was on the bridge for the midwatch that night, and when he called Evans on the sound-powered phone connecting the bridge with the captain's sea cabin to report a surface contact, he was startled when the captain answered the phone, "Sam Spade." It was common knowledge among the officers—as learned from the stewards—that the captain often read one of his many mystery novels for a time before finally going to sleep, and apparently this night was no exception. It was one more reassuring sign to Digardi. There was no doubt that Evans was very serious about his business, that he seemed to know everything a wartime captain should know, yet he was confident and relaxed enough to escape into a novel and maintained a sense of humor despite the awesome responsibility that came with his shoulder boards.

Johnston rejoined the other Squadron 55 ships after sunrise and spent most of the day conducting shore bombardment exercises before returning to San Diego during the second dog watch. At last she was moored at the destroyer base, starboard side to Pier 5, but any hope of a respite vanished at the sight of an ammunition lighter coming alongside. After about a half hour of moving ammo from the lighter to the magazines and the ready-service lockers, one of the exhausted members of the working party lost his grip while passing a 5-inch projectile. Trying desperately to keep the round from striking the steel deck, he suffered a compound fracture of one of the fingers of his right hand. As he was led below to the sick bay to get the necessary sutures and splinting, Bob Hollenbaugh heard one of the gunner's mates mutter, "Some guys will do anything to get outta work."

The next day brought more work. Divers had discovered that *Johnston*'s sonar dome had been seriously damaged, and the ship would have to be drydocked for the necessary repairs. At lunchtime, a warrant boatswain from the shipyard arrived and joined Evans on the bridge to conn the ship into the drydock. By 1400, *Johnston* was safely inside the dock, and the caisson was in place to close off the entrance. The rumble of massive pumps signaled the beginning of water removal, and the crew watched as their ship slowly sank into the dock. As the water receded, the ship settled carefully onto the keel blocks in the bottom of the dock. Once all the water had been removed, shipyard workers swarmed into the dock, their boots splashing in the remnant puddles as they began removing the sonar dome from the ship now towering high and dry above them.

Working through the night, the "sand crabs" finished replacing the dome by 0730 the next day. With all hands clear of the dock, massive valves were opened, and water rushed into the dock, refloating the ship. In time for lunch, *Johnston* was safely moored at Pier 3 and began loading "government supplied general mess stores [food]" and fuel, taking on 46,616 gallons to top off her massive tanks.

Finally the ship and crew were deemed ready for service in the fleet, and on 13 January 1944, *Johnston* left the continental United States in her wake as the ship rendezvoused with Rear Admiral Jesse B. Oldendorf's Task Group (TG) 53.5 off the coast of Southern California. (An entire fleet is too large to be used for most specific operations, but a particular task may require more than one ship. To better organize ships into useful groups, the Navy developed an organizational system that divides a fleet into task forces, and these can be further subdivided into task groups. If the task groups still need to be further divided, task units can be created, and these can be further subdivided into task elements. A numbering system is used to make it clear what each of these divisions is. The Seventh Fleet, for example, might be divided into two task forces numbered TF 71 and TF 72. If TF 72 needed to be divided into three separate divisions, they would be task groups numbered TG 72.1, TG 72.2, and TG 72.3. If TG 72.3 needed to be subdivided, it could be broken into task units numbered TU 72.3.1 and TU 72.3.2. [This "decimal" system might not sit well with high school math teachers, but it works for the Navy.] Further divisions of TU 72.3.1 would be elements numbered TE 72.3.1.1 and TE 72.3.1.2. This system can be used to create virtually any number of task forces, groups, units, and elements, limited only by the number of ships available.) Taking station in cruising disposition "3Love" with the heavy cruiser USS *Louisville* as guide, DD 557 proceeded with the other ships of the formation to cross the Eastern Pacific, headed for Hawaii.

The war was at last coming closer.

CHAPTER 2

"CHIEF"

When Ernest Edwin Evans was born in the town of Shawnee on 13 August 1909, Oklahoma had been a state for less than two years. Earlier attempts at making two separate states—"Sequoyah" embracing the Indian Territory and "Oklahoma" dominated by the largely white population that had arrived as the so-called Sooners and Boomers—had failed in Washington, so the people of the Indian and Oklahoma Territories voted to combine their lands into a single state in September 1907. The next month, President Theodore Roosevelt issued Proclamation 780, admitting Oklahoma as the forty-sixth state.

The so-called Five Civilized Tribes made up most of the Native American population in the new state. Ernest Evans' lineage included both Creek and Cherokee Indian blood, which was somewhat problematic because the two tribes were often hostile to one another. Mixed marriages were not uncommon, however, and his father was half Creek—the other half being mostly white—while his mother, Anna Birdsong, was apparently pure Cherokee. Young Ernest identified with the latter, which was probably preferable because the Cherokees often looked down on the Creeks.

In the days before statehood, the territorial property laws granted all land to the man in the case of divorce, which led Ernest's mostly white paternal grandfather—George Washington Evans—to marry two land-owning Creek women whom he subsequently divorced, then disinherited their offspring and kept their property. Ernest's father—William Charles Evans—was one of those disinherited children, and his life as an often-unemployed carpenter, retail grocer, or trolley operator was not an enviable one.

The family left Shawnee for Muskogee, a town on the North Canadian River, east-southeast of Oklahoma City. At the time, the town was on the rise, with much of its prosperity based on the "land grab" that was well underway, but the Evans family was relegated to the seedier side of Muskogee along the railroad tracks. Most of the children in that neighborhood attended the vocational school that emphasized manual training, but young Ernest had managed to attend the mostly white Central High School, graduating in 1926. Beneath his photo in the school yearbook are the words "the courage of his convictions." Sometimes prophecy appears in unlikely places.

During a quiet bridge watch in the dark of night, watch standers will sometimes lower those barriers that normally shield their private thoughts from the outside world and will confide in their shipmates things they would not ordinarily share. Perhaps the cloak of darkness provides a sheltering veil, or the vastness of the sea around them and the universe above alters their perspective, but it is not unusual for personal revelations to emerge as an antidote to the monotony of thrumming engines and the background hum of high-frequency radio receivers. On one of those occasions, Captain Evans, apparently unable to sleep, had emerged from his sea cabin halfway through the midwatch to join Ed Digardi, who was on watch as OOD. After a few minutes of Digardi briefing Evans on routine matters such as the state of the engineering plant and the current and predicted weather, the two men fell silent for a time. Evans was seated in his captain's chair; Digardi was standing a few feet away, habitually scanning the empty horizon through the binoculars that were the trademark of OODs everywhere.

When the captain's voice emerged from the darkness, addressing Digardi as "Ed" and asking how his family was back home, Digardi replied with a brief rundown of what the last mail call had revealed, aware that the recent letters he received had been written many weeks before and so he really had no idea how things were back home.

The two men fell silent again, and Digardi assumed the conversation was over. But then Evans quietly said, "I grew up in an Oklahoma town about fifty miles southeast of Tulsa. Could not wait to leave." There was something in the captain's voice that seemed to be evaluating as well as remembering. "A lot of us grew up admiring past warriors, and we were all very patriotic, so the military seemed like the obvious way out of Muskogee." He paused for a moment, his breathing steady but a bit louder than before. "I wanted to go to Annapolis to become a Marine officer, but I didn't stand much of a chance of landing a congressional appointment, so when that dream had evaporated, I enlisted in the Navy, hoping to land a fleet appointment to the Academy." Another pause. "I took the entrance exam and passed. Reported to Annapolis in the summer of '27." What sounded to Digardi like a small laugh preceded Evans' next words. "A lot of my classmates complained about the Annapolis heat and having to room together in 'Mother B,' but I thought I was living on the palace grounds. All that marble and those big brass cannons and . . ." His voice trailed off, and the moment had passed. Digardi scanned the horizon and checked his watch as he realized the captain was asleep.

Digardi would long remember that night when his captain momentarily stepped out of his command cocoon to wistfully recall his youth. Digardi often wondered whether Evans was lamenting the decisions he had made or was grateful for them. Knowing where those decisions had so far led him, he suspected Evans had few regrets that night. Looking back on what followed, Digardi wondered if Evans would change any of it if he could. He suspected not.

Like many young people who are less than enchanted with their childhood, young Ernest escaped through reading. Among the books he devoured were sea adventures, such as *Treasure Island*, *Moby Dick*, and *Midshipman Ready*. So it is not surprising that when he was old enough to make his actual escape, it was to the Navy.

Upon graduating from Central High, Evans was still sixteen, not yet old enough to enlist—a problem he solved by changing his birthday to a year before on his application for enlistment. For whatever reason, he also changed his place of birth from Shawnee to Pawnee, Oklahoma.

Once in the Navy, Seaman Second Class Evans was sent to San Diego. On a "personal history sheet" Evans answered yes to the question "Did you join the Navy with a view to entering the Naval Academy?" That aspiration led him to gain acceptance to the West Coast Preparatory Program, which had been set up to assist enlisted sailors who sought an appointment to the Academy. After six months of preparation, he took the entrance exam on 20 April 1927 and scored the highest grade among the sixty-two members of his preparatory class.

The exam mostly consisted of math problems and word associations. Amateur psychology must be taken with a grain of salt, but of the three questions that Seaman Evans missed, two of them tempt one to draw conclusions that they reveal who he had been and who he would become. The sixteenth question on the test asked, "A meal always involves . . . [?]" The choices offered were

1. a table
2. dishes
3. hunger
4. food
5. water

The drafter of the test felt that the correct answer was "food," as would most people who came from "normal" backgrounds. But to a Native American boy who had grown up on the wrong side of the tracks in Muskogee, Oklahoma, the answer was—not surprisingly—*hunger.*

Question 23 asked, "A contest always has . . . [?]" And the choices were

1. umpires
2. opponents
3. spectators
4. applause
5. victory

The Academy answer was "opponents," but had the test grader been able to see into the future, he would likely have understood why Ernest Evans' answer was *victory.*

Evans entered the Naval Academy on 29 June 1927, the same year that Joseph Stalin came to power in the Soviet Union, Charles Lindbergh made his historic flight across the Atlantic, and the Great Mississippi Flood inundated an area of 27,000 square miles, affecting ten midwestern states, including Oklahoma.

Midshipman Evans apparently had no serious problems in his four years at the Naval Academy, although a remark in his class yearbook—the 1931 *Lucky Bag*—hinted that his plebe year was not without difficulties, quoting him as remembering that year as "one bust after another." But the yearbook also recorded that he came through that first year with the philosophy that "life is what one makes it" and that he "established himself in the heart of every Middie."

IMAGE 6 • Photo of Ernest Evans as a midshipman in the 1931 *Lucky Bag*

In his second-class (junior) year, he ran into some trouble when he received an official letter from the superintendent (Admiral Samuel S. Robison) dated 23 November 1929, warning him, "You are deficient in physical training requirements for the term just completed" and urging him to expend "greater effort in order that you may become satisfactory." The letter goes on to warn him that if he did not comply, he "will not be permitted to go on Christmas leave but will be required to remain at the Naval Academy for extra instruction during that period." There is no record of whether he got home for Christmas that year. In any case, it is likely that Christmas would have been bleak for his family and so many other Americans that year (and others to come) because the stock market had crashed in October, plunging the nation into the Great Depression.

Remarks in the *Lucky Bag* indicate that his classmates were obviously aware of his Native American lineage and seemed to take it in stride. Nicknames were common—almost mandatory—among midshipmen, and Evans was known as "Cherokee," "Big Chief," and simply "Chief," the latter most commonly used. While "Chief" made sense in one context while at the Academy, it caused a few raised eyebrows in the fleet because there the term referred to chief petty officers, which were a wholly different entity.

His classmates apparently liked him, as evidenced in the *Lucky Bag*, which described him as "endowed with an exceptionally brilliant mind," adding that he had "a shining personality and pleasant nature, together with a knowledge of psychology, common religion, philosophy, love, or most any subject about which one desires to converse." As a "wife" (Academy slang for "roommate") he was "reliable, big hearted, and consistent, full of good jokes . . . never gripes, always ambitious." The *Lucky Bag* also described him—without further explanation—as "radical from birth."

In some ways, Evans' years at the Academy were well timed. In 1930, the year before his graduation, the Academy was accredited by the Association of American Universities, entitling it to confer the degree of bachelor of science. In the year after Evans graduated, the Depression caught up with the Academy. Due to drastic reductions in the Academy's budget, its administrators announced that only the top half of the class of 1933 would be commissioned. Described by his Academy roommate as practicing "a minimum of study and a maximum of reading and pleasure," Evans had ranked 322 of 441 in the class of 1931. History would have been significantly altered had Evans come to the Academy just two years later!

In the early 1930s aviation was still viewed as somewhat experimental and secondary to the surface Navy, with its big-gun battleships and cruisers. But it was also dangerous and attracted the more daring individuals. An early indication that he was one of the latter, Ensign Evans opted for aviation and was accepted into flight school early in his career. But more than courage was required. Poor hand-eye coordination washed him out early in the program.

In the surface fleet, he first reported to the battleship *Colorado* (BB 45) and then joined the crew of the destroyer *Roper* (DD 147). As a lieutenant, he served in another destroyer, USS *Rathburne* (DD 113), and the light cruiser *Pensacola* (CL 24), followed by service in the Far East in the transport *Chaumont* (AP 5) and the destroyer tender *Black Hawk* (AD 9).

Evans had married Margaret Bell in 1931. She remained in Long Beach during the years he spent in the Far East, raising their two sons, Ernest Jr. and Jerry. Because Evans was so often at sea, his family saw little of him. Even when he was home, Evans remained largely focused on being a naval officer. His eldest son recalled his father telling him about the great Battle of Jutland between the battle fleets of Germany and the Royal Navy. Despite the boy's youth, Evans would explain the tactics involved, including such practices as "following the splashes," in which a ship's captain would steer toward the points where the last enemy shells had hit the water, assuming that the enemy would not expend another round on a point that had just missed but would be adjusting his fire accordingly.

In 1941, Evans was promoted to lieutenant commander and was again far away, serving in the Western Pacific as part of the so-called Asiatic Fleet. For some time, the winds of war in that part of the world had been gathering momentum, and it did not take an accurate barometer to predict the storm that lay ahead.

CHAPTER 3

ABDA

When the United States Fleet was created in 1922, combining the assets of the Atlantic and Pacific Fleets, the Asiatic Fleet remained independent, and although much smaller in size, it was led by a four-star admiral (one of only four authorized at the time to hold that rank) and tasked with defending the U.S. possessions of Guam and the Philippines, as well as representing American interests in the so-called open door policy in China. Despite this outsized tasking and the presence of a four-star admiral at its head, it was clear to most actual and would-be strategists that if war came, the Asiatic Fleet would likely be unable to prevail against the Imperial Japanese Navy (IJN), which was becoming more and more formidable ever since its stunning victory in the Russo-Japanese War of 1904–5. Indeed, this diminutive American "fleet" was little more than a squadron, made up of aging ships that had been relegated to maintaining a tenuous American presence in the distant Western Pacific.

U.S. strategic planning recognized, although it did not specifically state, that the Asiatic Fleet would likely become a sacrificial lamb once hostilities commenced. Originally conceived by Admiral Raymond P. Rodgers in 1911, that strategic planning had been code-named War Plan Orange. Prescribing American actions in the event of war with Japan, Orange was one of many contingency plans developed by the Joint Army and Navy Board to prepare for war with various nations: Black represented Germany, Green prepared for a "Mexican Domestic Intervention," and there was even a War Plan Red that prepared for war with Britain and Canada.

Central to both Japanese and American strategic thinking was the idea of a decisive battle between the main fleets of each nation, a concept derived from the writings of the American maritime strategist Alfred Thayer Mahan. This was particularly true for the Japanese, who were influenced by their stunning success at the battle that took place in the straits of Tsushima in 1905, when they shocked the world by annihilating a Russian fleet. But it was also a centerpiece of American strategic thinking because the Orange plan envisioned the Asiatic Fleet holding out against the Japanese in the Western Pacific until the main U.S. Fleet could arrive for that decisive battle.

For the sailors of the Asiatic Fleet, this was a less-than-inspiring prospect. The Imperial Japanese Navy had been growing in strength at an alarming rate, and the idea of holding the IJN at bay while waiting for the U.S. Fleet to get underway and make the five-thousand-mile transit from Pearl Harbor to Asiatic waters seemed improbable at best. Virtually no one considered the possibility that the fleet at Pearl Harbor might be removed from the equation on the very first day of the war.

In mid-1941, although no Americans knew that the Japanese would attack the United States Fleet at Pearl Harbor in December of that year, there was little doubt that war with Japan was coming. Diplomatic attempts at preventing conflict were stalled, and there were strong indications that the Japanese were preparing for a war with the United States and her allies.

In August of that ominous year, Ernest Evans had been serving in the destroyer tender USS *Black Hawk* (AD 9) in the Asiatic Fleet when orders arrived to report as executive officer in the destroyer USS *Alden* (DD 211). With his warlike temperament, he must have been gratified to leave *Black Hawk*, a support ship tasked primarily with repairing destroyers, and headed to a warship as her second-in-command. But he likely also felt some disappointment at that warship being *Alden*. She was old, having been built during the Great War (as it was still called in those days) and commissioned a full year after the armistice had been signed. Her geriatric status had much to do with her being assigned to the hapless Asiatic Fleet.

Kemp Tolley, who had been serving in various roles in the Asiatic Fleet since 1937, later described its destroyers in an oral history interview: "The United States had thirteen destroyers out there. Those four-pipers had one three-inch gun with iron sights. In other words, it was about as close to useless as anything you could imagine, even against close-in aircraft. [They] tended to jam after about the third shot. . . . It was not a war fleet. It was strictly a fleet for showing the flag." (Because these early destroyers had four very prominent smokestacks, they were often referred to as "four-pipers." Captain Tolley's derisive assessment of the ships' guns was probably reasonably accurate [although he is referring to the one 3-inch/23-caliber antiaircraft gun and is ignoring the four 4-inch/50-caliber deck guns], but he may have been somewhat unfair in ignoring the ships' batteries of torpedoes. Those weapons were, after all, the most potent component of a destroyer's armament, the

IMAGE 7 • USS *Alden* (DD 211). Ernest Evans was serving as her executive officer when the Japanese attacked Pearl Harbor.

main reason that such ships had come into being in the first place.) In terms of increased responsibility and mission potential, Ernest Evans' career had taken a turn for the better by his assignment as XO in *Alden*, but in terms of relevance and survivability, being second-in-command in a "sacrificial lamb" was less than ideal.

Alden's captain was Lieutenant Commander Lewis E. Coley USN. Like Evans, he was a graduate of the Naval Academy, earning his commission in 1924, making him Evans' senior by seven years. Also like Evans, Coley had grown up in Oklahoma—just ninety miles from Muskogee in Oklahoma City—after his family had left his birthplace in Alabama when he was ten years old.

By the time Evans reported as Coley's XO on 9 August 1941, the Japanese had been fighting in China for four years and had moved into French Indochina less than a year before, when the French had become preoccupied fighting (and losing to) the Germans in Europe. With tensions rising in the Western Pacific, the Asiatic Fleet commander (CINCAF), Admiral Thomas C. Hart, had withdrawn his destroyers from Chinese waters. For many months, *Alden* and the other ships had been operating primarily out of the Philippines, much of the time alternating between maintenance periods at Cavite naval base in Manila Bay and training exercises designed to prepare for the war that many thought inevitable.

At first, the hidebound traditions of the "Old Navy" had prevailed in the Asiatic Fleet. Officers wore "white service" uniforms at sea and carried their swords with them when going ashore in any official capacity. The age-old Navy mandate for "spit and polish" kept sailors busy with shining, painting, and swabbing. But as the specter of war loomed larger, attitudes and actions began to change. There was less concern for the impractical and more emphasis on preparing for combat.

When Admiral Hart had ordered the sailors' families to be sent home in the fall of 1940, there was general agreement that this was a wise precaution under the circumstances. But as time went on and the war did not materialize, attitudes regressed. William P. Mack, a lieutenant serving as gunnery officer in USS *John D. Ford* (DD 228) in the Asiatic Fleet at the time—and

IMAGE 8 • Admiral Thomas Hart, commander of the U.S. Asiatic Fleet at the beginning of the Pacific War

later a renowned vice admiral—recorded the following in a Naval Institute oral history:

> In a sense the morale was good because you knew you were ready to go to war. On the other hand, morale was very bad because we'd been there for more than a year and Admiral Hart had given no sign of changing our tours. I had been there for two years in November and was going into my twenty-fifth month. My wife had been evacuated for thirteen months, and it was particularly tough on the officers who were married to stateside girls. The enlisted men didn't care because they were married mostly to Filipino girls, but the officers were pretty unhappy because they saw no signs of relief in sight. . . . Admiral Hart didn't seem to be considering shortening the tour and to keep up the rotation every two years and give you a chance to get back to the States since there was not a war and a tour of over a year was unheard-of in those days.

On 24 November, because of the "tense and unpredictable" situation in the Far East and concerned that the Japanese might cut off some of his forces from British and Dutch bases, Admiral Hart formed Task Force 5, consisting of the cruiser *Marblehead* (CL 12), the tender *Black Hawk*, and two destroyer divisions (57, which included *Alden*, and 58) and ordered them all to head for various ports in Borneo, the large island on the north side of the Dutch East Indies.

Alden got underway at 0830 the next day and headed for Balikpapan on the east coast of Borneo. The voyage was uneventful, but tensions ran high. On the 27th, she and the other U.S. ships received the following message from the Navy Department:

> This dispatch is to be considered a war warning. Negotiations with Japan looking toward stabilization of the conditions in the Pacific have ceased and an aggressive move is expected within the next few days. The number and equipment of Japanese troops and the organization of the naval task forces indicates an amphibious expedition against either the Philippines, Thai[land's] Kra Peninsula, or possibly Borneo. Execute an appropriate defensive deployment preparatory to carrying out the tasks assigned in War Plan 46. Inform district and Army authorities. A similar warning is being sent by the War Department.

"War Plan 46" cited in the message referred to the Navy's implementation of "Joint Army and Navy Basic War Plan–Rainbow no. 5," the result of an overhaul and consolidation of the earlier colored war plans. In the event of overt hostilities initiated by Japan, the plan called for CINCAF to coordinate "in the planning and execution of operations" with the "British Commonwealth and Netherlands East Indies" and to "raid Japanese sea communications and destroy Axis forces."

Arriving in Balikpapan on the morning of 30 November, *Alden*'s crew was elated to hear that they were to proceed to Batavia on the north coast of Java, the capital of the Dutch East Indies, "for supplies and liberty." The ominous warnings from the Navy Department seemed to have temporarily subsided, but as they headed southeastward across the Java Sea with the tender and the three other destroyers of Division 57—*Whipple*, *Edsall*, and *John D. Edwards*—new orders directed them to proceed instead to Singapore,

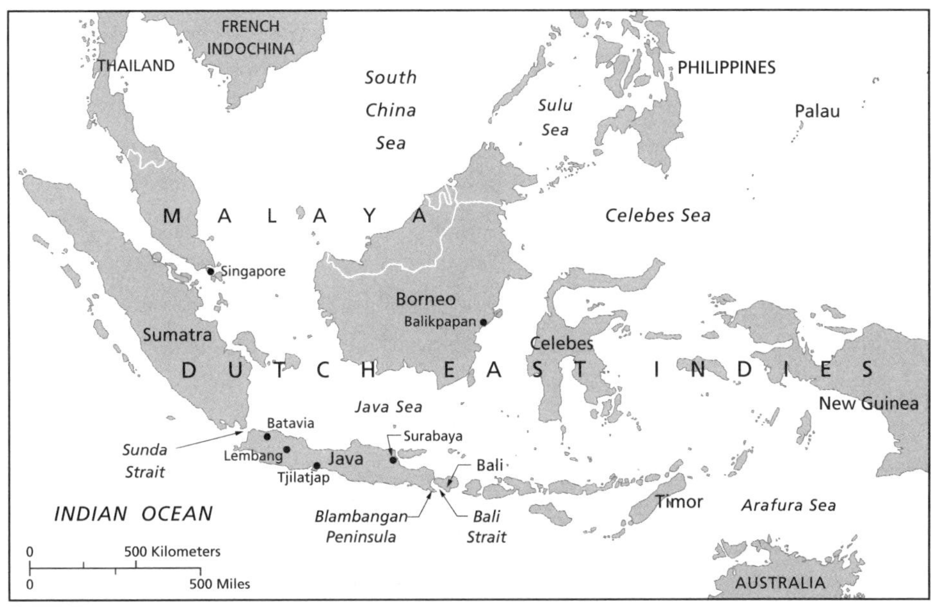

MAP 1 • Dutch East Indies in relation to Philippines and Malaysia

where they were to join a combined force of Royal Navy ships commanded by British Admiral Sir Tom Phillips, the newly designated Commander in Chief, Eastern Fleet. (When forces of different services [Army and Navy, for example] of the same nation operate together, they are called a "joint" force; when forces of different *nations* operate together, they are referred to as a "combined" force.) No one was surprised that the British and the Americans were joining forces in these foreboding times.

Leaving the tender behind, *Alden* and the other ships headed northeast at best speed. During the midwatch on 8 December, the officer of the deck woke Coley from his slumber to tell him an alert message had arrived saying, "Japan has commenced hostilities; govern yourselves accordingly." That news was not particularly surprising, but that the war had started over six thousand miles to the east at Pearl Harbor, Hawaii, was a substantial shock. Already feeling that they were a long way from home, serving on the fringes at or near the front lines of the coming war, the Americans serving in the Asiatic Fleet now felt as though they were more likely serving *behind* those lines.

With Pearl Harbor in flames, there remained some reassurance in knowing that they were headed for Singapore—the so-called Gibraltar of the East—at the southern tip of the Malay Peninsula. Bristling with artillery, protected by minefields, and with a jungle-covered peninsula to its north that was deemed impenetrable, this British bastion of the Far East offered an anchorage big enough to hold an entire navy, four square miles of shore facilities including huge cranes and well-equipped repair facilities, capacious warehouses loaded with food and ammunition, and the oil wells and refineries at nearby Sumatra. In the midst of an exploding Southeast Asia, Singapore seemed ready to stand against whatever the Japanese chose to bring to bear. Even more reassuring to the sailors of Division 57 was the presence of the Royal Navy, including the battleship HMS *Prince of Wales* and the battlecruiser HMS *Repulse*, both of which had seen action in European waters against German naval forces.

As the destroyers continued their northwesterly trek toward Singapore, the war that had seemed possible for so long was now reality, and every mast that climbed over the horizon was at first mistakenly perceived to be that of a Japanese warship. Stopping several merchant ships to make sure they were not Japanese, the Americans warned the ships' masters that war had broken out.

Alden and the others arrived at Singapore on the morning of 10 December. Met by a small British patrol craft that led the way through the defensive minefield, the ships proceeded in column with *Alden* third in line. From the bridge, Coley and Evans surveyed the harbor as they moved slowly toward their assigned berth and noted that there were several heavy and light cruisers present, including the Dutch light cruiser HNLMS *Java*, but there was no sign of *Prince of Wales* or *Repulse*.

Soon after *Alden* was securely moored alongside a fuel ship in the naval dockyard to take on fuel, Evans appeared on the quarterdeck to greet a Royal Navy lieutenant and four signalmen who were to embark in *Alden* to assist with communications in the combined force that was rapidly forming in anticipation of more hostile actions by the Japanese. Evans handed the signalmen off to *Alden*'s chief quartermaster, then escorted the lieutenant to the wardroom, where they were joined by the captain.

IMAGE 9 • The British Royal Navy cruiser HMS *Repulse* *Official U.S. Navy photo*

As Coley, Evans, and their British guest sat at the dining table in the wardroom over cups of steaming tea and coffee, the lieutenant informed the American officers that two days earlier a Japanese convoy had been spotted heading for British Malaya, probably intending to invade. He told them that Admiral Phillips decided to try to thwart the Japanese invasion and had left Singapore with Force Z, which consisted of *Prince of Wales* and *Repulse*, accompanied by the British destroyers *Electra*, *Express*, and *Tenedos* and the Australian destroyer HMAS *Vampire*. Ever since their departure, Force Z had maintained radio silence to prevent the Japanese from knowing their position, so nothing was known about their location or what they were doing.

Coley asked about air cover, and the lieutenant rolled his eyes. He informed them that there was little available and that the new aircraft carrier *Indomitable*, which was supposed to have been part of Force Z, had run aground in Kingston Harbor while working up in Jamaica. She was currently undergoing repairs in Norfolk, Virginia, and no replacement had yet arrived.

The messenger of the watch appeared at the wardroom door and informed Coley that a conference had been called on board *Whipple*. Leaving the British lieutenant to get settled in, Coley and Evans hurried to the conference. As Coley crossed the quarterdeck of his ship, two bells sounded on the ship's 1MC, and the words "*Alden* departing" followed by a single bell as Coley set foot on the adjacent fuel ship. Naval customs and traditions remained intact despite the commencement of hostilities.

Minutes later, the two men entered *Whipple*'s wardroom, which was crowded with officers from the other ships and two captains, one British and the other American. The air in the wardroom was thick with the smell of perspiration and fuel oil as the Royal Navy captain informed the group that Admiral Phillips had recently broken radio silence, reporting that Force Z was under attack and making an urgent plea for support. The U.S. Navy captain spoke next, informing them that he represented Admiral Hart and then relayed the order that Division 57 was to get underway as soon as they were refueled and to proceed up the coast of Malaya to rendezvous with Force Z. He warned them to be wary of submarine attacks and to anticipate an air attack at dawn the next day, adding that the British were working to provide some air cover from their land bases. After discussion of various operational details, including radio frequencies and recognition signals, the meeting adjourned.

Upon returning to their ship, Coley and Evans informed the department heads of what they had learned, for further dissemination to the crew. The chief engineer told Coley that because the pump pressure on the fueling ship was very low, the refueling was proceeding at a snail's pace. After several attempts to right the situation—punctuated by some salty terminology that did nothing to help—Coley decided that rather than delay their departure, they would get underway with their fuel tanks only half-full—about 63,000 gallons shy of *Alden*'s 123,000-gallon capacity.

At 1500, the Division 57 destroyers got underway with *John D. Edwards* leading the column out of Singapore Harbor. As they made their way through a safe lane in the defensive minefield, one of *Alden*'s lookouts nervously reported several objects in the water dead ahead, but they were soon identified as near-empty paint cans and what appeared to be some deck awnings that crewmembers of the lead ship had jettisoned as they zealously "stripped ship," the practice of removing any items deemed merely convenient and not necessary in wartime.

Once clear of the harbor, they secured the sea and anchor detail and set the underway watch. Now at Condition III for wartime steaming, men on deck for other reasons became additional, unofficial lookouts as they furtively scanned the sea around them and the sky above, anxiously searching for a Japanese periscope or an incoming flight of enemy aircraft. Both sea and sky remained empty as the sun slowly made its diurnal descent to the horizon. At dusk, several masts caught the waning rays of sunlight as they pierced that horizon ahead. A mixture of relief and disappointment pervaded as they soon recognized the approaching ships as Royal Navy destroyers, apparently headed for Singapore, rather than IJN ships. Henry Eccles, commanding officer of the *Edwards* later recorded that the two groups "merely exchanged calls and proceeded" on their reciprocal headings. Later events would prove that the Americans might have benefited from more information from their British counterparts.

Arriving at the last known position of Force Z after dark, Evans and the other men who crewed the ships of Division 57 experienced their first encounter with the reality of war. The sea was flat calm as they made their way at bare steerageway through what one sailor described as a "floating cemetery." It was indeed an eerie scene, made more so by a light mist that served as a gossamer shroud, diffusing the pale light of the moon as it illuminated a large field of detritus. Strewn across the glassy surface were life jackets, burned-out hulks of what had been boats, and small and large pieces of unidentifiable objects, most with jagged edges telling of violent forces at work. A few floating sailor caps and numerous empty life rafts were particularly haunting, and as the destroyers' searchlights probed here and there, colorful rainbows appeared on the mirrored surface, explained by the pungent, eye-watering smell of fuel oil.

This was not the rendezvous that the Americans had expected when they departed Singapore to join forces with the *Prince of Wales* and *Repulse*. Just hours before, those two Royal Navy leviathans—one of them more than once described as unsinkable—had succumbed to a Japanese air attack. Overcome by swarms of land-based aircraft delivering bombs and torpedoes, the two ships had been sunk in just a little over two hours of intensive attacks, taking with them 840 men, including Admiral Phillips. It was another devastating blow delivered by the Japanese, with more to come as they began a rampage across the Indo-Pacific that would expand their empire to dimensions once thought impossible. The loss of those two great ships was militarily significant, to be sure, but it was also a terrible blow to British morale: Winston Churchill later recalled, "In all the war, I never received a more direct shock. . . . As I turned over and twisted in bed the full horror of the news sank in upon me. There were no British or American ships in the Indian Ocean or the Pacific except the American survivors of Pearl Harbor. . . . Across this vast expanse of waters, Japan was supreme, and we everywhere were weak and naked."

Churchill's assessment was largely accurate but did not account for the Asiatic Fleet and those British, Dutch, and Australian ships that were still afloat and operating in Southeast Asian waters and still had some fight left in them. The question to be answered was whether they had enough fight to stop or at least slow the Japanese juggernaut. The next few weeks would answer that question as the great sea war got underway.

As the American destroyers combed the debris-covered waters, they did not find any survivors. All had been recovered by the British destroyers they had encountered earlier as they headed south to Singapore. Near the end of the midwatch, a message arrived informing them that the promised British air cover would not be coming, so before daylight could make them vulnerable to returning Japanese aircraft, the destroyers departed the area, making best speed for a return to Singapore.

Along with the attack on Pearl Harbor just three days before, this tragedy served as a lesson—learned the hardest of ways—that surface ships alone no longer dominated war at sea. Almost overnight, theory had been replaced by axiom that without air cover, even the most powerful ships were vulnerable to air attack. Even though this attack had been delivered by land-based aircraft, the long-running "battleships versus aircraft carriers" debate had been settled for all but the most obstinate members of the so-called gun club, who remained convinced that the big guns of the surface ships would deliver the decisive blows in forthcoming naval engagements. From this time forward, many of the major battles to come—and there would be *many* to come—would be decided by aircraft.

But for Ernest Evans and the other destroyermen, this did not mean that they—as surface warriors—had become irrelevant. Far from it. While the seasoned battleships would be largely relegated to protecting the upstart "flattops" and providing gunfire support for amphibious operations, the "tin cans" would spend the next several years of the war ubiquitously participating in a wide variety of operations, including those same roles of force protection and gunfire support performed by their larger sisters, but with many additional ones, including reconnaissance, search and rescue, antisubmarine warfare, and even surface combat. For Evans, his first encounter with the latter would come in less than three months as British, Dutch, Australian, and American forces struggled against superior Japanese forces in Indonesian waters. It would be a harrowing and edifying initiation into the unique world of naval combat and a personally formative experience for this Native American naval officer, now so far from Oklahoma.

Having left the "floating cemetery" behind, *Alden* returned to Singapore, arriving on 11 December and immediately mooring alongside the Royal Fleet Auxiliary *Franco* to replenish her fuel, which had gotten dangerously low. With little fuel for ballast, she had been difficult to handle toward the end of her voyage, bucking awkwardly even in a moderate seaway, especially when she and *Edsall* had briefly left the formation that morning to investigate reported torpedo wakes; finding nothing, *Alden* briefly overshot her station when returning to the formation.

As they made their final approach alongside *Franco* and prepared to shift colors to the in-port configuration, Captain Coley told Evans to lower the flag and jack to half-mast in tribute to the men lost in *Prince of Wales* and *Repulse*—over eight hundred in all. A Royal Navy lieutenant on the auxiliary saluted, then nodded toward the fantail, where the flag fluttered slightly in the morning breeze, apparently expressing his appreciation for the gesture.

Alden remained in Singapore until the morning of 14 December. After disembarking the Royal Navy liaison team, she took in her mooring lines and shifted colors to get underway along with the rest of Division 57 to make the one-day transit to Surabaya on the north coast of Java, the large southernmost island where Admiral Hart had moved his headquarters. There she joined other ships of the Asiatic Fleet, including the cruiser USS *Houston* (CA 30), the largest and most powerful combatant that the U.S. Navy had sent to the Asiatic Fleet, a ship that was popularly known as the president's favorite ship because Roosevelt had embarked in her on four separate occasions. A sailor named Red Reynolds recorded one of those embarkations with a great sense of awe, not just because the commander in chief was boarding his ship but also because of the physical strength and courage that FDR displayed as his limousine arrived at the foot of a steeply inclined forty-foot-long brow that extended from the ship's quarterdeck down to the pier:

> To my amazement, I watched [the president] lean from the back seat, reach out, grab the brow rails with both hands, and, hurtling through the air, draw himself to an upright position. Then hand over hand, he slowly progressed up the brow, his feet dangling inches above the deck of the brow. . . . As he reached the top of the brow, he reached out, grasping the arms of his wheelchair, swinging his body into the air. Raising his right hand to a smart sailors' salute to "Old Glory," as she waved back from her station on the main deck aft. As he dropped the salute, all honors were rendered and his first words were, "It's good to be back home again, Captain."

Little wonder that members of the other services often grumbled that Roosevelt was unfairly partial to the Navy! But it was that partiality that had kept a bad situation from being far worse, and that would ensure ultimate victory for the United States Navy in the coming sea war.

The nation that Franklin Roosevelt led in the 1930s was largely isolationist, wanting no part of the war that had (once again) broken out in Europe or the one being waged in the Far East. But FDR had correctly predicted the future and was able to get bills through Congress (with the immense help of members like Representative Carl Vinson and Senator David Walsh)

IMAGE 10 • Painting of USS *Houston* (CA 30). She served as flagship of the U.S. Asiatic Fleet and fought at the Battle of the Java Sea as one of the ABDA ships.

that had prepared the Navy for its eventual involvement in the coming war. The Two-Ocean Navy Act was passed in July 1940, not in time to prevent the setbacks that the Navy would endure in the early days of the war, but in time to ensure that the ships needed to turn the tide and achieve eventual victory were on the way—ships like USS *Johnston* and the other *Fletcher*-class destroyers, as well as the *Essex*-class carriers and hundreds of amphibious ships and submarines. Without the passage of that bill—the largest naval procurement bill in history, which increased the size of the Navy by 70 percent—the war would likely have gone on for several more years, with an even higher toll and more tragedy than it eventually inflicted.

For now, *Johnston* lay in Evans' future (construction would not even begin for several months), and for him and the other men of the Asiatic Fleet, it was time to make do with the ships they had, to do their duty despite the unfavorable odds.

Despite reports of Japanese advances in numerous locales, including Malaya, North Borneo, Hong Kong, and several of the Philippine Islands, *Alden* and the other ships at Surabaya enjoyed relative quiet for the next several days. On 20 December, in company with *Whipple* and *Edsall*, she departed Surabaya as part of a screening force for *Houston*. The small group was soon joined by the oiler USS *Pecos* (AO 6), the submarine tender USS *Otus* (AS 20), and the cargo ship USS *Gold Star* (AK 12), and all headed for Port Darwin in Australia.

Alden spent Christmas Day refueling from *Pecos*. As they heaved on their lines, manned their pumps, and carried out the many mundane but necessary tasks of keeping a ship at sea, many of the sailors no doubt felt the pathos of their situation, their families on the other side of the world trying to celebrate the sacred holiday as unopened presents lay beneath the decorated tree and prayers in church took on new significance. It would be the first Christmas at war for the Americans, with more to come. For too many, it would be their last.

The group arrived safely at Port Darwin on 28 December, and for the next two months, *Alden* escorted troop and supply convoys from Australia back to East Indies waters to support operations defending the Malay Barrier (a notional line running down the Malayan Peninsula, through Singapore and the southernmost islands of the Dutch East Indies).

Other elements of the newly formed ABDACOM were engaging the enemy, mostly with disappointing results, but for *Alden* and her sisters, these transits were largely uneventful. One exception occurred on the morning of 20 January, when *Alden* and *Edsall*, in concert with an Australian minesweeper and two aircraft, dropped depth charges on a suspected submarine. It is probable that they killed a large Japanese mine-laying submarine whose mines had already sunk three Allied merchantmen. It was Evans' first combat experience, with more on the horizon.

On 22 December, President Roosevelt and British Prime Minister Winston Churchill convened a conference in Washington, DC, code-named Arcadia, that lasted until 14 January and included the top military leaders of both nations. Many important strategic decisions were made during Arcadia, including giving the war in Europe precedence over the Pacific (the so-called Germany First policy), the promise that neither nation would negotiate a separate peace with their enemies, a system for coordinating shipping, and the principle of unity of command that established the Combined Chiefs of Staff. (The Combined Chiefs of Staff consisted of the American Joint Chiefs of Staff [the Army's Chief of Staff, the Navy's Chief of Naval Operations, the Chief of the Army Air Forces, and, later, the president's Chief of Staff] and the British Chiefs of Staff Committee [a representative of the prime minister in his capacity as minister of defence, the First Sea Lord, the Chief of the Imperial General Staff, and the Chief of the Air Staff, or the Washington representative of each]. These combined staffs coordinated allied actions of the two nations throughout the war.) They also agreed to appoint an allied supreme commander for each theater. For the Southwest Pacific area, it was agreed that the supreme commander would be British Field Marshal Sir Archibald Wavell and that he would command all American, British, Dutch, and Australian forces, which led to the acronym ABDA. Wavell was tasked with defending a huge area extending from Burma in the west to Dutch New Guinea in the east. (While the Philippines were theoretically included in ABDACOM, American General Douglas MacArthur maintained actual control there until the islands fell to the Japanese in May 1942.)

Wavell arrived in Singapore in early January and remained there until 1 February, when he moved his headquarters to Lembang in the mountains of West Java, a move that proved prudent when Singapore fell to the Japanese two weeks later. The naval forces available to ABDACOM, dubbed ABDAFLOAT, fell under the command of Admiral Conrad Emil Lambert Helfrich of the Royal Netherlands Navy, who had relieved Admiral Hart in the new command structure in mid-February and also set up his headquarters in Lembang.

ABDAFLOAT suffered from a confusing and inefficient command structure, divergent interests among the nations involved, and serious coordination problems, which led to a series of engagements that resulted in mostly disappointing results. One exception was a small "victory" that received more favorable attention in American newspapers than it probably deserved. In the predawn darkness of 24 January, four U.S. destroyers—*John D. Ford* (DD 228), *Pope* (DD 225), *Parrot* (DD 218), and *Paul Jones* (DD 230), under Destroyer Division 59 Commander Paul Talbot—infiltrated a Japanese invasion force near Balikpapan, off the east coast of Borneo, and fired forty-eight torpedoes at twelve anchored Japanese transports, sinking only four.

But overall, the various clashes occurring in January and February were indecisive and unimpressive as far as the Allies were concerned. *Alden* did not participate in any of these engagements but continued escorting convoys to various ports in the Dutch Indies as the Japanese continued to close in.

On 19 February, Japanese forces occupied Bali, immediately east of Java, where they captured an important airfield. It was evident that they were likely to move on Java itself very soon. Losing Java would give the Japanese control of the Malay barrier and the whole of the Dutch East Indies.

In the grand scheme of Japan's strategic thinking, economic resources were the main goal. Chief among them were the tin and rubber in Indochina and the oil in the Dutch East Indies. Although Pearl Harbor took center stage in American thinking, to the Japanese it was a virtual "side show." None of their ambitious imperialist goals could be realized without the oil needed to drive their ships and aircraft. Because the Philippines lay between Japan and the East Indies, the Japanese felt compelled to neutralize the American presence there. And because they were aware that U.S. strategy included sending the main battle fleet from Pearl Harbor in the event the Philippines came under attack, the Japanese decided to counter that response by sinking the U.S. Fleet at its moorings in Pearl Harbor.

ABDACOM's only hope of thwarting Japanese ambitions in the Dutch Indies was to maintain control of the Java Sea north of Java and prevent the capture of the island. Short of a miracle, that hope was largely futile considering the relative strengths of the forces committed to the struggle, thereby degrading the mission to merely slowing the Japanese advance.

Despite that gloomy appraisal, there was no shortage of determination or courage. For their part, the Dutch had been in control of the East Indies for centuries, and defending those territories was little different from defending their home nation, which by then had fallen to the Nazis. The British had similar interests, and the fate of the Australians and the Americans in the region had been decided in Washington during Arcadia.

On the morning of 22 February, *Alden* left Tjilatjap on the south coast of Java and, in company with the cruiser *Houston* and the destroyer *Paul Jones*, headed for Surabaya on the north coast, where the remainder of Allied ships were gathering for what was shaping up to be a showdown.

Arriving at the entrance of Surabaya on 24 February, the American ships were guided in by a tower of black smoke, the aftermath of one of the bombing raids the Japanese were inflicting on the hapless port several times a day. As *Alden* headed for the fueling facilities in Holland Basin, Coley and his crew saw warehouses ashore on fire and USS *Stewart* (DD 224) lying at a sickening angle in a drydock, having been knocked off her blocks in an earlier raid. A merchant ship lay on her side, gutted and aflame, as the pungent smell of her burning cargo of rubber drifted across the water.

Soon after mooring, Captain Coley was summoned to a meeting with his new boss, Commander Thomas Binford, who led Destroyer Division 58. Coley left Evans to supervise the refueling and to review the few charts available for their new operating area and made his way to USS *John D. Edwards* to meet with Binford and the commanding officers of the other destroyers in the division. Binford informed the group that they were now part of the so-called ABDA Strike Force, a title that exuded more hope than confidence among most of the ships' commanders. The multinational group included the remnants of the U.S. Asiatic Fleet and the Royal Netherlands Navy and was commanded by Dutch rear admiral Karel Doorman, whom Admiral Helfrich had placed in tactical command. Helfrich had apparently concluded that the only hope of deterring Japanese landings on Java was to attack the enemy's landing forces believed to be en route. Aware that his cobbled-together force was most certainly outmatched by the advancing

Japanese ships and aircraft that would surely be protecting those landing forces, but seeing no alternative, Helfrich had ordered Doorman to locate and engage those forces, which were expected to show up soon. There were murmurs and a few diverted glances as Binford continued. Facing the obvious communication problem among allies who spoke different languages and worked from different tactical manuals and maneuvering instructions, Binford informed them that Doorman had ordered contingents of British and American signalmen to embark in the admiral's flagship, the light cruiser HNLMS *DeRuyter*. These English-speakers would relay his commands to their own ships. Coley caught the eye of one of the other American destroyer captains, who smiled resignedly before returning his attention to the division commander, who was then updating the group on the latest reports of Japanese sightings. These were ominous and inconclusive at best and did more to confuse than inform.

Coley returned to *Alden* and briefed the officers on what he had learned. The rest of the day and the one following were uneventful except for the continued bombing runs, which required the ship to unmoor and move out into the sound for maneuvering room. It was a strange baptism by fire for the crew as they watched Japanese aircraft swooping and pirouetting about the sky, occasionally dropping bombs in what appeared to be haphazard patterns. The Japanese bombers maintained a high altitude for their runs, making it impossible for *Alden*'s antiquated 3- and 4-inch guns to reach them. The sound of explosions was disconcerting, and for the sailors on deck the concussive effects that made uniforms seem to stretch tight across their bodies was a new experience for most. A few of the usually gregarious youngsters were uncharacteristically quiet, and others seemed determined to fill the gaps in the cacophony with running commentaries, their voices—laced with adrenaline—slightly higher pitched than usual. Seaman Rodney Guidry complained that it "was really demoralizing to lay down on the deck and watch the bombers come above our antiaircraft fire while crawling under a coat of paint, praying and scared as hell. I say crawling under a coat of paint because there were no foxholes on the camber of a deck." Once the all clear had been sounded, many felt the exhilaration that often follows when the specter of death passes close aboard but has moved on.

At dusk on 25 February, Admiral Doorman—responding to Helfrich's pressure to find and engage the enemy—ordered his force to sea to conduct a sweep off the northern coast of nearby Madura Island. Not making any contact, the Allied force returned to Surabaya early the following morning.

Later that day, as the all-clear siren sounded after one of the Japanese air raids, music carried across the water as *Houston*'s band began playing swing tunes to buck up morale. As welcome as that little distraction was, it paled in light of the arrival of several British and Australian ships. At 1430, three British destroyers paraded into the harbor, followed by the heavy cruiser HMS *Exeter* and the Australian light cruiser HMAS *Perth*.

The new arrivals barely had time to get properly moored before Doorman again ordered all available ships to sea that evening. In other circumstances it might have been an impressive procession as the multinational force steamed out of Surabaya, but considering what was expected to be coming their way, few enjoyed much hope. These fourteen ships from four different nations and speaking two different languages were mostly old and badly needing some maintenance time. Their crews were exhausted, and their officers were making decisions based on little intelligence reporting—much of it faulty. Perhaps worst of all, they had no air cover, a fact that was both psychologically and pragmatically alarming in light of the recent disastrous loss of *Repulse* and *Prince of Wales*.

Many men, women, and children—probably relatives of the Dutch sailors—waved from the shore as the ships began unmooring. Whether it was a display of optimistic encouragement or a gesture of final farewell was indiscernible, but it was certainly dampened when Doorman's flagship *DeRuyter*—the first to get underway—almost immediately collided with a tug and water barge, sinking both of the smaller vessels.

Despite this rather inauspicious—some called it ominous—beginning, *DeRuyter* headed up the channel, leading the way out. Notably missing were her two floatplanes that normally resided amidships just aft of the stacks. As *DeRuyter* passed *Alden*, still anchored and waiting her turn to get underway, Evans questioned why Doorman would leave his reconnaissance aircraft behind, and Coley speculated that it might be because the admiral was anticipating a night action where the planes would be useless, adding that, with their gasoline engines, the aircraft could prove to be a fire hazard when the shooting started. Still, with so few Allied air assets in the region, it seemed a rather myopic decision.

Houston was next underway. Her main battery normally bristled with nine 8-inch guns in three turrets, but her after turret had been disabled during the Battle of Makassar Strait on 4 February, which reduced her firepower by a third and meant that Doorman would not be able to use her in the rear of his formation. In the interwar years, she had been a handsome vessel, fit for presidential visits, with her brightworks glittering in the sunlight and snow-white macrame-like Turk's head and chain sinnet knots serving no purpose other than cosmetic enhancements of her natural beauty. Now the old girl was showing her age and the effects of the travails she had endured in these first weeks of the war. Jagged wounds marred her once-smooth lines, streaks of running rust bled from her scuppers, and a sickly green verdigris tarnished the once-gleaming brass fittings. Despite these wounds and blemishes, she still exuded an aura of power as she weighed her anchors and twisted smartly about to follow the Dutch flagship, her forward 8-inch guns pointing ahead as though daring the unseen enemy to come within range.

Falling in astern of *Houston* was the heavy cruiser HMS *Exeter*. Her six 8-inch guns were fully functional, and both she and HMAS Perth were armed with torpedoes.

The last of the cruisers was the Dutch light cruiser HNLMS *Java*. Her main battery of 5.9-inch guns were mounted on the open deck rather than in enclosed turrets, supplemented by an array of 40-mm and .50-caliber guns. Many considered her obsolete the day she was commissioned in 1925, and she seemed particularly diminutive as she followed *Perth*, who was nearly 60 feet longer and whose Australian ensign was much larger than that of the Dutch ship.

At last it was the destroyers' turn. Three were British (*Encounter*, *Electra*, and *Jupiter*) and two were Dutch (*Kortenaer* and *Witte de With*). As *Alden* fell into the long column wending its way through the channel toward the open sea, Coley noted that his sailors were carrying out their duties well, but many of them showed outward signs of fatigue, a notable sluggishness in their movements, slack jaws, and prolonged blinking of the eyes. He knew that the sailors on the other ships had to be exhausted as well. The previous night's sortie and the Japanese air attacks had caused many of the men to remain at their battle stations for far too many hours with only occasional respites that were too few and far too short.

Despite this exhaustion and the uncertainty of what lay ahead, there were valiant efforts to keep up morale. As the ships emerged from the Surabaya channel and into the open waters of the Java Sea, *Exeter* suddenly hoisted a large white battle ensign—twelve feet across—and surged forward, exhaling a dark gray cloud of smoke from her twin stacks as she charged ahead. Watching the huge ensign billowing in the wind, one sailor pointed out the apparent contradiction of displaying such a visible element from a ship that was covered in a rather complex pattern of camouflage! (In both World Wars, the U.S. and Royal Navies painted a number of their warships with geometric patterns that were intended to confuse enemy gunners and pilots as to the ship's size, distance, direction, or heading, thereby compounding their targeting calculations. "Dazzle" patterns were particularly chaotic and gave ships an especially odd appearance.)

Overtaking *Houston* to port, *Exeter* moved up in the column, falling in directly astern of *DeRuyter*, supplanting the American cruiser in the number two position. As she made this rather ostentatious move—apparently on her own volition, since no signal had come from the flagship—*Exeter*'s flamboyance was compounded by her playing the song "A-Hunting We Will Go" over her external loudspeakers. This bravado was welcomed by those whose blood was up and were anxious to engage the enemy, even if only to end the uncertainty and the draining routine brought on by Doorman's persistent quest to carry out his orders. Others saw the gesture as inappropriate and feared it might prompt the gods of war to retaliate for their hubris. All knew that a reckoning was coming and that it was only a matter of time.

As night fell on the Java Sea, the fourteen ships of Admiral Doorman's Combined Striking Force headed east along Madura Island. This close to the equator, there was little wind or sea to contend with as the ships prows easily tilled the obsidian-like surface of the sea, making the voyage an easy one even for the destroyers. A moderately heavy cloud layer shrouded the sea below, so the lookouts peered into charcoal blackness, their weary eyes searching vainly for some glimmer of light.

Intelligence reports, contradictory and sparse as they were, made it clear that Japanese forces were converging on Java, but it was unclear where they were and where they were headed, so Doorman had no choice but to steam randomly along the Java coast, hoping to stumble onto the phantom enemy. Helfrich kept up his pressure to engage, and Doorman, acutely aware that his crews were near the end of their endurance, was determined to locate and engage the Japanese while his multinational sailors still had a modicum of fight left in them.

The voyage eastward was uneventful, and at 0100 Doorman ordered his force to turn north for a time, then headed westward back toward Surabaya, before reversing course and heading east again. On through the midwatch and into the next, the mind-numbing routine continued. Desperate for distraction, some of the crew listened to the Japanese propagandist Tokyo Rose as she sardonically broadcast, "Poor American boys. Your ships are being sunk. You haven't a chance. Why die to defend foreign soil which never belonged to the Dutch or British in the first place? Go home, before the slackers steal your wives and girls." While no one said it, to some the sound of a female voice—even that of an enemy—was soothing, despite her taunting script.

At last, a nearly indiscernible glow due east on the horizon signaled the approach of sunrise. With the welcome light of dawn came the unwelcome sound of droning engines from above the blanket of clouds. At just after 0900, a Japanese plane emerged from the overcast and dropped several bombs that fell harmlessly into the sea near HMS *Jupiter.* She was about five miles ahead of the flagship, where Doorman had positioned her in the van of his formation as part of an antisubmarine screen made up of the British and Dutch destroyers.

No more bombs fell, but the continuing sound of engines above and the occasional glimpse of an aircraft through a break in the clouds made it clear that the Japanese were shadowing the ABDA force and were no doubt reporting their location to the Japanese fleet, wherever it was.

Helpless to do otherwise, Doorman steamed as before until noon, when the destroyers began reporting that their fuel consumption was becoming a concern. Ordering the force to return to Surabaya, the admiral reluctantly reported his decision to Helfrich. After an exchange of messages that made it clear that Helfrich did not fully comprehend Doorman's tactical situation and was continuing to pressure his subordinate to find the enemy and attack, Doorman revealed his frustration when he responded, "This day the personnel reached the limit of endurance. Tomorrow the limit will be exceeded." Doorman turned his force southward and headed for the Surabaya channel.

In midafternoon of 27 February, *Alden*, following in the wake of *John D. Edwards*, was about to enter the protective minefield in the Surabaya channel when Admiral Doorman's flagship suddenly reversed course and signaled, "am proceeding to intercept enemy unit. follow me. details later."

It seemed clear that Doorman had received some new intelligence. His intentions were less clear, but Coley dutifully came about and headed back out of the channel. Once out in the open sea, Doorman ordered the ships into a battle disposition that placed the cruisers into the same column as before (DeRuyter in the lead, followed by *Exeter*, *Houston*, *Perth*, and *Java*), headed on a northwesterly course of 315 degrees true. Doorman sent the destroyer *Jupiter* five miles ahead of the flagship to give him eyes over the horizon and placed the other two British destroyers—*Electra* and *Encounter*—three miles ahead, 45 degrees off his starboard bow. The two Dutch destroyers, *Witte de With* and *Kortenaer*, were placed equidistant off his port bow.

As *Alden* cleared the headland, the shrill whistle of a boatswain's pipe sounded over the 1MC, followed by the words "General quarters, general quarters. All hands man your battle stations." There was an immediate cacophony as boondockers hit the decks at a dead run and ladders clattered as men climbed up those on the starboard side while others descended those on the port side to avoid collisions. It was fast and it was smooth, the result of frequent drilling under Coley's demanding eye.

It was pretty clear that Doorman must have expected the Japanese to be somewhere near due north; the northwesterly advance would unmask the guns of the cruisers in the column should the Japanese be encountered in that direction. Further, his positioning of the more capable British destroyers along that axis, and his relegating the Dutch destroyers—which had been hampered by engineering problems—to the more sheltered position, seemed to support that thinking. Evans had remained a student of naval tactics since leaving the Academy, and his reading about naval battles in the past might have caused him to wonder why Doorman had kept his cruisers in a single column that mixed the heavy and light cruisers and did not account for their different gun ranges. The likely answer was that Doorman anticipated problems maneuvering the bilingual force in combat and wanted to keep things as simple as possible.

The wind was blowing out of the northeast at no more than Force 1 or 2 on the Beaufort scale (between two and nine knots). (The Beaufort scale is a "seaman's eye" system of estimating wind speed based on telltale signs, such as "ripples with appearance of scales, without foam crests" and "edges of crests break into spindrift; foam is blown in well-marked streaks along the direction of the wind.") But the sea was now running with ten-foot swells off *Alden*'s starboard beam. Coupled with her rapidly diminishing fuel state, she and the other destroyers were rolling uncomfortably. The whining of her forced draft blowers testified that she was laboring to keep up the ordered speed as she followed *John D. Edwards*, with *John D. Ford* and *Paul Jones* astern, so it was disappointing but not surprising that Doorman had placed the aged American destroyers in a column off his port quarter. There, on the anticipated disengaged flank of the formation, they would be less likely to get in the way if the cruiser column needed to maneuver quickly. Despite their speed limitations and the small caliber of their guns, the old tin cans did have torpedoes that could be used to advantage once the forces were engaged, but their positioning would make it difficult to bring those weapons to bear.

Like the day before, a cloud cover masked much of the sky, and Japanese aircraft occasionally emerged from the woolly blanket to drop a few unsuccessful bombs among the Allied ships before again merging with the clouds. Given that the Japanese controlled several airfields in the region, this was not particularly revelatory, but about midafternoon a more telling sighting occurred when *Alden*'s after lookout reported three aircraft near the horizon astern, noting that through his binoculars he could see bulky floats on their undercarriages. This told Coley they were likely scout planes from either cruisers or battleships, rather than land-based aircraft. It was becoming more and more apparent that a Japanese surface force was nearby and tracking them.

At 1615, the starboard forward lookout reported that *Jupiter* had reversed course and was heading back toward the formation. Through binoculars, geysers were visible leaping out of the sea around the zigzagging destroyer, indicating that she was under fire. Her signal lamp was frantically winking as she headed back toward the friendly formation, reporting two enemy heavy cruisers, three light cruisers, and many destroyers at twelve miles, 35 degrees true.

From *Alden*'s bridge, puffs of light brown smoke could be seen at the northern horizon, apparently the result of the Japanese guns firing. Before long, the distinct pagoda-like masts of the larger Japanese ships pierced the horizon, and it appeared that they were headed on a westerly, gradually converging heading. The two heavy cruisers, *Houston* and *Exeter*, opened fire with their long-range 8-inch guns, which were elevated for maximum range. Yellow flames flashed from their barrels, and the reverberation arrived several seconds after. A shroud of thick smoke enveloped the firing cruisers, and minutes later the pungent smell of cordite drifted across the water. The Japanese immediately shifted their fire to the Allied cruiser line in response, and splashes appeared on the sea ahead of *DeRuyter*.

As expected, the American destroyers were at this stage mere observers, too far away from the firing to participate either as shooters or targets. From their perspective, it was difficult to make complete sense of the tactical picture. There was a great deal of smoke from the exhalations of the many propulsion plants churning away at high speed, the great clouds of burned propellant blossoming from gun barrels hurling projectiles at one another, and the deliberate laying of smoke screens to mask and confuse and provide temporary refuge as many of the combatants dashed about in a chaotic choreography of evasive maneuvering. With their relatively low height of eye, the destroyer sailors' view was very different from the bird's-eye views that the battle diagrams in the history books would later afford.

The gunnery officer in the lead ship—Lieutenant Commander William P. Mack—enjoyed a more advantageous view of the developing battle from his elevated gun director in *John D. Edwards*. He later recalled what he observed in an August 1943 *Proceedings* article, one of the earliest accounts of the battle:

> I could see the changing dispositions of both forces, and the positions of our ships and the enemy's ships in formation. I was reminded vaguely of my classroom days at Annapolis where the fleets of Germany and England had battled on our blackboards. This scene in the Java Sea was similar but there were sinister differences. Here was no chalk dust, but powder smoke and flying spray. Salvos of eight to 15 shots were rising about our ships. ["Salvo fire" is the simultaneous firing of all guns ready and aimed at the same target.] In the distance I could see the tops of similar splashes temporarily blotting out the enemy. The formation of these flashes was impressive. They rose slowly, remain suspended for seconds, and then collapsed.

Having all the cruisers in one column rendered the shorter-range guns of the light cruisers impotent until the distance could be closed. The only way to correct that rapidly would be to turn the formation toward the Japanese, but that would make them vulnerable to a classic "Crossing the 'T'" tactic. (Because ships are necessarily proportionately long and narrow, they can carry many more guns along their sides than at the bow and stern. Consequently, if one ship is able to maneuver to place her broadside across the bow [or stern] of her opponent, she gains a tactical advantage by bringing more guns to bear. The resulting configuration looks something like the letter "T" when viewed from above, hence the name "Crossing the 'T'" [or sometimes "Capping the 'T'"]. The same principle applies [even more so] when dealing with columns of ships, where a column of ships crossing their opponent's column is able to bring many guns to bear on the lead ship of the other column, who can respond only with her forward mounts.) Doorman kept the column intact but adjusted the heading to a more westerly tack, still converging with the Japanese force. As the combatants drew closer, the tactical picture clarified a bit. Although the Japanese had a numerical advantage and their ships were generally more modern, the Allies were fortunate that there were no Japanese battleships in the force; had there been, the shooting would have commenced at a much greater range, with a one-sided barrage of much heavier-caliber shells raining down on the ABDA force long before they could have responded.

The two sides continued to exchange salvoes without scoring any hits, although there were some near misses. Based on the limited but fairly consistent intelligence, it seemed likely that the Japanese combatants were keeping themselves between Doorman's ships and the troop transports that were reportedly bound for Java. If Doorman were to carry out his orders to attack that invading force, he would have to fight his way through that wall of combatants. Accordingly, he turned his battle line more to the north, and the light cruisers at last came into range of each other, causing the exchanges between the two sides to intensify.

As the firing continued, several Japanese aircraft dropped through the overcast and began circling the battling ships below. They were no doubt providing spotting information to their ships, giving them a considerable advantage over the Allied ships, which were limited to their optical range-finders. This disparity soon took its toll as *Exeter*, *DeRuyter*, and *Java* were hit. Apparently none of the hits on the Dutch ships were lethal or even significantly debilitating, as they continued steaming and firing. But *Exeter* was less fortunate. A mix of black smoke and white steam erupted from her starboard side, telltale signs that her engineering plant had been struck. She began to slow, and her captain ordered a turn to port to get out of the way of *Houston*, who was coming up astern, still at ordered speed. But *Houston*'s captain assumed he must have missed a signal from Doorman and followed in *Exeter*'s wake instead of proceeding on course. *Perth* and *Java* followed as well, leaving *DeRuyter* to steam on alone. With the formation thrown into confusion and the poor communications system lagging in sorting it out, it took some time for Doorman to get control of the situation and re-form his column.

When Doorman had re-formed his cruiser column, he turned northward toward the enemy force. With *Exeter* limping away to the south, taking half of Doorman's 8-inch guns with her, his firepower was seriously weakened. *Houston* continued firing, but at a diminished rate, either from waning ammunition or crew exhaustion.

Several reports of torpedo wakes in different languages further complicated the chaos. *Alden*'s after lookout reported an approaching torpedo on her port quarter, his normally baritone voice an octave higher than usual. The deadly fish passed them by, and many of the crew began breathing again.

At about the same time, the Dutch destroyer *Kortenaer* was not so fortunate. Now off *Alden*'s starboard bow, she was hit by one of the torpedoes. The speed of her demise was shocking to these sailors who had no combat experience. She broke in two, and the amputated after half went down in less than thirty seconds. The forward half lingered briefly, her prow pointing toward the sky as though trying to escape the pull of the sea, and then that too plunged into the roiling water. Several men could be seen clinging helplessly to her lifelines as she disappeared from view.

Those torpedoes that had missed their targets began self-destructing at the end of their runs. These explosions provoked several unsubstantiated reports of Japanese submarines in the area.

Undeterred by the overwhelming forces arrayed against them, the British destroyers *Electra*, *Encounter*, and *Jupiter* surged toward the Japanese forces and disappeared into a cloud of smoke. Flashes of gunfire could be seen strobing inside the cloud as destroyers from both sides engaged one another at close range. The British attack caused some of the Japanese forces to turn away toward the north. But not without cost: *Electra* suffered severe gunfire damage and would eventually sink.

Evasive maneuvering had again left Doorman's force in chaotic disarray, and now the American destroyers—still in column—were positioned between Doorman's cruisers and the oncoming Japanese forces. It seemed it was at last time for the American destroyers to join the fray. Doorman ordered them to counterattack, but soon after signaled "cancel counterattack," then "make smoke." From these confusing signals, Commander Thomas Binford conjectured that Doorman must be attempting to disengage and wanted his destroyers to screen his withdrawal. Anxious to commit his ships to battle, he further concluded that the best way to accomplish that would be to launch a torpedo attack. So he ignored the "cancel" order and carried out the other two. Making smoke, he turned his column almost due north and, with *Edwards* in the lead, charged ahead as fast as weary engines would allow. Heavy black smoke billowed from *Alden*'s four stacks as she labored to keep up, and the whole ship seemed to be trembling as she followed in *Edwards*' white wake. A sailor clinging to a binnacle on *Alden*'s bridge drew a nervous laugh from his shipmates when he said, "I always knew these old four-pipers would have to go in to save the day."

Japanese salvoes intended for the cruisers passed overhead as the destroyers climbed up and over the swells, slamming down into the troughs, foaming white waves at their bows and greenish-white trails churning in their wakes. Sheets of spray cascaded over the crews on deck at their torpedo stations as they struggled to maintain their footing while preparing their weapons for launch.

The Japanese either did not see the American destroyers in the waning dusk light or preferred to concentrate their fire on Doorman's cruiser column, so the advancing destroyers were able to continue closing the range unmolested. Binford remained calm as he continued to weigh the situation, aware that the closer he got, the more he improved the chances of their torpedoes striking their targets, but knowing that with each passing second their own vulnerability increased logarithmically. If he waited too long, enemy fire could rip the charging tin cans to pieces before they could deliver their fish.

The lead Japanese cruiser had a tall superstructure that loomed taller as they drew closer; her flared bow with the bright white bow wave below looked like a wolf baring its teeth. Suddenly, her forward guns flashed much brighter than before, a sure sign that she had shifted her aim toward the destroyers. Several plumes of water erupted dead ahead as Japanese rounds fell mercifully short. At that moment, Binford ordered his ships to commence launching their torpedoes. On *Alden*, a sailor shouted into his sound-powered phone set, repeating Coley's orders: "Salvo fire! Fire 1! Fire 3! Fire 5! Fire 7!" Each of the ships likewise emptied their starboard tubes, and twenty-four torpedoes splashed into the churning sea. Binford immediately ordered a 45-degree turn to starboard to unmask the tubes on their port sides. Coley ordered "right full rudder," and as the bow swung rapidly about, more shell bursts could be seen off the port quarter, marking the areas where the destroyers would have been had they maintained course a minute longer. Once the column was steadied up on the new course, Binford ordered another salvo, and *Alden*'s torpedoes 2, 4, 6, and 8 leaped into the sea bound for the oncoming Japanese force.

With all their torpedoes expended, on Binford's order *Alden* and her sisters turned away from the Japanese force and wisely beat a hasty retreat. In his after-action report, Commander Coley wrote, "The rear ship of the enemy column appeared to be on fire aft, and to have a fire in her high forward turret or superstructure." Whether that was accurate reporting or a product of wishful thinking, the important thing was that the enemy's main force turned away to evade the oncoming torpedoes, and that gave the remaining ABDA force time to retreat into the gathering darkness.

Despite all the ordnance that had been expended, *DeRuyter*, *Houston*, *Java*, and *Perth* had suffered little damage. *Exeter*, now farther south, remained afloat and was slowly making way, but she was clearly of little combat value. Doorman ordered his able cruisers into the familiar column formation and headed south toward Java. It appeared that the Japanese had decided not to pursue, although the unsettling droning of engines above continued.

The four American destroyers were left trailing behind. From *Alden*'s bridge, the cruisers were invisible in the darkness except when Japanese aircraft occasionally appeared, sporadically dropping flares to illuminate the column. It was a strange sensation to be plowing ahead in utter darkness, then to suddenly see the formation ahead bathed in the eerie light of flares, strobing as they neared the end of their descent, then winking out as they plunged into the dark waters.

Edwards' captain later reported, "We followed the main body endeavoring to regain station, and not having the slightest idea as to his [Doorman's] plans and still only a vague idea of what the enemy was doing." One of the other destroyer captains reported, "There were no more signals, and no one could tell what the next move would be. Attempts were made to communicate again with *Houston* and *DeRuyter* with no results."

As they neared the Java coast, without explanation Doorman turned his force westward to skirt the coast, perhaps in a last attempt to intercept the impending Japanese invasion force. It was unclear whether Binford had received orders from Doorman or had taken it upon himself to break off from the formation, but he now ordered his destroyers to retire to Surabaya. It seemed the only logical option because their fuel state had reached the critical point, and that became their foremost priority.

Only later would the Americans learn that separating from Doorman's remnant force had proved fortuitous.

The Battle of the Java Sea was the biggest surface engagement since the Battle of Jutland, nearly thirty years before. Unlike Jutland, where both sides claimed victory with some justification, this battle was clearly a Japanese victory: The ABDA force failed in its primary mission to thwart the Japanese invasion of Java. There had been no shortage of courage, but poor communications and incongruent battle doctrines had severely hampered the ABDA ships in their attempt to stop the Japanese assault. Even with the best tactics, the result would likely have been similar. It was a lopsided battle from the outset; the Japanese had the upper hand in both quantity and quality.

Despite these disappointing results in the Western Pacific, the formation of ABDACOM at the Arcadia Conference in Washington had set the important precedent of combining Allied forces, something that would improve with time in terms of both cooperation and more efficient operations.

Coley and Evans would not learn the fate of the other ABDA ships until much later, and it would not be good news. Except for the American destroyers, all of Doorman's ships that had survived the battle on 27 February were lost; Doorman himself went to the bottom with *DeRuyter.* As if that news were not tragic enough, many of those who had survived the sinking of their ships were subsequently captured and would spend the duration of the war in terrible conditions as prisoners of war.

A Dutch hospital ship was dispatched to recover survivors of *DeRuyter* and *Java*, but she likely never arrived on the scene. Radio contact was lost with the ship, and an observer in an aircraft reported that he believed he had seen her steaming in company with two Japanese destroyers. She was not heard from again.

The once-proud *Houston* went down fighting, and when her loss was reported in the American press back home, it caused a strong public reaction. In Houston, Texas, more than a thousand young men volunteered to replace the ship's crew and were sworn into the Navy on Memorial Day in an impressive twilight ceremony on a downtown street, a replica of the cruiser in the background. Houston's mayor read a message from President Roosevelt, who had once declared the ship his favorite:

> On this Memorial Day all America joins with you who are gathered in proud tribute to a great ship and a gallant company of American officers and men. . . . I knew that ship and loved her. Her officers and men were my friends. When ship and men went down, still fighting, they did not go down to defeat. . . . The officers and men of the USS *Houston* drove a hard bargain. They sold their liberty and their lives most dearly. . . . Our enemies have given us the chance to prove that there will be another USS *Houston*, and yet another USS *Houston* if that becomes necessary, and still another USS *Houston* as long as American ideals are in jeopardy. Our enemies have given us the chance to prove that an attack on peace loving but proud Americans is the very gravest of all mistakes. The officers and men of the USS *Houston* have placed us all in their debt by winning a part of the victory which is our common goal. Reverently, and with all humility, we acknowledge this debt. To those officers and men, wherever they may be, we give our solemn pledge that the debt will be paid in full.

Arriving in Surabaya after midnight, *Alden* waited nearly two hours for her turn at Holland fuel pier. When the ship finally pulled alongside, the weary crew found that the pumping stations that were normally manned by Javanese workmen had been abandoned. Barely able to walk by now, some exhausted sailors dragged the heavy fuel hoses on board, while others figured out how to operate the Dutch pumps. After a frustrating delay, the black hoses finally pulsed as fuel began to flow into the cavernous tanks. With nothing more to do while the fuel flowed, several of the men dropped to the deck, falling instantly asleep.

Her fuel at last replenished, *Alden* detached from the fuel pier and anchored just before sunrise. Coley had slept briefly in his captain's chair on the bridge while Evans supervised the refueling. An hour into the morning watch, both men were red-eyed as they leaned on the starboard bridge wing rail and conferred over lukewarm cups of black coffee. As the heat of the day set in, they watched as a pair of boatswain's mates sprayed water over the sunlit forecastle and clouds of steam rose from the deck.

In the aftermath of the fruitless battle it was not at all clear what was to be done now. *Alden* had fuel, gun ammunition, and some depth charges, but no torpedoes. Food was becoming a concern. With Doorman and the remainder of the force gone God-only-knew-where, there were no ships to screen, and any offensive actions against the Japanese seemed suicidal at best. It seemed their best chance was to try to get through to an Allied base, but with the noose tightening around Java, that option was diminishing quickly. The shocking news of Singapore's fall and their recent experience in the Java Sea made it obvious that all the East Indies would soon join the burgeoning Japanese Empire. The Philippines was out of the question, since there were reports that the American and Filipino forces had abandoned Manila and retreated to the Bataan Peninsula and the island of Corregidor. With no hopes of a relief force, it seemed clear that it was only a matter of time before the Philippines would fall. So that left Australia.

While the two officers pondered their situation, Japanese aircraft droned in from the east yet again, and from high altitude they dropped bombs in random patterns around the port. Both men remained on the bridge wing watching, because they were either by now inured to the danger or too fatigued to move.

When this latest reminder of Japanese air superiority had subsided, a radioman appeared, stomping across the wooden gratings on the bridge-wing deck in a cacophonous clatter. While rendering a half-hearted salute, he handed Coley a clipboard with a message. As Coley read the message, it appeared that he and Binford were of like minds. No longer in communication with Doorman, Binford had appealed to Admiral Glassford, who was responsible for the remaining American forces in ABDAFLOAT, and asked for permission to get underway that night, taking his four destroyers eastward for a run south through Bali Strait and then on to Australia for rearming and further assignment. Binford was awaiting approval from Glassford, but he told his captains to make preparations accordingly. It was clear that retreat was now the only sensible option, no matter how distasteful. Coley smiled slightly as he handed the message to his executive officer. Evans did not return the smile.

Glassford gave his approval later that afternoon.

It seemed like a good plan, though by no means a foolproof one. The Bali Strait was a good choice because it was deep enough to allow passage for the destroyers but too shallow for cruisers and battleships. Once through, they would emerge into the Indian Ocean, where they might still be subjected to air attacks, but it was hoped they would not encounter any enemy surface forces there, since it seemed likely the Japanese would be preoccupied with the final conquest of Java.

The destroyers would wait until dark to make their eastward move and would be able to transit the strait before the sun rose again. But the weather forecast and the Nautical Almanac predicted a cloudless night with a bright waxing moon, just a few days short of full. They would have to hug the land as close as they dared on the west side of the strait, hoping to avoid being silhouetted by the moon, which would be hovering on their port beam as they dashed southward.

After some brief but desperately needed rest and the first of many meals of canned Spam, the boatswain's mates of First Division began painting over any brass fittings that might reflect the anticipated moonlight in the coming night. Gunner's mates fussed over their weapons, reapplying lubricants that had lost some of their viscosity in the searing East Indian sun and reinserting tampions into the muzzles after yet another inspection of the still-pristine inner barrels. Two signalmen on opposite ends of the signal bridge lazily exchanged semaphore messages about real and imagined encounters with members of the opposite sex. Seamen apprentices scrubbed greasy pans in the scullery, while others in the ship's laundry hefted loads of dungarees—still wet with accumulated perspiration—into the gaping maw of the large washing machine. Two of the junior officers who would be standing bridge watches that night studied the Dutch chart of Bali Strait, while a freckle-faced quartermaster carefully wound the chronometers nearby. In the tiny sick bay, a pharmacists' mate organized battle dressings according to size, then prepared a batch of salt pills for issue to the crew at the next meal.

In the early afternoon, the chief storekeeper took a small working party ashore on a scavenging foray and returned with two crates of papayas and a freshly slaughtered emaciated chicken. They reported that they had seen another American *Clemson*-class destroyer—USS *Pope* (DD 214)—moored about a mile away around a bend in the docks. *Alden*'s sailors had asked *Pope*'s crew if they would be joining them for the planned escape that night but had been told that because her torpedo tubes were still full, Admiral Glassford had ordered them to escort *Exeter*, which had managed to limp into Surabaya and was undergoing emergency repairs not far away. Because of Exeter's deeper draft, they planned to use the Sunda Strait between the western end of Java and Sumatra, and then continue on to Colombo, Ceylon. Only later would the *Alden* sailors learn that both *Exeter* and *Pope* were sunk before they even reached the strait.

Despite the momentary excitement generated by more Japanese air raids, for many of *Alden*'s crew the hours seemed to crawl by as they watched the blazing sun imperceptibly but inexorably descend toward the western horizon. For others, these few hours of reprieve before they would again venture into hostile waters were escaping their grasp at too rapid a rate. The young men's desire to prove themselves in combat had already been satisfied, and they were eager to trade the Java Sea—now for all intents and purposes a Japanese lake—for the relative safety of the Indian Ocean and the continent of Australia, more than a thousand nautical miles to the southeast.

At last the waiting was over, and the destroyers of Division 58 got underway and headed to sea. *Edwards* and *Alden* shifted colors at 1700, followed by *Ford* and *Paul Jones* a half hour later. In the remaining daylight, Binford chose to use the western channel in case any Japanese aerial snoopers were watching—hoping they would conclude that he would be heading west across the Java Sea—before doubling back and heading out the eastern channel toward the oncoming darkness and Bali Strait.

As predicted, it was a clear night, and the bright moon cast its unwanted light over the area, its reflection presenting a shimmering path that would be welcome under other circumstances. A light breeze from the southeast barely stirred the placid waters as the ships crept along at bare steerageway, trying to keep their telltale wakes from further revealing their presence.

A Dutch patrol craft prowled along the southern edge of the minefield as they passed. The Dutch captain had either not spotted them or recognized them for who they were. In any case, the small craft moved on, steady on its original course.

Shortly after midnight, the skulking destroyers left the minefield behind and entered the narrows of Bali Strait. Almost immediately, *Alden*'s forward lookouts reported several craft ahead, but binoculars revealed the soft glow of white sails, a good sign that they were merely local fishing boats, presumably no threat.

The men on deck wore kapok life jackets and had blackened their faces and hands with shoe polish. With their sleeves rolled down and their trousers tucked into their boots to protect them from flash burns, dark rivulets of perspiration trickled down their faces and necks, staining their buttoned collars.

The ships hugged the Java shore as closely as they dared, all placing their faith in *Edwards*' navigator as his ship led the way, relying on a mix of old Dutch and American charts whose data was suspect at best. The tension was palpable as the men on watch scanned the waters ahead, hoping not to see the telltale froth of a coral reef that had grown up in the years since those charts had been printed.

The moon was now about 45 degrees above the horizon and only occasionally shrouded by a passing cloud. At 0115, as the strait began to widen, Binford ordered his ships to increase speed to twenty-five knots. The acceleration brought a relative wind that was welcomed by the sailors sweltering on deck.

Nearly an hour passed uneventfully, and many began to hope they were going to make a clean escape. But those hopes were suddenly dashed when a dark shadow appeared ahead off the port bow. As the distance closed, the shadow took on the form of a destroyer that appeared to be patrolling the southern end of the strait. For several tense minutes nothing happened. Then, from farther south, flashing lights shone dimly as they winked out coded messages. Soon, two more destroyers emerged from the darkness, their distinctive outlines leaving no doubt that they were Japanese.

It seemed they had not spotted the Americans against the dark shoreline. But at about 0230, the navigator's chart showed a reef off the eastern tip of Blambangan Peninsula looming ahead, and Binford had no choice but to lead the column eastward to prevent running aground, closing the distance to the enemy destroyers. The Japanese at last spotted their adversaries and opened fire. The night was lit up by the flashes from the Japanese guns, and the first salvo straddled *Ford*. Several more rounds landed close aboard, but she was not hit as she heeled over in a sharp evasive turn, aiming for the splashes of the unsuccessful rounds in hopes that the Japanese would be adjusting their fire and not hitting the same spot. This was the established tactic that Evans had once explained to his young son while reading to him about the Battle of Jutland years before. Now he was seeing it in action.

Binford ordered twenty-seven knots and "commence firing." By now the range to the Japanese destroyers was about five to six thousand yards, and *Alden* and the others responded with their 4-inch guns, using a continuous fifty-yard "rocking ladder" (i.e., "walking" the point of aim back and forth across the target at predetermined increments). With the exception of *Edwards*, who did not use her forward guns for fear of the flashes blinding the lookouts from seeing navigational hazards ahead, the American ships put out a high volume of fire. None of the shots found their targets, but the continuous barrage kept the Japanese from closing the range. Binford later reported, "An attempt was made to keep up a rapid volume of fire rather than an effective fire . . . to keep the enemy outside effective torpedo range." Although none of the American ships had torpedoes, the enemy did not know that, so the torpedomen fired blank torpedo impulse charges in their empty tubes, hoping the Japanese would see the flashes and assume torpedoes were on the way. On *Alden*, several sailors furthered the ruse by retrieving empty shell casings from the deck and tossing them overboard in front of the torpedo tubes hoping the Japanese would think the splashes were from torpedoes hitting the water. Whether it worked or not, the Japanese ships came no closer but continued to hammer away with their guns.

For Binford, it was tempting to press the attack, since the Americans had a four-to-three advantage, but their lack of torpedoes, the uncertainty of the navigational picture, and the possibility that more Japanese ships might be in the area to join the fray caused him to choose escape over further engagement. He turned his destroyers southward again and left the enemy ships behind in the Bali Strait. Eventually both sides ceased firing and the flashes of gunfire gave way to the steady light of the placid moon.

Lieutenant Commander Mack later recorded in his 1943 *Proceedings* account,

> Every hour that passed put 30 miles between us and the nightmare on Java. We had done all we could. Now we could only hope to escape to fight another day. Dawn found us 120 miles south of Java still racing southward. Anxiously we searched the sky for aircraft. Down below in the radio shack, reports were coming in of attacks by Jap carrier aircraft on other ships fleeing from Java. Somehow they missed us, as we steamed on and on without slowing. All that day and night and the next day we kept going until we knew that we were safe. . . . The old US destroyers which fought so well will probably never fight again. They have since been retired to pasture, to honorable retirement. . . . The officers and men who fought on them have gone to other duties on other ships where they will someday help to avenge their comrades who were less fortunate during those last fateful days of February 1942. They fought a losing campaign but not a lost cause.

CHAPTER 4

PURGATORY

Few would question that Thomas Heggen's *Mister Roberts* is a classic in every sense of the word: The novel has not only enjoyed a long life but has also spawned a hit play, an enduring feature film, a television series, and a TV movie. Besides being a masterful piece of short fiction that at first glance appears to be a comedy, *Mister Roberts* is actually a brilliant study in leadership, a series of case studies in what to do and what not to do when entrusted with the authority and awesome responsibility of rank. It serves as inspiration, warning, and challenge and is made real by the intrusion of human frailties and palatable by the embellishment of humor.

Mister Roberts is a "war story" in that it takes place in the midst of the greatest conflict in history, yet in many ways it is the antithesis of the normal war story. For all but a brief moment, the Japanese enemy is distant and vague, and another enemy is much more immediate, personal, and complicated. The normal terrors of war are supplanted by tedium and frustration. And it is that frustration that drives Doug Roberts to make the fateful decision that will cost him his life.

In the opening scene of the movie, we see a powerful fleet silhouetted on the tropic sky as it makes its way westward to find and destroy the enemy in titanic battles, and we can sense Lieutenant Roberts' disappointment as he must remain behind in a kind of purgatory, continuing to serve in the backwaters of the war in a purely logistical role. He is terrified that the war will pass him by, that this great dramatic moment in history will play on center stage while he can only watch from the wings, waiting for the final curtain.

Ernest Evans would likely have felt great empathy for Doug Roberts had he lived to read Heggen's work. In the months following *Alden*'s escape from the Java Sea, Evans shared that terrible frustration of watching from the wings, of being excluded from the epic struggle of good versus evil then playing out on so many waters of the world, of being trapped in those same backwaters that so tortured the cargo officer of USS *Reluctant*.

Like Lieutenant Doug Roberts, Commander Ernest Evans would get his chance to participate, to at last find his way to the "front" and to pay the ultimate price of admission to this expensive play we call "war." But it would be more than two and a half years before the curtain would rise for that final act, and in the interim, Evans would more than once preview the courage that would reach legendary dimensions in one of the greatest sea battles in history in a previously little-known place called Leyte Gulf.

Alden and the other destroyers of Division 58 arrived in Fremantle, Australia, on 4 March 1942. At this point in the war, it was not clear whether the Japanese would continue their rampage by attempting to invade Australia, but Fremantle was far to the south, and in any case, compared to their ordeal in the Java Sea, the Americans now enjoyed the relative safety and hospitality of their Aussie allies.

There were decidedly mixed emotions among *Alden*'s crew. Overall, there was great relief at having escaped, but for some there was also a feeling that they had run, that perhaps they should have stayed and fought, that there is no glory in retreat. As more and more information trickled in—telling of the loss of all the ships they had shared battle with and left behind in the Java Sea—a pall of survivor's guilt settled in. So many others had perished or had become prisoners of war, and it seemed somehow unfair that they were now relatively safe in Fremantle. There was talk of revenge against the Japanese, and some felt resentment that they and the other ships of the Asiatic Fleet had apparently been abandoned by the Navy to face that ordeal alone.

There was uncertainty about the future, and anxiety about the present. They were so far from home, and it would be a while before mail would catch up to them. They had no idea whether loved ones were safe and well, or even alive—some had friends and relatives serving elsewhere in the war, and there was not a lot of comforting news from other theaters.

For Ernest Evans, whose bellicosity had been enhanced rather than diminished by the limited combat and forced retreat he had experienced in the Java Sea, there was news that was both good and bad. Lewis Coley had apparently impressed his boss, Thomas Binford, during *Alden*'s time in Division 58, and Binford had recommended Coley for a more favorable assignment (and for a Navy Cross, which he later received in October 1942). (Coley's citation reads, "The President of the United States of America takes pleasure in presenting the Navy Cross to Lieutenant Commander Lewis Elliot Coley, United States Navy, for extraordinary heroism and distinguished service in the line of his profession as Commanding Officer of the Destroyer U.S.S. ALDEN [DD-211], in a torpedo attack against superior enemy Japanese forces in the Java Sea on 27 February 1942. Skillfully maneuvering his ship, torpedo hits were scored on Japanese cruisers in the face of heavy gunfire from the enemy, marking a courageous and determined handling of his ship. Lieutenant Commander Coley's aggressive spirit and high type of leadership in action are in accord with the best traditions of the United States Naval Service.") Orders arrived directing Coley to turn over command of *Alden* to Evans.

Command is the dream of most naval line officers, so that was the good news. But USS *Alden* was not a dream command. Having been laid down in October 1918, less than a month before the armistice that ended World War I, she was old, and her weapons and other forms of technology were far from state of the art. Short of another last-ditch stand under unfavorable circumstances, she had most likely seen her last combat.

But as most realistic military officers know, who fights and who supports is largely a matter of luck, and "defend[ing] the Constitution of the United States against all enemies, foreign and domestic"—as stated in their oath of office—can take many forms, requiring that they must "well and faithfully discharge the duties of the office" with little regard for their own personal desires.

So it was that Lieutenant Commander Ernest E. Evans assumed command of USS *Alden* (DD 211) on 14 March 1942, very near to and yet very far from the combat operations that would ultimately determine the outcome of the Pacific War.

Any concerns that Evans had regarding his new command's subsidiary role in the war were soon confirmed. In late March, *Alden* reported to Commander, Australia–New Zealand Area, and operated in South Pacific waters on routine missions until late April, when she was ordered to go to Mare Island Navy Yard in California for a much-needed overhaul. With a brief stopover in Pearl Harbor, she arrived at Mare Island on 7 June, and there she remained until early August.

No sailor enjoys a maintenance period, particularly in a shipyard where privations are many, as electrical power and hot water can be fleeting commodities, civilian workers (known as "sand crabs," without affection) intrude and disrupt, and the noise levels routinely exceed cacophonous. For Ernest Evans it must have been a particularly trying time, as reports of the ongoing war constantly reminded him of where he was not. Since he had taken command of *Alden*, the war was being fought all over the Pacific theater. In April, in sharp contrast to Division 58's flight from the Java Sea, U.S. forces had launched a daring raid on Tokyo itself in the militarily inconsequential but tremendously morale-boosting operation known as the "Doolittle raid." In May, Japanese and American task forces clashed in the Battle of the Coral Sea, which would be evaluated as a tactical victory for the Japanese but a strategic victory for the United States because it prevented the Japanese from taking Port Moresby on the southern side of New Guinea, which would have endangered Australia. In June, four Japanese aircraft carriers were sunk at the Battle of Midway, a clear victory for the U.S. Navy. As part of the Midway operation, the Japanese had invaded the Alaskan Aleutian Island chain, further broadening the geographic reach of the Pacific War. In July, fighting continued in the Southwest Pacific as Japanese and Allied forces clashed in and around New Guinea. And as *Alden* was completing her purgatory in the Mare Island shipyard, the struggle for the Solomons was getting underway at a heretofore little-known place called Guadalcanal, a yearlong campaign that would see a great deal of destroyer surface action.

Evans' frustration grew over the next eight months as *Alden* shuttled back and forth between San Francisco and Hawaii on escort duty. In April 1943, Evans was sent even farther away from the Pacific War when he was ordered to report to Commander, Caribbean Sea Frontier, and, after transiting the Panama Canal, spent the next two months shuttling convoys between Trinidad and Guantánamo Bay, Cuba.

In June, more salt was rubbed in Evans' wounds as he was ordered to take *Alden* to the New York Navy Yard for repairs and alterations. By now it had been nearly a year and a half since he had seen combat in the ill-fated Battle of the Java Sea, and purgatory must have seemed to have devolved into hell itself as the enervating sound of chipping hammers and deck crawlers continued to supplant the terrifying but exhilarating sound of gunfire.

At long last, Evans was thrown a lifeline by the Bureau of Personnel when, in late June, he received orders to report to Pacific Todd Shipyard to assume command of a new destroyer then under construction. While a return to combat action was still a long way off as he waited for his ship to be built, Evans was at last relieved of the prosaic duties that came with command of an archaic ship, and his penance was rewarded by his being given a state-of-the-art destroyer, one of the many *Fletcher*-class vessels that were emerging from shipyards around the United States.

Such things are of course arguable, but many veterans and historians agree that the *Fletchers* were the best class of destroyer ever built. Whether that is true or not, the "marriage" of soon-to-be USS *Johnston* with Ernest Edwin Evans would prove to be one of the most famous combinations in U.S. Navy history.

CHAPTER 5

GREYHOUND

John Vincent Johnston of Cincinnati, Ohio, entered the Navy in September 1861 as first master in gunboat *St. Louis*. He assisted in the Union gunboat attacks that captured strategic Fort Henry on the Tennessee River on 6 February 1862, and on the night of 1 April 1862, he was the Navy commander of a combined Army-Navy boat expedition from St. Louis that landed and spiked the guns of Fort No. 1 above the Confederate stronghold of Island No. 10. For his gallantry, he was promoted to Acting Volunteer Lieutenant and was given command of the stern-wheel steamer Forrest Rose to patrol the Mississippi and its tributaries. On 15 February 1864, his gunboat repelled an attack by Rebel raiders, saving the town of Waterproof, Louisiana, and its federal garrison. Lieutenant Johnston resigned from the naval service on 23 June 1864, and died on 23 April 1912 in St. Louis, Missouri.

Thirty-one years after John Johnston's death, the U.S. Navy christened the latest *Fletcher*-class destroyer in his name. One hundred and seventy-five *Fletchers* would be built and would serve in the war. Once commissioned, this one would serve just two days short of a year. But the brief service of this "Greyhound of the Sea"—as destroyers are often called because of their speed and agility—would loom large in the annals of American naval history, her name synonymous with courage and sacrifice, and her legacy a soaring standard of conduct for all who would subsequently earn the title "United States Navy sailor."

Lieutenant (jg) Ed Digardi, the junior officer of the deck and conning officer for the morning watch, surveyed the seemingly endless sea ahead as *Johnston* trekked westward across the Pacific. The sea was a translucent blue, speckled by tufts of white. "Beaufort 3," he deduced, referring to the mariners' use of the Beaufort scale. A glance at the anemometer confirmed that the wind was blowing from dead ahead and registered twenty-three knots; combined with the relative wind generated by the ship's ordered speed of fifteen knots, that left about eight knots—definitely a 3 on the Beaufort scale!

Ahead lay 2,171 nautical miles of ocean as the ship headed for Hawaii in the ordered "cruising disposition 3L," accompanied by seven other destroyers in various stations, three of them *Fletchers*, the others of older vintage. With shakedown completed, *Johnston* was finally a full-fledged member of the fleet, heading westward to catch up with the war as part of Task Force 53, designated the Northern Attack Force for an operation yet to be identified. Even here, in the relatively safe waters of the eastern Pacific, the threat of submarine attack could not be discounted, and many of the crew found the pinging of the sonar somewhat disquieting as the ship swallowed the miles between San Diego and Lahaina, Territory of Hawaii.

Captain Evans emerged from his sea cabin and stepped out onto the starboard wing. Peering aft, he could see the formation guide, heavy cruiser *Louisville* (CA 28), off *Johnston*'s starboard quarter. She looked menacingly large, even at this distance. Evans moved closer to Digardi and quietly told him to open the range another hundred yards. "Aye, sir," Digardi responded, and through the open port behind him, he gave the appropriate order to the lee helm. Soon Digardi could feel a slight surge as his ship increased speed to carry out the order. A hint of that characteristically enigmatic smile appeared on Evans' face.

The time Ernest Evans had spent in USS *Alden* must have made him especially appreciate his new command. The *Fletcher*s had come a long way from the *Clemsons*. At 376.5 feet long, *Johnston* was 62 feet longer than *Alden*, and her beam—at just under 40 feet—was 8 feet wider. Her full load displacement (weight) of 2,924 tons was more than double that of *Alden*, requiring very powerful engines to drive her at the needed flank (top) speed of thirty-six knots. (Because destroyers spent much of their time escorting the new battleships and aircraft carriers that could race across the Pacific at thirty-three knots, they needed to go even faster to be able to move around within a large formation of ships or to move out ahead of the ships they were defending. *Fletcher*s were originally designed to be capable of thirty-eight knots but were slowed somewhat as more weapons and other systems added to their displacement.) This was accomplished by a very large engineering plant that took up about a third of the ship's total interior space, leaving another third for fuel and ammunition stowage and the final third for all else, including a relatively small amount for the crew's living space.

Four massive boilers located in two separate firerooms provided the steam needed to drive the turbines located in the two engine rooms that delivered 60,000 shaft horsepower to the ship's two screws (propellors). These boilers had divided furnaces that allowed the burners in the larger segment to control the generated steam pressure at six hundred pounds per square inch (psi). Containing the steam at that high pressure required sturdy piping, since a rupture could be deadly—even a pinprick in a pipe would release a jet of steam that could instantaneously remove fingers, or worse. The burners in the smaller furnace operated separately to control the steam temperature, which could be raised to a maximum of 850°F at a rate of 50 degrees every five minutes (about a half hour total). This arrangement provided more precise control at high speeds but placed limitations at lower speeds that required the officers conning the ship from the bridge to be aware that they could not reduce the speed too quickly without risking damage to the piping that carried the high-pressure steam.

It is significant to note that while Naval Academy graduates came to the fleet with an excellent engineering education—acquired over several years in Annapolis—the vast majority of officers manning the ships during World War II arrived on deck with significantly less preparation, having gone through accelerated training at quickly improvised schools that earned them the sardonic sobriquet "ninety-day wonders." Many of these "officer candidates," like Ed Digardi and Bob Hagen, entered the Navy with nontechnical educations that prepared them little for mastering even the rudiments of marine engineering. It was up to the Navy to take these complete neophytes and, in a very short period of time (many of the officer accession programs were even less than ninety days in duration), teach them enough engineering basics to be able to handle powerful and complex engineering plants safely and efficiently. And that was only a portion of the candidates' curriculum, which also included navigation, seamanship, weapons systems, communications, wardroom etiquette, and how to salute properly! It is one of those miracles of World War II that this abbreviated system worked so well, a favorable testament to both the Navy's trainers and the officers they produced.

The forward fireroom—located directly below the forward stack—contained boilers 1 and 2. The forward engine room was immediately aft, followed by the after fireroom, containing boilers 3 and 4, and finally the after engine room, which was farthest aft. The forward fireroom and engine room could be operated as a completely independent engineering plant, as could the after fireroom and engine room. This redundancy increased the ship's ability to continue to operate after sustaining battle damage. Survivability was also enhanced by watertight bulkheads isolating each of these spaces, with access provided only from the main deck. This configuration required a sailor wanting to move from one engineering space to another to climb up to the main deck before descending to the other space. This "up, over, and down" configuration was inconvenient but worth the trade-off because it prevented the spread of fire or flooding.

For normal steaming (up to twenty-eight knots), only two boilers were required, and the ships could cover sixty-five hundred miles at fifteen knots without refueling. These "long legs" were further extended as the Navy improved its underway replenishment techniques, allowing fuel, ammunition, and other stores to be transferred while at sea rather than a ship having to return to port.

Other important components of the engineering plant were the electrical generators and the distilling plants. The latter converted salt water to fresh, which both the boilers and humans needed to function. When there was a conflict in those needs, the boilers took precedence (except for drinking water). To preserve fresh water, showering was limited when underway. If not banned altogether, showers were restricted to wetting down, turning the water off, soaping, and then a quick rinse. Not ideal under normal circumstances, this practice was particularly vexing in the South Pacific, where the hot climate elevated bathing to a higher priority. The smell of aftershave and other olfactory masks were largely unsuccessful antidotes to the smell of perspiration in the berthing compartments and other close quarters about the ship.

A significant portion of the 273-man crew who manned the *Fletcher*s worked in the engineering spaces. Sometimes referred to as "the black gang"—a reference to their soot- and coal-dust-covered faces in the days when coal was the source of energy for creating steam—they were more frequently called "snipes" after John Snipes, one of the earliest marine engineers, who is reputed to have improved the lot of those early landsmen who came from steam plants ashore to man those installed aboard ships. (The John Snipes story is perhaps apocryphal, since Snipes has never been linked with a specific Navy ship, but it maintains that when the captain of his ship refused his pleas for better working conditions for his men, Snipes simply shut down the plant until his demands were met!) The "firemen" (junior sailors working in the engineering department) and their petty officer supervisors (boilermakers, machinist's mates, water tenders, and electrician's mates) enjoyed a better working environment than their predecessors who had shoveled coal directly into the gaping maws of fearsome furnaces, but they still inhabited a infernal world of intense heat and the deafening roar of forced draft blowers, a place where the sun never shines and only the clocks distinguish night from day. Little wonder that Bob Hollenbaugh's father had advised his son to "stay topside" and avoid becoming a snipe.

"Topside" was the realm of many of the nonengineering sailors manning the ship, most especially the boatswain's mates, sometimes called "the deck gang" (or even less formally "deck apes") because they spent much of their time maintaining the ship's exterior as well as operating and maintaining the ship's boats, anchors, and mooring lines. Much like the perspiration that so often coated the snipes below, the ship's topside areas were frequently glazed with ocean spray that transmuted into running rust on exposed surfaces. The dissonant sound of chipping hammers and deck crawlers often signaled that the boatswains were at war with this ubiquitous enemy during normal operations. When the ship went into battle mode ("general quarters," in Navy argot), boatswain's mates manned many of the weapons stations.

The other ratings needed to keep a destroyer functioning were quartermasters, who assisted the navigator; yeomen, who were virtual secretaries handling the ship's paperwork under the supervision of the executive officer; storekeepers and ship's servicemen, who tended to supply needs; cooks, who supervised the preparation of the crew's meals; stewards, who cared for the officers; radarmen and sonarmen, who maintained and operated those electronic sensors; radiomen and signalmen ("skivvy wavers" in mocking sailor argot), who were responsible for the ship's communications; and pharmacist's mates, who cared for the sick and wounded. These and other ratings, under the leadership of their officers and senior petty officers, ensured that the ship could operate independently or in support of other ships for significant periods of time.

As *Johnston*'s gunnery officer ("gun boss"), Bob Hagen was one of the ship's three department heads (the other two led Operations and Engineering). He was responsible for the teams of sailors who manned and maintained the various weapons that gave "GQ Johnny" her punch. The gunner's mates ("cannon cockers"), fire controlmen, and torpedomen made up many of the men in his department and were supplemented by the boatswains and other ratings when all the battle stations were manned. In a postwar interview, Hagen was quick to credit *Johnston*'s enlisted sailors, many of whom "were mere boys, still wet behind the ears" who "did their duty as the men they quickly became."

Johnston's main battery consisted of five "5-inch/38 guns." (Large-caliber guns were designated by the interior diameter of the barrel [5 inches in this case] followed by a number [38] that represented the length of the barrel by multiplying the diameter times that number [5 × 38 = 190 inches, or nearly 16 feet long].) They were rated as dual purpose (surface-to-surface and antiair) and were in boxlike mounts on the ship's centerline—two forward of the bridge and three aft the stacks—and were numbered consecutively (51, 52,

53, 54, and 55). They could fire up to eighteen rounds per minute, with an effective surface range of just over 17,000 yards at 45 degrees elevation, and at 85 degrees they could reach an altitude of 32,250 feet. Although the preferred method of fire was automatic control, they could also be aimed and fired individually by Bob Hollenbaugh and the other gun captains in local control.

When the crew was at their battle stations, Hagen was in the gun director of the ship's Mk 37 fire control system, crowded in with six other men. ("Mk" is an abbreviation for "Mark." The Navy's Mark and Mod system, still in use today, describes many types of equipment: guns, torpedoes, bombs, fire control systems, etc. The Mark number, assigned sequentially, is a means of distinguishing one similar item from another. If the Navy accepts a modified version, that is indicated by the Mod [modification] number. The original version is designated Mod 0, and the first modified version is Mod 1. "Mark" is often abbreviated "MK" as well as "Mk." In some contexts, the Mod number is important, but in common use, the Mod portion is often omitted: for example, the Mark 46 Mod 5 torpedo is often referred to simply as the "Mark 46 torpedo.") Mounted above and just aft of the pilot house, the gun director's boxlike structure with an angled front face looked much like the gun mounts below (without the protruding gun). Sitting atop a barbette, one level up and just aft of the pilot house, it was the highest manned station in the ship. (Originally the term "barbette" described a mound of earth or a platform that allowed guns to fire over a parapet, but when adopted for naval use it described a cylindrical housing—often armored—on which a gun mount or a fire control director was mounted.)

From his perch inside the gun director, Hagen could control all five of the ship's 5-inch gun mounts. The Mk 37 included an optical rangefinder that was still often used despite the system's more modern radar, which had started the war as a curiosity for many but had made rapid improvements as the war progressed. The system also included a kind of electromechanical device that was an early form of analog computer, which significantly enhanced the ship's ability to deliver accurate fire.

When engaged in battle, two men in the gun director mount—the trainer who controlled the mount's bearing (horizontal motion) and the pointer who controlled its vertical orientation (elevation)—would keep the crosshairs in their telescopic sights fixed on the target. When Hagen was satisfied that they were aiming properly, he would order the crews in the gun mounts to "match pointers," and the guns would align with the director through a system of electronic synchros. From that point on, all five guns would perform a synchronized dance that was controlled by the director.

Hollenbaugh and the other four gun captains—all senior petty officers—were each supported by a team of more than twenty men, the majority of whom worked below the mount itself, manning the upper and lower handling rooms to pass ammunition from the ship's powder and projectile magazines up to the mount; mechanical hoists did some of the work, but much of it was done manually.

Inside the gun mount, Hollenbaugh was perched halfway up the back on a platform that he called his "throne." He could raise his head and shoulders out through a hatch for a view of what was going on outside the rotating box that housed all but the barrel of the gun.

From his "throne," Hollenbaugh also had an excellent view inside the mount. Next to him was a voice tube that allowed him to speak to the men down in the upper handling room, and within easy reach were various switches that controlled other communication circuits and emergency lighting. Beneath a specially designed helmet, he wore a sound-powered headset that allowed him to communicate with Hagen and others on the firing circuit.

When the mounts were in automatic control, Hollenbaugh's primary function was to ensure safety and efficiency among his gun crew, but when the mount was turned over to him in local control, he became the gun's director, giving orders to his crew who would manually aim and fire the gun. Around his neck he wore a pair of binoculars that included a reticle of angular milradians (mils) to aid him in comparing shot groupings or to count the number of mils a shot was off target. With those gunnery binoculars, he estimated the range to the target and its bearing rate, and then mentally converted these into range and deflection orders to his sight setter, who entered the information by turning two hand cranks that moved the prisms in the gunsights used by two other members of the gun crew, the pointer and trainer. After firing, Hollenbaugh would observe the fall of the shot and make sight corrections as necessary for the next salvo.

Besides the sight setter, who was stationed in the mount at Hollenbaugh's left, the mount crew consisted of six other men. Seated in the right forward corner of the mount on something akin to a metal bicycle seat, the pointer controlled the gun's elevation and, on the gun captain's order in local control, was the "triggerman," normally firing the gun by using an electrical firing key or, as a backup, using a percussion foot pedal to manually fire the gun through a mechanical linkage. Seaman First Class Bobby Chastain was the trainer controlling the horizontal positioning of the mount and sat on the opposite side of the gun. "It was like one of those carnival rides when the mount spun around," he told an interviewer after the war. "Might have made some people sick, but I was okay."

The powder man lifted the twenty-five-pound powder case being passed up from the upper handling room through a scuttle in the deck and loaded it into the gun's rammer tray. For those projectiles that included mechanical time fuses, the fuse setter set the time as the projectile man received the fifty-six-pound projectile from the mechanical hoist that brought it up from below. The projectile man placed it into the rammer tray in front of the powder case before pulling the rammer lever to send both into the gun's chamber. With the breech block in place sealing off the gun's barrel, the powder could safely be ignited, the resulting explosion hurling the projectile out the open end of the barrel and (hopefully) on to its intended target.

The intended targets determined the type of projectile to be used. High-capacity (HC) projectiles were designed for use against unarmored surface targets, shore installations, and personnel, while armor-piercing (AP) projectiles included special delayed fuses that allowed them to first penetrate armor before detonating. Other specialized projectiles included illumination rounds that shed light in nighttime engagements by lofting parachute-equipped flares into the night sky, antiaircraft rounds designed to spread clouds of shrapnel among enemy aircraft, dummy rounds for drill purposes, and others.

After the gun fired and the empty powder case was ejected, the hot case man, wearing a bulky pair of asbestos gloves, would retrieve the now very hot case and dispose of it through an opening in the rear deck of the mount.

With these casings pouring out of the bottom of the mount, the weather deck could soon become crowded with empty cases during a prolonged engagement, sometimes requiring sailors to jettison them while exposing themselves to hostile fire.

Below the gun mount was the upper handling room and, below that, the magazines. Third Class Gunner's Mate Lloyd Campbell, whose battle station was in the upper handling room below Bob Hollenbaugh's Mount 54, remembered that "hefting those projectiles could really take it out of a fella. It could get mighty hot in there and it was no place for anybody with claustrophobia." (Author's note: As a seventeen-year-old gunner's mate striker, I spent time in the powder magazine deep in the hull of a destroyer similar to *Johnston*, where I was acutely aware that a layer of steel was all that separated me from the ocean's depths, and where the pungent odor emitted by the powder combined with the ship's considerable motion as she climbed and plunged through a heavy sea made retaining my lunch a notable challenge.) When the gun fired, Campbell recalled, "you could feel it in your bones, but I figured it was even scarier for the poor bastards who were on the receiving end."

Besides the five mounts that made up the main battery, *Johnston* bristled with 40-mm and 20-mm guns in open mounts at various locations around the ship. Bill Mercer worked in the ship's laundry as his "day job," but when the ship went to general quarters, his battle station was the trainer on the twin 40-mm gun on the port side, just forward of and one level below the bridge. It was a vantage point that allowed him to hear some of what was happening on the bridge, including the captain's or the officer of the deck's orders and some of their conversations if they were out on the port bridge wing. When much of the crew often had little or no idea what was going on, Mercer could collect some scuttlebutt (a Navy term for "rumors") to share with his chums in the laundry or on the mess deck. While he enjoyed having this vantage point, he also realized that his battle station might not be the best place to be during battle, since he assumed the bridge would be one of the prime targets for enemy guns or bombs. After the war he recalled, "Unlike the 5-inch guns, we had no mount to hide in. We were out there in the open, which was a swell place to be in good weather when nobody was shooting at you, but sometimes I wished I could trade places with Chuck [Gunner's Mate Third Class Lloyd C. Campbell], who at least had some steel around him."

Besides the pointer and trainer, the gun was crewed by five other men: the gun captain, two first loaders, and two second loaders. Like the 5-inch guns, Mercer's 40-mm could be controlled locally or by Mk 51 directors perched on the roof above the pilothouse. In local control, Mercer and the pointer would work together to control the gun with individual handwheels, aiming through gunsights mounted at eye level. "It wasn't so hard—although pretty damned scary—when the Jap planes were coming right at us, but when they were moving sideways, we had to really crank those wheels to keep up with them."

When the two-man director crew took control of the guns, Mercer and the pointer had nothing to do but be ready to serve as backup should the director fail. The loaders, however, would remain very busy during the firing of the guns, whether in local or director control, feeding the two-pound rounds in clips of four as fast as they could.

Each of the twin 40-mms fired 160 rounds per minute, per barrel, with an approximate effective range of about four thousand yards. Ready service ammunition was held in nearby lockers and in racks welded to the inside of the "gun tub," which had a low steel bulwark built around the gun.

The ship's seven 20-mm guns had no directors and relied solely on the solitary gunner for aiming and firing. Purely mechanical weapons with no power requirements, these relatively small guns—known as "Oerlikons" after the Swiss manufacturer that made them—could be bolted to the deck almost anywhere there was a space for them. Primarily used to shoot down enemy aircraft at close range, by mid-1943 they were gaining a reputation for ineffectiveness against heavier attacking aircraft. Back in San Diego, Bill Mercer had shared a few drinks with a sailor he knew only as "Jake," a second-class gunner's mate from a tin can that had seen action in the Solomons. Jake had said, "When the Oerlikons start firing, it's time to dive for cover."

Understandably biased, Bob Hollenbaugh would often argue that the 5-inch guns were the most important weapons on the ship, but he had to admit that the torpedoes "gave more bang for the buck." Unlike the guns, which could only hit those parts of enemy ships that were above the waterline, *Johnston*'s Mk 15s could deliver a "wallop below the waterline where the damage was most likely to be fatal." *Johnston* carried ten torpedoes—five in each of the two mounts that were located on the centerline, one between the two stacks and the other just aft of after stack. They could be trained out to either side of the ship and could be fired individually or in salvo. Despite his concession to the effectiveness of the torpedoes, Hollenbaugh would be sure to point out that "ten of them could run out quickly, but we gunners had a lot more stamina."

In the wardroom one evening after the evening meal back in San Diego, Ed Digardi listened as the captain and the gunnery officer discussed the importance of torpedoes. Evans was sitting at the head of the table, something he did not always do. Bob Hagen had once remarked that Evans was unusual in that regard—that most destroyer captains consistently sat at either the head of the table or, "like Jesus at the Last Supper," in the middle. But Evans often took the nearest seat upon entering the wardroom or sometimes took the one closest to the coffee pots on the narrow counter next to the galley door. Hagen thought that said something good about Evans—that he was not too impressed by his exalted station. Very different from his previous experience.

Evans recalled that in the Java Sea, *Alden*'s guns ("peashooters," he called them) were all but useless against the Japanese, and it was her torpedoes that had at least gotten the Japanese to turn away. Hagen said that at Guadalcanal, he had seen the *Barton* (DD 599) get hit by two Japanese long-lance torpedoes, break in two, and go down with 80 percent of her crew. His ship, *Aaron Ward*, had been unable to get her torpedoes off before being disabled by Japanese gunfire, something he often thought about with regret. "We thought we had a shot to port," he recalled, "but then a lookout spotted [the heavy cruiser] *San Francisco* [CA 38] too close to the target to risk a shot. And then *Sterrett* [DD 407] appeared out of nowhere, forcing us to turn hard to port to keep from colliding with her. A real SNAFU [Situation Normal, All Fouled Up—and sometimes "fouled" is replaced by another word]," he concluded.

Digardi felt a sense of comfort listening to these two combat veterans. He was glad that the number one and number three officers in the ship were not "amateurs" like himself. He also understood why GQ Johnny made countless mock torpedo runs under Evans' watchful eye.

The last components of *Johnston*'s weapons package were the depth charges, designed to kill submarines. Two racks on the ship's fantail each held eight 600-pound depth charges that were rolled down the racks and dropped into the ship's wake, where they would explode at predetermined depths. Two adjacent storage racks held five more.

Abreast the after superstructure were six "K-gun" throwers, three on each side, with five 300-pound depth charges ready to be hurled away from the ship's side before descending to destroy their prey.

All these weapons—guns, torpedoes, and depth charges—gave *Johnston* an impressive offensive capability under the right circumstances. But as Chief Burnett often told his men, "She's no battleship, boys. They don't call these buckets 'tin cans' for nothing. All that paint we slapped on her is not the same as armor. When the shooting starts, keep your helmet on and your life jacket handy."

CHAPTER 6

FIRST CONTACT

By early 1944, the U.S. Navy had amassed a substantial amount of hard-fought combat experience. The aerial clashes at Coral Sea and Midway had finally stopped the forward progress of the Japanese juggernaut and were followed by the yearlong close-run campaign in the Solomons, in which the Americans under Admiral William F. "Bull" Halsey had ultimately won the war of attrition that cost both sides many ships, aircraft, and men. With the Japanese retreating in the Solomons and General Douglas MacArthur continuing his separate campaign in the Southwest Pacific, Admiral Chester Nimitz began his Central Pacific campaign by first taking Tarawa in the Gilberts, a very bloody and costly assault from which many hard-earned lessons were gleaned. As January ushered in the new year of 1944, it was time to move on to a new chain of islands.

On the morning of 21 January 1944, the sound of anchor chains rattling through hawsepipes carried across the water as *Johnston* and the other ships of TF 53 dropped their anchors in Auhu channel off Lahaina, Hawaii. The eight-day transit from the West Coast had been largely uneventful. When not taking part in exercises conducted by the task force or screen commanders, GQ Johnny continued to train and drill under the critical eye of Bob Hagen.

Johnston's war diary recorded that the drills were "excellent" and "made impression on crew of the seriousness of our mission."

Once anchored, Evans disappeared into his cabin for a time, emerging just before lunch in a fresh uniform. After eating, he lingered in the wardroom for a time, sipping coffee and thumbing through a six-month-old *Life* magazine with cowboy Roy Rogers and his palomino Trigger on the cover.

Ed Digardi, who was seated at the other end of the wardroom table with a stack of papers in front of him, wanted to ask him what he should do with a box of radio tubes that had arrived addressed to the destroyer *Dale*. But Digardi had grown accustomed to seeing his captain on the bridge, always calm but ever vigilant, and seeing him now, apparently relaxing, Digardi could not bring himself to interrupt that unusual moment.

Digardi was clearly in awe of Evans. But he also liked him. Beneath that aura of self-confidence, he detected a man who was aware of his own limitations, always striving to improve on them while tolerant of the shortcomings of others, as long as they too were striving to improve. He was often loud when giving orders, but it never sounded like yelling. Digardi had heard the tales of junior officers from other ships describing their captains as "screamers," but it would never have occurred to him to describe Evans that way. His self-assuredness never seemed imperious and was reassuring in its own way. By now Digardi was aware of the reality of the dangers that might lie ahead, but he felt his odds of surviving were enhanced by serving under Ernest Evans.

After another quarter hour, Evans put down the magazine, looked over at Digardi with a wry smile, and said, "Off to see the Wizard." Digardi knew from reading the message traffic that morning that Evans was actually headed for the light cruiser *Santa Fe* for a commanders' conference with Rear Admiral Laurence DuBose, Commander of Task Unit 53.5.2. Wanting to let Evans know he was staying up on things, Digardi said, "Headed for *Sante Fe*, sir?" and immediately regretted it, feeling it was transparent what he was up to. But Evans smiled and nodded as he said, "Admiral DuBose was teaching at the Academy when I was there." Picking up his cap and heading for the wardroom door, he added, "We'll see how much the old man has aged since then." Two minutes later, the 1MC announced, "*Johnston* departing," and a subsequent bell signaled that Evans had left the ship.

The war in the Pacific had come a long way by the time USS *Johnston* was about to see her first combat. Since Evans had barely escaped from the Java Sea in those early days when the Japanese so thoroughly held the upper hand, the U.S. Navy had rebounded. Of special significance, the American war machine had ramped up into full gear, producing ships, aircraft, and weapons at astounding rates. At Midway, Rear Admirals Frank Jack Fletcher and Raymond Spruance had only three carriers available for that crucial battle; now—just eighteen months later—Vice Admiral Spruance commanded the Fifth Fleet, which included twelve carriers as well as many battleships, cruisers, and destroyers and countless transports and amphibious vessels.

Despite these impressive changes, there was still a lot of war to be fought. For those who consulted them, maps of the Pacific did not alleviate that anxiety by revealing how many Japanese-held bastions lay ahead on the road to Tokyo.

Indeed, as Admiral Nimitz met with his subordinates to plan the next step in the campaign, he was met with a notable degree of caution as they urged him to proceed conservatively. With Nimitz contemplating a move into the Marshall Islands, Vice Admiral Raymond Spruance, Marine Major General Holland Smith, and Rear Admiral Richmond Kelly Turner pointed out that unlike the Gilberts, which had been occupied at the beginning of the war, the Marshalls had been in Japanese possession since 1914, giving them much more time to build up their defenses there. Whereas the Japanese had built only one airstrip in the Gilberts, in the Marshalls they had built six.

While Kwajalein Atoll was a tempting target, it was also a daunting one. Roughly shaped like Florida, it was the world's largest coral atoll, containing nearly a hundred islands and islets surrounding a massive lagoon of 839 square miles. The Japanese had located their principal naval base on Kwajalein Island at the southeastern tip of the atoll and had constructed a major airbase on the connecting islands of Roi and Namur on the northeastern end, as well as a seaplane base on Ebeye just north of Kwajalein Island. Nimitz's three advisers urged him to hold off invading Kwajalein until they could first seize two of the smaller outer islands, Wotje and Maloelap. Nimitz, however, was

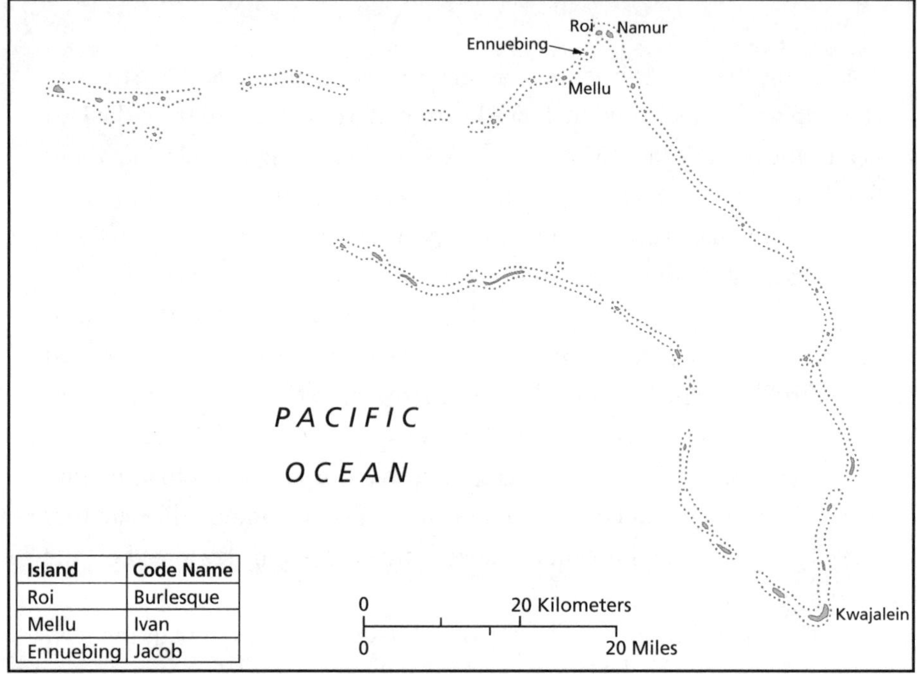

Island	Code Name
Roi	Burlesque
Mellu	Ivan
Ennuebing	Jacob

MAP 2 • Kwajalein Atoll

not swayed by their concerns and ordered them to go straight to Kwajalein, pausing only to take undefended Majuro Island, about 350 miles southeast of Kwajalein; the lagoon there would provide an anchorage for the mobile service squadron (oilers, ammunition ships, and others needed for logistical support). Nimitz told Spruance and the others to then proceed to attack the strongholds at the northern and southern ends of the atoll.

The Southern Attack Force (Task Force 52) would take Kwajalein Island and the nearby island of Ebeye. The Northern Attack Force (Task Force 53)—which included *Johnston*—was tasked with taking Roi and Namur Islands to neutralize the air facilities there. The Fifth Fleet's four fast carrier task groups would attack and neutralize those Japanese airfields in the eastern Marshalls that most threatened the planned assault on Kwajalein Atoll. Plans made, it was time for Task Force 53 to leave Hawaiian waters and make the two-thousand-mile transit to the designated targets in the Marshalls.

Two hours after his departure for the conference in *Santa Fe*, Evans returned to the ship and disappeared into his cabin briefly before calling a meeting of the officers in the wardroom. His mood was obviously good as he started off with a joke—something about Marines and sailors on liberty together. The story was lost on Bob Hagen, who was keyed up thinking about the coming operation. He focused when Evans said, "Gentlemen, it looks like we are going to finally bring our weapons to bear on the enemy." He was looking at his gunnery officer as he spoke.

"We have been ordered to a place called Kwajalein in the Marshalls, to participate in an amphibious landing," he said. "Code name is Operation Flintlock. We'll be screening the Northern Attack Force against subs during the transit to the objective area, and then we'll be shelling Jap defenses before and during the Marine landing. The flyboys have been hitting the Jap air bases for some time now, so we don't expect many problems from Jap aircraft, but you never know . . . I expect you to urge upon your men that this is the real thing. We will continue to take advantage of the time during transit to exercise and go over the operation order"—he nodded toward the XO, who waved a stack of paper—"but when we get to the objective, the time for training will be over and the time for killing will have arrived." With that, he took a moment to make eye contact with each man in the room—Hagen remembered it as "intense"—then left the wardroom without another word.

That evening, *Johnston* shifted colors and made the short trip to moor alongside the oiler *Chikaskia* to refuel. Evans had the conn as *Johnston* approached the oiler's port side with a light wind just off the starboard bow. Ed Digardi noted that even though *Chikaskia* appeared to be pretty new—no telltale streaks of rust at her scuppers—the smell of fuel oil was strong as they closed the distance. He saw a young ensign standing at one of the fueling stations, his khaki uniform speckled with dark stains that he assumed were splashes of oil, and Digardi was glad to be serving in a destroyer.

The refueling began as soon as they could get the hoses across and lasted nearly two hours. With Evans again at the conn, *Johnston* returned to berth A-31 in the Auhu Channel to spend her last night in Hawaiian waters.

The next day Evans attended another conference, this one convened by the screen commander, that met on board the destroyer *Morris* (DD 417). When he returned to his ship, he again called the officers to the wardroom and this time explained what to expect during the two-thousand-plus-mile voyage from Hawaii to Kwajalein. Most of it centered on antisubmarine warfare (ASW), but he also told Hagen to use the transit time to have the gun crews run loading drills as much as practicable.

That night Evans optimistically confided to his official war diary that the crew "is in capable condition and the ship ready to do its part. It is surprising how fast the crew has shaken down." Three days later—in contrast to his war diary entry of 2 January, which had described his crew as "slow in becoming war conscious"—Evans now recorded that "much anxiety reigns, but the crew is conscious of the importance of this operation."

Seaman Harley Chronister was one of those crew members who felt that anxiety Evans had acknowledged in his war diary, but he also wanted to "do something that counted." Like many of his shipmates, he was anxious to see "some real action," to trade all those countless hours of training for the chance to do "something *real*." He knew all the practice was a good thing, but he was weary of the mind-numbing repetition and the lack of tangible results. He had never cared much for studying for tests while in school, preferring to "just get it over with." But he also knew that failing a math test in school was not the same thing as failing to perform in battle; both were undesirable, but failing in battle had much more serious consequences.

Besides his not wanting to die or suffer serious injury, there was something else at stake, something he was surprised he felt. "I didn't want to let down my shipmates," he recalled years later. "Some of them were my pals, so of course I felt like that, but some of them I didn't even like very much, but I had somehow changed since going through boot camp and becoming part of GQ Johnny's crew. I knew we had to stick together if we were going to make it." He also felt a kind of obligation to Chief Burnett, who had always treated him kindly while pushing him to do better. "And then there was the captain," he added. "In a way, he was kinda scary—all the officers were somewhat—but he also made you feel safe because he seemed so capable. You felt like he would know what to do if things got bad."

Ed Digardi had similar feelings about Evans, but Bob Hagen—who had seen serious combat before coming to *Johnston*—had once confided that even though he agreed that the captain seemed completely competent, he worried about Evans' determination to "go in harm's way" as he had promised during the commissioning ceremony. Hagen told Digardi that when Evans had followed up that promise by pointing to the ship's gangway and inviting anyone who did not want to go with him to leave the ship now, there was a part of him that wanted "to take the skipper up on his invitation." Digardi acknowledged that Hagen's combat experience gave him a different and certainly valid point of view, but he said he was glad to have Evans in command, adding, "Whether we like it or not, it's our lot to be caught up in this war, and I would much rather face it with Evans than some of the other men I've seen wearing three stripes." Hagen agreed but said, "I just hope that the skipper remembers what happened to Custer." Realizing the irony in light of Evans' Native American heritage, both men laughed.

It seemed to Chief Burnett that "there were ships everywhere" as they made their way from Hawaii to the Marshalls. As part of the Northern Support Group (TG 53.5), *Johnston* was one of nine destroyers escorting three battleships, two heavy cruisers, three light cruisers, and nine LCIs (landing craft, infantry). Burnett marveled at the latter vessels that an admiral had once called the "waterbug Navy," a nickname that stuck. Indeed, these diminutive vessels were less than half *Johnston*'s length, and during amphibious landings they scurried about, transporting two hundred troops to the beach, extracting casualties, and ferrying supplies. Their small size and flat bottoms made them barely seaworthy, and as a boatswain's mate, Burnett admired but did not envy the sailors who crewed them.

A half hour into the morning watch on 31 January, Burnett had given up on sleep and, armed with two cups of hot coffee, entered the pilot house. *Johnston* was steaming independently, en route to her assigned station off Mellu Island—code named Ivan in Operation Order A157-44—to provide naval gunfire support to the Marines who would be landing there. As he expected, Burnett found Evans awake in his captain's chair on the starboard side of the pilot house and offered him one of the coffees, which the captain took, nodding his thanks.

As *Johnston*'s senior enlisted man, Burnett regularly kept Evans apprised of the crew's morale. He told the captain that the men were keenly aware that they were in enemy territory, alert to the possibility of air or submarine attack, but handling it well. Most were eager to "lose their virginity" (as one of the gunner's mates put it) by firing on the enemy. He was a little concerned that a few of the younger men seemed a bit too keen, but he had assigned several of the more senior petty officers to keep an eye on them. Evans listened, responding "Good" only once as Burnett continued to report.

As Burnett retrieved the captain's empty coffee cup and prepared to leave, Evans asked, "How's Chronister doing? Keeping his meals down?"

One of the things that Burnett admired about Evans was his detailed knowledge of the crew. "He's doing fine, Sir. Carries a stack of saltines with him a lot of the time."

Evans smiled but said nothing more. Burnett left the pilot house in pursuit of more coffee.

In radio and radar silence, the ship had been steering southeasterly since 0255, when they had been detached from screening the larger ships of the task group. Weapons stations were manned, all four boilers were on line, and battle dress was the prevailing fashion. The wind had been rising and was nearing twenty knots as the ship neared the westward side of Roi Island. "Looks like the Marines are going to have a rough ride," Evans said to Ed Digardi, who had the conn. Both men were on the port bridge wing scanning the sea off the port bow.

"Yes, sir," Digardi agreed, peering through his binoculars. A gibbous moon provided enough light for him to see shapes forming on the water ahead. He could make out a half-dozen ships he presumed to be the landing ships (LSTs) strung out on a north–south line, and he did not care for what he saw. He requested Evans' permission to light off the radar. "Granted," Evans replied, and a minute later Digardi was leaning over the glowing scope, where he saw Roi Island blossoming brightly on each pass of the rotating radar beam. He also saw a line of short blips on the scope, corresponding to the shapes he had assumed were the LSTs. Returning to the port bridge wing, he reported what he had seen to Evans. "Captain," he said, "I don't believe those LSTs are as far west as they are supposed to be. They aren't leaving much room for us to get by Burlesque [the code name for Roi Island] to take our firing position off Ivan [Mellu]."

Mellu Island was about three and a half miles southwest of Roi. If *Johnston* steered east of the landing ships, they would come perilously close to the westward side of Roi, within easy range of the Japanese shore batteries that aerial reconnaissance had sighted there. But if they went around to the safer westward side of the LSTs, they would not arrive on station on time for their assigned gunfire support mission. To Digardi, it was evident that they were going to have to be late, and he recommended coming right to a new course of two-six-zero.

"Negative," Evans said. "Come left to one-niner-five," he added.

Digardi did as he was told, then moved to the small plotting table on the port side of the pilot house. Wielding his dividers and parallel rulers on the nautical chart taped to the tabletop, he calculated that they would pass within three thousand yards of the westward side of Roi. He passed that information to Evans, who matter-of-factly replied, "Very well."

As the ship drew closer to the island, Digardi joined the captain on the port wing of the bridge and could see faint white lines off to port as the sea washed over the coral wall that marked the outer edge of the atoll. He couldn't believe how close they were, and he felt sure the Japanese guns would commence firing at them any second now.

Evans stepped into the pilot house and lifted one of the sound-powered handsets from its cradle. Speaking to Bob Hagen in the gun director just above them, he said, "Train all five mounts to port." Almost immediately, Digardi saw the forward two mounts swing rapidly around so that their barrels were pointing eastward. He felt certain that other barrels were pointed in the opposite direction, and he wanted very much to duck below the solid metal apron in front of him. But he remained upright and, using the brass speaking tube in front of him, needlessly said, "Mind your helm" to the young seaman who was steering the ship inside the pilot house. "Helm, aye," the sailor replied, his eyes locked on the compass before him and his voice sounding no different than usual. There was something reassuring in that brief exchange, and Digardi, realizing that he had been holding his breath, forced himself to take a healthy draught of the salt-laden air.

"I guess the Japs are still asleep," Evans said, his voice calm as ever. "Maybe too much sake last night."

"Maybe so, sir," Digardi replied, not believing it but trying to match his captain's placidity. Through his binoculars, he could make out the dark shape of the island but could discern no details. He thought he saw a glimmer of light at one point but decided he had imagined it.

Dropping the binoculars to his chest, he scanned the sea ahead and then peered aft. He was reassured by *Johnston*'s churning wake, a sign that the ship was moving at good speed. But then he felt uneasy as he realized the frothing water was reflecting the ambient light, leaving a glowing white streak on the black water, something the enemy could use in targeting the ship. He turned to scan ahead, trying to ignore the looming dark shape to port.

A quarter hour passed with no enemy gunfire. Digardi couldn't believe their luck. They were so close and yet the Japs had held their fire. Maybe they could see *Johnston*'s 5-inch guns and were chastened by them. He really doubted that they were asleep. Whatever the reason, Digardi was not disappointed. He felt a rush of exhilaration as he watched Roi receding off the port quarter, still quiet.

As they continued heading southward, gradually coming right to avoid the atoll that now extended southwestward, Digardi looked to starboard and, seeing the LSTs west of them, he wondered what their crews must be thinking, watching this crazy destroyer in so close to this island incongruously called "Burlesque." Nothing funny or alluring about that place, he thought.

As he watched Evans scan the sea ahead, that half-smile bending the edges of his dark mustache, Digardi realized that his exhilaration had been replaced by a more sobering thought that this captain had been entirely honest when, back in Seattle a few long months ago, he had told his crew, "I intend to go in harm's way."

The sun pierced the horizon at 0602 on 1 February, its rays fanning out in a way that was a bit too suggestive of the Japanese naval ensign. Soon after, the sun was absorbed into a low-hanging overcast that threatened rain. After clearing the LSTs, *Johnston* took up her position in Fire Support Area 6. As they drew closer to the western side of Ivan, it was apparent that it was a mere islet. Digardi noted that it was cloaked in green with palm and breadfruit trees shading a thick undergrowth that looked like the shaggy carpet in his grandmother's living room.

At 0652 the quartermaster's deck log entry read, "Commenced firing on Mellu Island bearing 128° 3300 yards." Indeed, all five of *Johnston*'s 5-inch guns fired in unison as Bob Hagen closed the firing key in his director. The ship shuddered markedly as the broadside erupted, hurling high-capacity rounds at the hapless little island.

Bob Hollenbaugh raised his head out of the hatch on top of Mount 54 and, through his binoculars, watched for the fall of shot. His nostrils filled with the pungent smell of cordite, and he felt heat on his face and hands. Puffs of smoke popped up from the island's undergrowth, and seconds later he heard the muffled thump of the exploding rounds come back across the water, in contrast to the sharp bang of the outgoing blast. He felt the mount jerk suddenly to the right as Hagen made his adjustments for the next salvo. Someone on the sound-powered circuit said, "We're in the war now, fellas."

On the bridge, both Evans and Digardi likewise peered through their binoculars. Countless drills were at last vindicated as GQ Johnny delivered ordnance on the enemy, and Digardi felt an electric exhilaration as he saw the rounds impacting Ivan. He suspected that the captain felt something similar. For a brief moment, he felt a trace of shame for feeling so happy about raining such violence on other men, but it quickly passed as he countered with the knowledge that they were the enemy by their own choosing and had earned his retribution. He also knew they would not hesitate to do the same to him and his shipmates.

Robert Clare, a member of repair party 1, was not so much impressed by his own ship's firing at the enemy shore; he was much more concerned about

IMAGE 11 • Fires burning on one of the Marshall islets in the Kwajalein Atoll as U.S. forces attack early in the Central Pacific campaign

the high-caliber rounds passing overhead as the battleships, farther out, had joined the fray. He later remembered "hoping those gunners knew what they were aiming at because we were in so close to the beach."

Despite having been in combat before—much more serious combat than this—Bob Hagen was glad to be shooting without fleet training observers looking over his shoulder and not having to worry about his rounds coming too close to a target-towing tug or straying off a practice gun range. It was a liberating feeling to be "focusing on hitting things without having to worry about *not* hitting things."

From his seat on the port side of Mount 54, Bobby Chastain peered out through the small port in front of him as the mount swiveled slightly to the right. He couldn't see much but noted that, in contrast to the gloomy interior of the mount, it was very bright outside despite the overcast. Behind him, he heard a projectile being slammed into the gun tray and the telltale *whoosh* as it and the powder case were rammed home. Seconds later, he could feel a powerful jolt and heard the loud clap as GQ Johnny delivered a second salvo. He glanced over his right shoulder and saw the freckle-faced hot case man lunge for the powder case as it leaped from the now-open breech and clattered onto the mount's deck. Having seized the hot metal in his asbestos-gloved hands, the boy quickly dropped it through the open trap door to the weather deck outside.

Johnston closed to two thousand yards off the beach while continuing to fire her main battery of 5-inch guns. Through his telescopic sight in the director, Hagen saw two Japanese breastworks disintegrate under his fire. He continued the barrage—pausing only once for eight minutes while a carrier-based air strike pummeled the island. At 0749, he ceased firing the 5-inchers and turned the show over to the 40-mm guns. They pounded away for about ten minutes, giving the 5-inch gun crews a brief rest. Then Hagen recommenced the barrage with the bigger guns.

There did not appear to be much to shoot at on the island—just a few minor structures scattered at uneven intervals. The Japanese did not return fire, and only one secondary explosion occurred when an observation tower on the south end of the island received a direct hit from a 5-inch round. Digardi saw what he was sure was a human body thrown upward from the blast; it sailed over some nearby treetops before disappearing into the dunes.

At 0825, Evans ordered ceasefire and brought the ship about to clear the area for the scheduled landing of Marines at H-Hour. Although they were an hour late arriving and there was initially considerable confusion, waves of landing craft filled the sea approaches to Ivan. The roar of diesel engines replaced the cacophony of gunfire. Evans had been right in his earlier prediction that the Marines were in for a rough ride to the beach. The nineteen-knot wind had kicked up significant swells that reduced the speed of the LVTs (Landing Vehicle, Tracked) to about half and made for a bone-jarring, nausea-inducing trip.

The area now crowded with landing craft, *Johnston* withdrew and joined the ships of Fire Support Unit 2. The ship secured from general quarters and set Readiness Condition 2-M. (Conditions of Readiness specify a ship's readiness for battle in terms of what stations are manned and the state of the ship's weapons. In World War II there were three main conditions and several modifications for specific circumstances. Condition 1 was the highest condition of readiness, with all battle stations manned and alert, and ammunition ready for instant loading or preloaded as ordered of the commanding officer. Condition 2 specified one-quarter to one-third [depending on arrangements of batteries and personnel available] of main, secondary, and antiaircraft gun and automatic weapon batteries manned [on a rotational basis], and fire control, combat information center, and communications manned for immediate use. Condition 3 assumed a lower level of risk—allowing main and secondary batteries to not be manned but requiring that antiaircraft gun and automatic weapon batteries be manned on a rotational basis. Conditions could be modified depending on circumstances; for example, "Condition 1-A" applied to loaded transports, freighters, landing ships, and landing craft and added requirements pertaining to disembarkation, while "Condition 1-AA" appropriately lessened the Condition 1 requirements except for the possibility of air attack. "Condition 2-M" as indicated in *Johnston*'s after-action report does not appear in the tactical doctrine of the time, but some sources indicate it may have applied to the possibility of gas attack.) For the rest of the day, she screened the main body as the small aircraft carriers (CVEs) assigned to the group launched and recovered aircraft to provide air support to the ongoing landing. In the relative quiet of screening duty, many of the crew were besieged by a postadrenaline lethargy that made it difficult to stay awake as they patrolled the open sea around the larger ships. More than once during the afternoon watch, Lieutenant (jg) Ellsworth (Els) Welch caught himself drifting off even though he was on his feet. His mind kept drifting back to his home in California and to that first night in Washington when the crew had turned the commissioning ball into a brawl. How far they had come since then! How long ago that seemed!

As the day wore on, the ship got a freshwater washdown as she passed through several intermittent squalls. Visibility was temporarily reduced to the extent that some of the crew felt all alone on the vast sea, despite the knowledge that they were part of a great armada.

As night fell, the moon could not penetrate the overcast, so it was very dark except for occasional flashes of lightning and the flicker of gunfire from one of the destroyers up to the north of them. It was unclear what she was firing at, but it continued intermittently for several hours into the midwatch. Some of the crew found it unnerving, but Seaman Harley Chronister found it somewhat reassuring, as he assumed the Japanese were getting the worst of it. The baritone rumble of the distant gunfire mixed with the sporadic thunder to create an unusual low-frequency chorus that could be felt as much as heard. All in all, though, it was a quiet night compared to the raucous gunfire and deafening roar of landing craft engines during the day.

At 0652 daybreak brought a new assignment. *Johnston* was ordered to follow a line of LSTs into the lagoon in preparation for an assault on Roi and Namur from the lagoon side of the islands. The Japanese had fortified the seaward side of the island more heavily than the lagoon side, so attacking from there made good tactical sense. After seizing Ivan and Jacob (another islet in the chain delineating the westward side of the lagoon) the day before, the Marines had set up artillery on the two islets to ensure a safe passage through the two passes of the same names.

Johnston followed the group of LSTs entering the lagoon through Ivan Pass. After a delay caused by some of the LSTs stopping in the narrowest part of the channel to offload their amphibious tractors (amtracs), Evans took his ship into the passage, relying on his sonar to locate and avoid the reefs that hid beneath the surface. As they passed from the open sea into the lagoon at about 0815, the color of the water changed to a much brighter blue, reminding Digardi of the swimming pool where he spent part of his summers while in high school. It was inviting but harrowing when he could clearly see some of the menacing reefs dangerously close in the clear water. He was glad that Evans had the conn, the captain calm as ever as they snaked their way through the narrow passage.

Once in the lagoon, Evans headed the ship to their assigned station in Fire Support Area Five Alpha, five thousand yards south of Namur Island, the easternmost of the two objective islands. As they crossed the lagoon, Evans continued to rely on his sonar and ordered Lieutenant Elton Stirling, the officer of the deck, and the XO, Lieutenant Commander Howard Baker, to position themselves on top of the bridge to give them a good perch from which to spot the numerous coral heads in the area. As the ship threaded its way among those obstacles, other lookouts scanned the beach watching for enemy fire.

When the ship was within forty-seven hundred yards of the Namur beach, Evans gave the order to commence firing, and with all five mounts in director control, Hagen began to pummel the Japanese coastal defense and antiaircraft guns that he could see through his range finder. The destroyer *LaVallette* was about five hundred yards off *Johnston*'s stern, and she also opened fire.

Reconnaissance photographs taken earlier by carrier aircraft showed a small blockhouse east of a pier extending into the lagoon. The photos revealed what appeared to be a 90-mm gun bearing into the lagoon, and this had been designated as the first target. Hagen scored a direct hit on his third salvo, and the blockhouse was destroyed. He then turned his attention to other structures visible along the south shore of the island and worked his way to the southeast point, destroying several other blockhouses and a number of pillboxes.

At just before 1000, Hagen poured a full salvo into a blockhouse with no apparent results. As he peered into his rangefinder preparing to deliver another salvo, the blockhouse "exploded in my face." It literally disappeared in a tremendous explosion that was so powerful that the *Johnston*'s official report recorded, "It is believed that several of the battleship and cruiser spotting planes were knocked out of the air." This was later refuted by Admiral Oldendorf in his endorsement as commander of Task Force 53.5, saying that it was several palm trees that had been blown into the air and were mistaken for low-flying aircraft.

Another blockhouse seemed impervious to the half-dozen direct hits that Hagen delivered, while yet another could be seen burning through holes in its walls. This one eventually exploded as well, but not with the same force as the earlier one.

Calling a temporary ceasefire at 1002 while U.S. aircraft bombed and strafed the island, Evans maneuvered *Johnston* even closer to the beach and dropped anchor a mere two thousand yards from the enemy-infested

IMAGE 12 • A Japanese signal tower projects above the thick foliage on one of the islets in Kwajalein Atoll. U.S. Marines can be seen on the beach.

shore. Although anchored, he continued to use his engines to keep the ship parallel to the shore.

During the lull in firing, a sailor in the radio shack played a big band song, "Sleepy Lagoon," on the 1MC for all to hear. Evans smiled.

At one point, from his flagship USS *Appalachian*, Rear Admiral Richard L. Conolly, CTF 53 (Commander Task Force 53—Northern Attack Force), called for counterfire on enemy forces that were operating from the southeast point of Namur. Evans complied, again using *Johnston*'s engines to keep the ship broadside to the beach so that all the 5-inch guns were unmasked and able to deliver rapid, continuous fire until the enemy's guns fell silent.

While serving in the Mediterranean theater, Admiral Conolly had earned the nickname "Close-In Conolly," and it was clear that Evans took that to heart. Crew members stationed topside could see how close they were to the enemy shoreline, and some were nervous. From his battle station as trainer on the twin 40-mm gun just below the bridge on the port side, Bill Mercer felt "very naked and exposed as the skipper kept us broadside to the beach. Seemed like we must've made one big, tempting target for the Japs. I wanted to crawl up inside my helmet."

Mercer was soon distracted from those harrowing thoughts when, at 1114, the 5-inch guns fell silent and his 40-mm slewed around to face the shore. Hagen, now in control of the smaller-caliber guns, began firing at human targets who could be seen scurrying about among the piles of rubble that had been pillboxes and buildings just two hours before. With their twin barrels pumping in and out, alternately spewing rounds at a furious rate, the "pom poms" (as they were sometimes called) responded to Hagen's aim from his Mk 37 director, causing Mercer's mount to lurch violently at times as the gun boss adjusted his fire in pursuit of rapidly moving targets ashore. With Hagen in control, Mercer had little to do, and he felt sorry for the loaders who were laboring mightily to feed the hungry guns.

Many of the crew were getting into the moment, some of them anxious to participate beyond their normal duties. The men manning the 20-mms on the engaged side of the ship opened up as well. With Chief Burnett's approval, the men in his repair party broke out rifles and, lying prone on the main deck, joined the fray, firing at anything that moved and many things that did not. Els Welch, the junior officer of the deck, unholstered his .45-caliber handgun and began firing toward the beach as well. Evans watched as though amused but said nothing.

At 1120, the 5-inch guns resumed their barrage. A Japanese officer bravely—some would say foolishly—stood up in plain sight and began waving his saber in an apparent attempt to rally his troops. Hagen slewed his director, putting the officer squarely in his sights and closed the firing key. All five guns of the main battery erupted, and the Japanese officer was obliterated. Hagen was pleased when Evans looked up at the director from the bridge wing and said, "Mr. Hagen, that was very good shooting." Still smiling, Evans added, "But in the future, try not to waste so much ammunition on one individual."

Enemy retaliation was not heavy, but the occasional sound of shrapnel rattling against *Johnston*'s superstructure was disconcerting to those who heard it. Bobby Chastain described it as "like hail on a tin roof."

Even here, inside the lagoon, the wind had built a choppy sea and, as the first boat waves loaded with Marines passed by *Johnston* on their way to the island, it was evident that the landing craft were struggling to prevail against the chaotic waves. Chief Burnett watched with empathy as the small craft climbed and lurched and plunged among the rollers and breakers, guessing that many of the Marines would prefer enemy gunfire ashore to the torment of seasickness out there in the angry waters.

Chief Yeoman Joe Woolf, standing next to the captain and taking photographs for the official record, voiced his own and Burnett's thinking by saying aloud, "Why are the jarheads getting out of those amtracs so soon? Wouldn't it be safer to stay inside and let those tractors take them farther across the sand?" Still peering through his binoculars, Evans responded, "Could be they can't wait to get out after that rough ride to shore." Turning to face Woolf, he added, "More likely there is some kind of obstacle like an anti-tank ditch there that we can't see."

As the barrage continued, a few 8-inch rounds from some of the bigger ships farther out fell short of the island and struck the water uncomfortably close to *Johnston*, causing someone on the JL sound-powered phone circuit to mutter, "Whose side are those guys on?"

At 1150, *Johnston* suffered her first casualty. Seaman Second Class Lee Burton was out on the weather deck clearing away shell casings that had accumulated during the heavy firing when he was hit by a shower of shrapnel. Fortunately his wounds were minor, and he was back in the galley preparing meals the next day.

At 1152, Evans ordered all of *Johnston*'s guns to cease firing, and five minutes later the first wave of Marines landed on Namur's beach. There appeared to be little or no resistance as the Marines moved across the beach toward the vegetation line. Most remained upright as they moved forward, and none fell.

As the Marines reached the vegetation line and began disappearing into it, the crackle of small-arms fire and the thump of mortars drifted across the water signaling that the enemy had begun to resist. With the fight moving inland, there was little for *Johnston* and the other fire support ships to do but wait for calls for fire should the Marines need it. As it happened, they would need more than fire support.

At twenty-five, Coxswain Ed Block was older than many of *Johnston*'s crew and had some experience under his belt. He had joined the Navy in February 1940, and after graduating from boot camp in May he was sent to Mare Island, California, to join the crew of a repair ship, USS *Medusa* (AR 1). In the months that followed, rumors of war were heard more and more, and Ed's mother was pleased when he told her that repair ships were not combatants. Almost two years later, *Medusa* had moved to Pearl Harbor, and on a bright sunny Sunday morning, bombs began falling from the sky. He watched through a porthole as planes were blown into the air on nearby Ford Island. On deck, he saw the water around the ship and men engulfed in flames.

He remained in *Medusa* for nearly two more years before receiving orders to *Johnston* six months before her commissioning. Shortly after reporting on board, he was summoned to an upstairs office in the SeaTac shipyard. Knocking on the office door, he heard a deep voice from within telling him to enter. Inside, he was surprised to see the captain sitting on a metal chair, dressed in a T-shirt and a pair of khaki trousers. Wondering if he was in some kind of trouble, he was relieved when Evans said, "I hear you were a barber on your last ship. I could use a haircut." Glad he was not in trouble but still feeling some trepidation, Block gave the captain a haircut, trying to keep his hands from shaking as he worked. Evans did not say much beyond asking what *Medusa* had been like and saying that he too had served in some auxiliaries. When Block had finished, Evans looked into a mirror on the back wall of the office and said, "You've given me a very good haircut." Block quickly replied, "I had to, sir. You're the captain," causing Evans to laugh.

Block had cut the captain's hair many times since that first encounter. Evans did not talk much while Block worked, often reading a mystery novel as the black hair fell onto the yellowed pages. On one occasion just before their arrival at Kwajalein, Evans confided that he had hoped to become a Marine when he was young. Block said he too had thought about joining the Corps but had decided on the Navy, mostly because of his mother. As Evans rose from the chair, brushing away a few stray hairs, he said, "Probably a good choice for both of us."

At just after noon on the day of the invasion of Namur, as *Johnston* lay anchored close in to the south shore of Namur waiting for calls for fire from the Marines ashore, one of the landing craft contacted the ship, reporting that there were six wounded Marines on board in need of medical attention. As the craft approached the ship's port side, the ship's doctor and Pharmacist's Mate Charles Bruce waited for the men to be hoisted aboard and then began caring for them on a triage basis. Five of the wounded Marines had treatable wounds and survived, but one PFC who had been shot in the head lingered unconscious for an hour before succumbing.

From his battle station at the Mk 51 gun director on the bridge, Ed Block could clearly see the wounded men below as they were brought on board and later confided, "To see those young kids laying there all shot up brought tears to my eyes and I cried. But for the grace of God, I could have been one of those kids."

On 4 February, with Roi-Namur secured, Admiral Oldendorf had authorized some of the captains of the bombardment group to go ashore to observe the damage they had done. Just after the noon meal, Evans and Hagen climbed down a Jacob's ladder to the waiting boat that would take them ashore. Chief Yeoman Joe Woolf was already on board, holding tight to a bulky camera as the boat bucked slightly in the swell. They shoved off, and the coxswain steered around *Johnston*'s bow, avoiding the starboard anchor chain that hung almost straight down from the hawsepipe, disappearing into the sparkling water of the lagoon. A school of minnows escorted them for a few yards, then darted away as the boat steadied up and headed toward the remnant of a pier near the southeastern tip of the island.

Evans led the way as they debarked and headed inland. Almost immediately, they had to step over and around the dead bodies of several Japanese that lay baking in the noonday sun. Crabs competed with flies to feast on the corpses, adding to the gruesomeness of the spectacle. Hagen was tempted to search the pockets of one of the less-mutilated bodies for a souvenir, but thought better of it as he drew closer and the unforgettable stench of death assaulted his nostrils.

In the aftermath of the assault, Namur Island was devastated. Where exotic palm trees had previously brushed their fronds against the bright Pacific sky there now remained only jagged stumps. Buildings that must have once seemed protective had been reduced to haphazard piles of rubble. Flames flickered in places and roared in others, the still-brisk wind mercifully dispersing the acrid smoke that rose from these random pyres.

Evans—who had recently been promoted to commander—was wearing his brand-new combination cover with gold braid on the visor. "I plan on staying close to you, sir," Hagen said to Evans, "in case there are any snipers still alive. I figure they are more likely to shoot at the guy with scrambled eggs on his cap." Usually Evans was quick to banter with Hagen, but if Evans heard him on this occasion, he did not respond. He seemed focused on the damage inflicted by *Johnston* and the other ships. As they moved among the shattered structures and the craters left by exploding ordnance, Evans appeared to be analyzing, occasionally looking out to the lagoon where the ships remained at anchorage. He seemed to be evaluating the fall of shot, and more than once pointed at a crater and told Hagen, "That's one of yours." Hagen was not convinced but did not argue.

Moving farther inland, they encountered a small group of Marines sheltering from the midday sun beneath a ragged tarp that had been rigged from the severed trunk of a palm to the side of what had been some sort of maintenance building. Several were eating from their mess kits, and one was cleaning his M-1 rifle. Most did not seem to notice the three sailors, but a baby-faced PFC closest to them jumped to his feet and rendered a salute. Hagen wondered if the boy had looked as terrified when facing the Japanese as he now did at the sight of a Navy commander.

At a little past 1500, they crossed paths with the captain and gunnery officer of the USS *Haraden*, another destroyer that had also bombarded the island. The two captains conferred for several minutes while Hagen wandered off. As he ascended a small berm and peered down the opposite slope, he was dismayed to see a Chevrolet sedan incongruously parked on the edge of what had been a road. Riddled with bullet and shrapnel holes and showing more rust than paint, the old car was nonetheless a nostalgic reminder of the very different world that Hagen had left behind. He climbed into the driver's seat and had Chief Woolf photograph him there, leaning out the window and smiling as though he were headed for a movie date back home.

Leaving the Chevy behind, he and Woolf found Evans, now alone, again surveying the pockmarked landscape. After a few more minutes, Evans had apparently seen enough, and the three returned to the boat waiting for them at the drooping pier. They were back on board *Johnston* in time for the evening meal. The XO was waiting for them at the quarterdeck holding the OPORDER for the next assault—another island in the Marshalls chain called Eniwetok.

The next day Evans submitted a report addressed to the Commander in Chief of the United States Fleet—Admiral Ernest J. King—via the chain of command, which required five endorsements on its way to the top. The day before, Hagen had "felt like a tourist" strolling around Namur Island with his skipper and Chief Woolf, but apparently Evans did not share those feelings. His report informed his superiors that he "had inspected the target area for this ship on Namur island," and it continued,

> Naturally a point of great interest was the scene of the explosion at 0952 on 1 February. At first great amazement was felt that 5-inch gunfire could penetrate such substantial fortifications. The walls of this structure, which seems to have been a magazine, appeared to be 18 to 24 inches thick of concrete, steel reinforced. After careful study, this command believes it has solved the mystery as to why 5-inch shell fire should have been so effective when the structure successfully withstood battleship and cruiser major-caliber gunfire.
>
> It appeared that only the seaward walls of this structure were of reinforced concrete, and that the enemy, with his usual conservation of metal, had constructed the walls facing the lagoon of non-reinforced concrete. It is believed that those non-reinforced walls were breached by the 5-inch gun projectiles fired into them.

Evans concluded, "It is suggested that this matter be investigated further by the forces at Namur in the belief that it may prove helpful in future operations."

The report did not provoke much interest as it climbed the chain of command. The endorsements gave no indication of reactions, either favorable or unfavorable, mostly simply forwarding the report with little or no comment. But along the way, the classification of the report was elevated from confidential to secret, so someone apparently thought the discussion important enough to safeguard it.

Evans' observations reveal a tactical mind and one that was intrigued by a mystery, something that was reinforced by his reported appreciation of mystery novels. While his deductions make sense, it is not clear what value they might have, since the circumstances were rather unique. But more atolls lay ahead, and it was possible that similar situations might repeat.

By 7 February, landings had been completed on thirty different islets around the Kwajalein lagoon. No U.S. ships were sunk or suffered major damage. The entire operation cost 372 soldiers and Marines killed (195 at Roi-Namur). Of 3,563 Japanese defenders on Roi-Namur, only 51 were taken alive, and in the south only 49 of 5,112 had been taken prisoner. The successful capture of the atoll at a relatively low cost vindicated Admiral Nimitz's decision to go straight to Kwajalein and would serve as an important component of his overall strategy.

For most of the men of USS *Johnston*, this had been their proverbial "baptism by fire," and they had made the transition from neophytes to combat veterans with the requisite courage and competence. They had delivered violence to the enemy and risked exposure to retaliation. *Johnston*'s after-action report recorded that they had fired a total of "652 five-inch AA common, 8 five-inch common, and 1500 40mm rounds," concluding that their barrage "appeared to have excellent results against enemy personnel." In his endorsement to the report, Admiral Oldendorf described *Johnston*'s performance of duty as "excellent." As the report made its way up the chain of command, Admiral Conolly's second endorsement agreed with Oldendorf that Evans' "use of high lookouts and sound gear to navigate within the lagoon shows good judgement and effective use of the equipment provided." But Conolly—considered by most to be a tough taskmaster—was less happy with Evans' performance the day before at Mellu Island (Ivan). In the longest paragraph of his letter, he asserted,

> *Johnston* left Fire Support Area No. 6 prematurely at 0825, which was just 2 hours and 9 minutes before the troops landed on Mellu Island at 1034. This was a serious error in judgment on the part of the commanding officer. If strong enemy opposition had actually been on the island, they would have certainly taken cover during the firing of *Johnston*, and just as surely they would have come out of their shelters during the exceedingly long absence of 5-inch support. Previously considered "nonexistent" batteries, even if just machine guns, could have then opened up and perhaps jeopardized the success of the entire operation. As it turned out, of course, there was no opposition on the island, but the fact remains that *Johnston*, with her 5-inch guns and close-range machine guns, was not at hand, and the assault waves moved forward covered only by the LCIs. It is absolutely vital that fire support units remember that they are supporting the landing of foot troops. Everything must be coordinated to get them ashore safely. If a ship is assigned to render close support until five minutes before the troops land, the commanding officer of the ship concerned must remain and provide that support, even if the landing time is delayed for hours at a time, unless specifically ordered otherwise by superior authority. Any other course of action may well be fatal to the troops landed. It is clear from the evidence at hand that the commanding officer of *Johnston*, was not aware of his responsibilities and was not sufficiently familiar with the requirements of the support ordered by the force commander.

There is no record of Evans' reaction to this report and no further elaboration on the incident. It is possible—even likely under the circumstances—that Evans never saw the endorsement, but it would likely have stung if he had. It is most likely that Evans' premature exit was the result of the "fog of war," a phrase Carl von Clausewitz coined in his seminal work *On War*. Knowing Evans' aggressive nature, he would never have departed early had he understood the situation as depicted by Conolly. Amphibious assaults are very complex operations, and though there is much to be admired in their planning and execution—which only got better as the war went on and lessons were learned—this one had its share of confusion and delays.

Yet when all was said and done, the capture of Kwajalein Atoll was an undeniable success. Operation Flintlock had applied many lessons learned during the costly (but ultimately successful) capture of Tarawa and had introduced many new elements of amphibious warfare—rocket-firing LCIs, flamethrower tanks, and UDT (Underwater Demolition Team) frogmen, among others—that would be employed time and again in the inexorable march across the vast Pacific, each step bringing the growing armada of American seapower closer to Tokyo and to ultimate victory.

As for *Johnston* and her captain, Bob Hagen concluded,

> I knew, after that show [Kwajalein], we had a good ship and captain who could strike fighting spirit from his men the way steel strikes sparks from a flint. Commander Evans was magnificent. I can see him now: short, barrel-chested, standing on the bridge with his hands on his hips, giving out with a running fire of orders in a bull voice. And once he gave us an order, he didn't ride us, but trusted us to carry it out the way he wanted it done. It was that quality of leadership which made us all willing to follow him to hell.

There remained many steps ahead, and USS *Johnston* would be one among the thousands of ships that would fight their way forward, far from home, with loved ones tethered only by the infrequent and often unreliable mail calls. Theirs would be a daily existence of seemingly endless tedium punctuated by moments of sheer terror. The same blue skies, warm seas, and resource-rich tropical islands that had long enticed explorers and would someday reward pleasure-seeking tourists were, for these men dressed in denim and khaki, realms of prospective danger and constant reminders of their mortality. Few doubted that their nation would triumph, but none were certain that they would witness that final victory. For the sailors who crewed GQ Johnny, many would and too many would not.

CHAPTER 7

PACIFIC ADVANCE

After the capture of Kwajalein, the Americans quickly moved on to Operation Catchpole—the capture of Eniwetok, another atoll in the Marshalls, 325 miles west-northwest of Kwajalein. With the Marshalls secured and General Douglas MacArthur continuing his drive in the Southwest Pacific, Admiral Chester Nimitz had to decide where to go next in the Central Pacific.

Almost due west—directly in the path to the Philippines—were the Carolines, where the Japanese had built a major naval base on the island of Truk. Northwest of the Marshalls were the Marianas, a chain that included the previously American island of Guam. The capture of those islands would put the Americans within striking distance of the Japanese home islands with the newly developed and highly capable B-29 Superfortress bomber.

Military leaders ultimately decided to bypass the Carolines and go to the Marianas, but not before neutralizing Truk using the massive striking power of the Fifth Fleet. Such was the power (still growing) of U.S. naval forces in the Pacific that the attack on Truk was conducted while simultaneously mounting the amphibious assault on Eniwetok.

The basic overall Pacific strategy of a two-front advance remained, with General Douglas MacArthur proceeding up the coast of New Guinea in the Southwest

> Pacific and Admiral Chester Nimitz continuing westward in the Central Pacific. The crew of USS *Johnston* would remain with Nimitz for the next several months, until MacArthur and Nimitz converged on the Philippines, ultimately fulfilling MacArthur's promise to return and resulting in the cataclysmic clash that would seal the fate of the Imperial Japanese Navy and place the men of GQ Johnny in a maelstrom they could barely imagine as they moved westward across the vast Pacific.

One evening after the evening meal, Lieutenant (jg) Els Welch was sitting on one of the bitts on the forecastle just aft of the anchor windlass, sipping at a cup of cold coffee. Before the war he had always put cream and sugar in his coffee, but he had since learned to drink it black—"regular Navy," as Chief Burnett described it. Condiments such as cream and sugar were not always available or handy, and more often than not, one had to resort to stirring with a pencil. It was simpler just to drink it black.

Bob Hagen was leaning on the lifelines a few feet away, peering out at the sheen on the placid water. *Johnston* was anchored at Kwajalein, and because the lagoon was so large, it seemed as though the ship was anchored in the open ocean. Hagen watched as a school of silver fish darted about in the water below, all of them in perfect unison as they turned this way and that. He wondered how they communicated so quickly and perfectly—so much more efficient than using signal flags or even radios to coordinate the movements of ships.

Hagen suddenly straightened and said, "Captain" as Evans suddenly appeared and began climbing the sloping forecastle toward the bullnose. Welch jumped to his feet in response. Evans seemed unaware of the two officers and continued his journey until he was standing just behind the jackstaff, peering out across the lagoon. He paused there for several minutes, then turned and headed back down, this time acknowledging the two men standing at attention with a nod and the words, "Carry on, gentlemen," then disappeared as he had come.

Once Evans was out of sight, Hagen said, "Els, you don't know how good we've got it. We've got a good one here."

Welch nodded. "Yeah. No psychological ploys. Just makes it clear what he expects of you." To Els Welch there was something about the captain's quiet

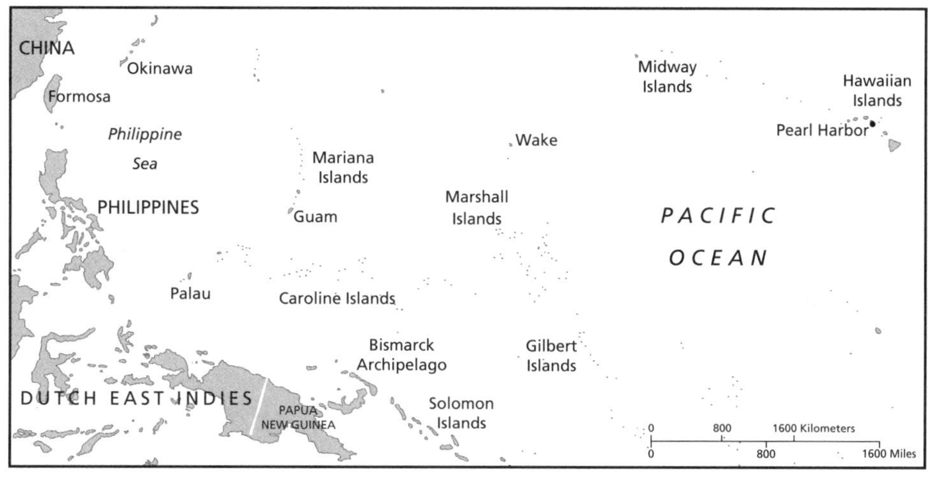

MAP 3 • Western Pacific

confidence that made it clear he was in command even without the oak leaves on his collar. In a postwar interview, Welch recalled that he had stood many bridge watches under the watchful eye of Evans, so he had seen the captain "up close and personal" and liked what he saw. There was nothing imperious about him, yet "you never doubted he was in charge, no matter what was going on."

Welch thought Evans was a good teacher who allowed his junior officers much leeway when they were conning the ship, allowing them to learn from their mistakes while helping them out when they got into trouble and patiently explaining how they could improve.

"My first skipper had somehow missed that leadership lecture that says, 'Praise in public; reprimand in private,'" Hagen said. It was not the first time that Hagen had complained about his first captain. Nor was it the first time he had sung Evans' praises. After the war, he recalled that Evans "trusted you to do what was expected and made you more afraid of disappointing him than any punishment he might inflict. But he was no pushover. He believed in second chances but took a dim view of those who did not learn from their mistakes."

After a few minutes of silence, Hagen said, "Definitely high class!" and started heading for the break, following the path of black "nonskid" that had been laid down on the smooth blue deck by the boatswains. Welch poured the dregs of his coffee over the side and followed.

This favorable evaluation of Evans was not confined to the wardroom. Similar thoughts were shared on the mess decks. Gunner's Mate Third Class Joseph Check thought Evans was "a great leader" whose example "helped me believe in myself." Quartermaster Third Class Neil Dethlefs, a relative latecomer to the crew, was impressed that the captain "kept us informed," adding, "I never found morale to be a problem in the *Johnston*." From his battle station in the port side 40-mm gun, Seaman First Class Bill Mercer could hear Evans' booming voice and felt it "somehow reassuring."

Those who had the misfortune of standing before the captain at mast found it distressing but most agreed that the punishments he handed out were not excessive, but neither were they overly lenient—especially for repeat offenders. Chief Burnett was often in attendance when the captain held mast and observed that "it was something he had to do to maintain good order and discipline, but the Skipper got no pleasure from it."

Evans did not like profanity from either the officers or the enlisted men. And while Chief Burnett held that Evans was no martinet when it came to uniforms, he nonetheless did not hesitate to point out when a crewmember was overly careless in his dress. "He seemed particularly bothered by shirt-tails, often telling the men to tuck them in," Burnett recalled. As senior enlisted man in the ship, Chief Burnett's assessment of Evans carried much weight. Years after the war, Burnett recalled, "As far as I am concerned, Captain Evans will be my idea of what a naval officer is supposed to be. I will feel that way as long as I live."

On 7 February, Lieutenant Welch had the conn for the second dog watch as *Johnston* made her way south from Kwajalein to Funafuti Atoll in company with the other ships of Task Unit 53.13.3. From the starboard bridge wing he could see a group of sailors building some sort of contraption on the main deck just forward of the break. Whatever it was meant to be, Welch knew

the "shellbacks" (sailors who had crossed the equator at least once) were constructing it to serve as part of a "Crossing the Line" ritual—an ancient tradition shared by seafarers the world over in which the shellbacks initiate the "pollywogs" (those who had *not* previously crossed the equator) by making the latter miserable in a hazing ceremony that would include such activities as crawling through a makeshift chute filled with garbage collected from the scullery or suffering beatings with "sailors' shillelaghs" fashioned from worn-out pieces of fire hose. (The Navy History and Heritage Command describes the Crossing the Line ceremony as "often involving varied events throughout which pollywogs, the term given to those who have not crossed the equator before, are put through a series of initiation rites involving harrowing and often embarrassing tasks, gags, obstacles, physical hardships, and generally good-humored mischief. Modern antics have been curtailed somewhat but remain a challenge between carrying on a bonding tradition and straying into a form of 'hazing.' After the ceremony, the sailors are inducted into the 'Solemn Mysteries of the Ancient Order of the Deep,' meaning that King Neptune had accepted them as one of his trusty shellbacks. With the pollywog to shellback transition complete, a certificate is often awarded to the new shellback as a rite of passage.")

Because Funafuti was 8 degrees south of the equator, many of *Johnston*'s shellbacks were anticipating the coming equator crossing and the attendant ceremony with much fervor, while pollywogs such as Els Welch were feeling more a sense of dread. King Neptune made no distinction between officers and enlisted men, requiring all pollywogs to suffer the hardships of initiation regardless of rank or relative seniority. Had Captain Evans not been initiated during his time in the Asiatic Fleet, even he would have been subjected to the privations and humiliations being planned by GQ Johnny's shellbacks.

As Welch watched the hammering and sawing continue on the forecastle below, it appeared to him that the object was beginning to look like a guillotine, and he had to smile when he saw one of the carpenters holding a piece of flat rubber that was apparently going to serve as the blade. The planned antics were silly at best, but they gave the crew something to do and to focus on—no small benefit as a counter to the mind-numbing routine of life at sea during wartime.

And, silly as it was in the grand scheme of things, Lieutenant Welch looked forward to becoming a shellback, one more checked box toward being a sailor. After just over two months since *Johnston*'s commissioning, he still had moments when he wondered if he had what it took to meet the challenges of being a naval officer, but he was growing more confident as time went on. He was very aware of his junior status in the wardroom but still marveled that men like Chief Burnett—who were older than he was and who had much more experience—were compelled to call him "sir." This military and nautical world was very different from the one he had left back in Long Beach, California.

Glancing at his watch, Welch saw it was nearly 1730. His relief as junior officer of the deck should be appearing soon, and he was looking forward to heading below to the wardroom for the evening meal—lunch had been nothing to write home about, and he was hungry.

As Welch peered through the starboard pelorus at the formation guide, making sure *Johnston* had not drifted off station, a light began winking Morse code from the flagship. Looking above to the signal bridge to make sure the signalmen were alert and receiving the message, he returned his attention to the flashing light, trying to read the incoming characters. He had made a valiant effort to learn how to read Morse code but could not keep up with the signalmen who were "fluent" in that language of dots and dashes, so he waited until they delivered the completed message to the captain attached to a weather-beaten clipboard.

Evans read it and passed it to Bob Hagen, the officer of the deck. "We've been ordered to detach from the task unit and head back to Majuro to refuel and rearm and then back to Kwajalein," Evans said.

Hagen replied, "Aye-aye, sir. I guess King Neptune is going to have to wait for his ceremony." Welch saw the boatswain's mate of the watch scowl and a simultaneous smile emerge on the helmsman's face; it was not hard to guess which man was a shellback and which a pollywog.

As ordered, *Johnston* left the formation and reversed course, now headed northward. Along the way to Majuro, they passed over an area where USS

Haraden had prosecuted a possible submarine contact, and Evans conducted his own sonar search of the area but, like *Haraden,* came up empty.

They arrived at Majuro the next morning (8 February), entering the lagoon through the north pass at 1036. Evans reported to the commander of Service Squadron 10 with the expectation of replenishing his fuel, ammunition, and general stores. Earlier in the war, when there were fewer ships, such a quest would have been straightforward and relatively simple. But now, with so many ships involved, simplicity was replaced by complexity, and Evans embarked on a frustrating saga that would prove that more is not always better.

As reported in *Johnston*'s war diary, "Our arrival was unheralded, and no facilities were ready for fueling or taking on ammunition. We were told to contact [the oiler] USS *Pecos* (AO 65) for fuel and [the ammunition ship] USS *Sangay* (AE 10) for ammunition." After sending flashing light messages to the two auxiliaries and receiving nothing more than acknowledgments, Evans received instructions from the senior officer present afloat (SOPA) to moor alongside the destroyer *Dortch* on the near side of the lagoon and wait for further instructions.

Having received no further orders by the forenoon watch the next day, Evans was growing impatient. Ed Digardi said Evans seemed like a caged lion as he paced up and down, periodically peering at SOPA's ship—the battleship *Washington*—through binoculars and grumbling something unintelligible but likely not pleasant. A few minutes after 0900, he noisily dropped his binoculars into the mounted receptacle just below the starboard bridge window and ordered the OOD to prepare to get underway.

When the last line was taken in and the colors were shifted from the jackstaff to the gaff, Evans maneuvered his ship across the lagoon, slowly approaching the oiler *Pecos*, the lion now out of its cage and stalking its prey. Acting as though he were under orders to do so, Evans sent a flashing light message requesting instructions for refueling. After *Johnston* had hovered about a hundred yards off the oiler's port quarter for just under an hour, *Pecos* signaled for her to come alongside. GQ Johnny took a long drink, gulping down black oil until her tanks were topped off, and the boatswains began scrubbing away at the viscous puddles left by the dripping hoses as they were detached and returned to the life-sustaining oiler.

As *Johnston* backed away from *Pecos*, Evans retrieved his binoculars and started scanning the lagoon in search of the ammunition ship *Sangay*, apparently planning a similar run on her. She was last reported to be moored in the northwest sector of the lagoon, and Evans headed that way.

Finding no ammunition ship in the northwest sector, Evans then conducted a search of the entire lagoon but could not find the ammunition ship. Queries of other ships in the lagoon eventually revealed that *Sangay* had departed the previous night. To add insult, Evans learned that *Sangay* was only able to provide bombs and aircraft ammunition and would have been unable to satisfy *Johnston*'s needs. One of the carriers suggested that Evans try USS *Mauna Loa* (AE 8), but when he requested permission to come alongside, she referred him to USS *Rainier* (AE 5).

It was now 1400, and Evans exasperation grew when *Rainer* informed him that all of her 5-inch ammunition, the kind *Johnston* needed, lay beneath her stock of 8-inch rounds. Evans then waited impatiently as the heavy cruiser *Minneapolis* moved alongside *Rainier*. He assumed that the cruiser would take on the 8-inch rounds and thereby clear the way to the 5-inch below. But when he asked *Rainier* permission to come alongside, he was informed that the cruiser had taken all of her 5-inch rounds as well. *Rainer* then suggested that Evans contact USS *Mauna Loa* . . . and Commander Service Squadron 10. With no small amount of irony, *Johnston*'s war diary recorded, "This is where we came in . . ."

Johnston's resupplying difficulty illustrates some of the logistical problems and challenges facing the U.S. Navy as it continued its march across the Pacific. By the time of the capture of Kwajalein in February 1944, the Pacific Fleet was huge and getting bigger. So many ships were a much-appreciated asset, but keeping them supplied with fuel, ammunition, and other supplies required a great deal of coordination, and often that desired harmony was lacking. In his introduction to *Beans, Bullets, and Black Oil: The Story of Fleet Logistics Afloat in the Pacific in World War II by* Worrall Carter (the commander of the aforementioned Service Squadron 10), Admiral Raymond

Spruance shed light on the changing circumstances in the Pacific by the time *Johnston* had arrived in Majuro seeking fuel and ammunition:

> In the early days of the war, when the fighting was principally in the South and Southwest Pacific, we had around our bases good-sized land masses, which permitted the construction of shore facilities. Shipping then was scarce and at a premium, and large numbers of ships could not be spared for conversion to the special purposes of a mobile floating base. Furthermore, our advance against the enemy then was not so rapid in its movement as it became later. Shore bases continued to be close enough to the fighting front to retain practically their full usefulness. When we started planning in the summer of 1943 for operations in the central Pacific, it was obvious that the geography of the area which we hoped to capture had characteristics very different from those of the South Pacific. We did not know how fast we would be able to move ahead, but we did know that in the Gilberts, Marshalls, and Carolines, many of the islands had splendid, protected anchorages in their lagoons. However, the land areas surrounding the lagoons were very small. These islands were only large enough, as a rule, to enable us to construct the always necessary airstrips and to take care of the requirements of the atoll garrison forces. . . . This geography meant that the logistics support for our fleet during operations in the central Pacific would have to be primarily afloat, in what developed into the mobile service squadron.

Seventeen fleet oilers had participated in the Kwajalein operation, and there were multiple tankers that had to shuttle oil back and forth to keep the oilers supplied with fuel for transfer to the combatants and auxiliaries. This sounds like a lot until one considers that there were 359 ships involved in the invasion. And then there was ammunition, food, medical supplies, spare parts, and much more to consider.

When one considers the daunting numbers of this challenge, it is not too surprising that *Johnston* ran into such complications and that Evans was understandably frustrated at Majuro. But the service squadron operating there was just getting its sea legs, dealing with a shortage of boats and tugs as well as a scarcity of charts mapping out the lagoon, which made it difficult for ships to find each other—likened by one ship's skipper as "trying to find a house address in a big city without a street map."

Worrall Carter's service squadron went from "hectic and chaotic" (his words) to much improved in a relatively short period of time. Carter initially operated from the battleship *Washington*, which was temporarily laid up after a collision with the battleship *Indiana*. But then he temporarily moved his flag to one of the tankers with an LST (landing ship, tank) moored alongside to provide feeding and berthing to his staff, before making another move to the destroyer tender *Prairie*.

Adopting the motto, "If we've got it, you can have it," Worrall's Service Squadron 10 lived up to that promise in the following months, sometimes sacrificing guns from his own ships to replace those needed by battle-damaged combatants, and once emptying all his storerooms of socks to accommodate a battle force that had come up short of the needed footwear. As things improved, Squadron 10 set up a fleet post office and a motion picture exchange and brought mine sweepers, floating drydocks, and sled targets for gunnery practice from Pearl Harbor. The survey ship *Bowditch* arrived and made a complete survey of the anchorage, producing hundreds of accurate charts that were distributed to every ship, boat, tug, and barge operating in the lagoon.

But all these improvements to Majuro were just beginning. Expanding logistical needs brought about the establishment of more advance bases, and the need for mobility drove the development of more proficient underway replenishment techniques, allowing striking forces to operate beyond the tethers of shore-based facilities. These efforts became so effective that the fast carrier force—the main striking power of the Pacific Fleet—did not return to Pearl Harbor until war's end, able to stay forward for the remainder of the war to keep up relentless pressure on the retreating Japanese forces.

With his magazines still near empty, Evans requested—and received—permission to proceed back to Kwajalein in hopes of finding some ammunition among the ships there. After a delay caused by large quantities of jellyfish clogging his main condenser intakes, Evans was able to get underway for Kwajalein the next day. Making landfall at 0630 on 11 February, *Johnston* was greeted by a radio report of a submarine contact near Gea Pass on the western side of the lagoon, near the southern tip. Evans reported to the senior officer present afloat (SOPA) and was immediately assigned to search the area.

GQ Johnny spent the greater part of the day conducting the search as ordered. On several occasions the pinging sonar returned an echo, causing some excitement among the crew, but each time, as they prosecuted the contact, it disappeared as quickly as it had been detected. After several hours of fruitless pinging, at 1645 Evans ordered his ship to abandon the search and to proceed into the lagoon to an anchorage assigned by the commander of Task Force 51.

Grateful for a respite from operations, much of the crew settled in for a rest once they were safely anchored and only the in-port watch remained on station. A sense of relative peace settled over the weary ship. In the engineering spaces, the ship's service generators hummed steadily away providing electricity to the destroyer, while the turbines in the engine rooms were dormant. In the galley, the mess cooks were securing "mid-rats" (midnight rations) as the watch standers for the coming midwatch departed the mess decks with full bellies. The berthing compartments, bathed in subdued red light to preserve night vision, were quiet except for the continuous drone of fans and some sporadic snoring. In the wardroom, two of the junior officers listlessly played one last hand of gin rummy, while Ed Digardi sat at the dining table composing an overdue letter home.

On the bridge, only the hiss of a high-frequency radio receiver intruded on the silence there. Els Welch was having difficulty staying awake as he alternately stood still then paced the steel deck, periodically lifting his binoculars to peer around the moonlit lagoon. He had drawn the midwatch, and it was just a little past midnight as he faced four more hours of the seductively quiet watch, trying to decide whether to fight his drowsiness with a cup of coffee proffered by the messenger of the watch. From the smell, he was pretty sure the coffee was less than freshly brewed.

Trying to focus on something that would distract him from the fatigue that was weighing down his eyelids, he looked across the water at a massive battleship silhouetted by the silver trail of moonlight behind. He marveled at the large guns that made up her main battery, the phallic barrels protruding from her otherwise graceful lines, and he wondered what it must be like to be on board when she let loose a full broadside. The first time GQ Johnny had fired her 5-inchers, he had been amazed—not so much by the sound, which he was prepared for, as by the concussive effect of the blast. It flattened his clothes against his body and seemed to resonate in the marrow of his bones. He could barely imagine that sensation magnified so greatly by the larger caliber of the battleship's guns.

Gazing at this floating behemoth, he felt somehow diminished and wondered what it would be like to serve in one of those colossal ships rather than this tiny destroyer. He imagined it would be a much more stable ride as the giant parted the oncoming waves rather than riding up and over them. The scuttlebutt ashore told him that the battleship navy was different from the tin can navy, that there was more spit and polish on the battlewagons, that the food was better, and that the berthing compartments and mess decks had more elbow room. But he was not sure how much he believed those claims, and he knew that the presence of so many more officers would make him that much more junior by comparison. He considered that in a sea battle, the Japanese were more likely to concentrate their fire on so large a ship and that his odds of survival were better in this much smaller target. He decided he was better off where he was.

Suddenly Welch's reverie was broken by the TBS radio, the anonymous speaker's slight southern drawl personalizing the electric voice that now demanded attention. SOPA was warning the ships in the lagoon that "several bogies" (unknown, possibly hostile air contacts) had been detected inbound and "all ships to make smoke" to confuse the enemy aircraft.

Evans appeared on the bridge within seconds of the alert and ordered the ship to go to general quarters. The previous placidity was replaced by a cacophony of activity as the crew relinquished their rest and quickly manned their battle stations. *Johnston*'s funnels began coughing out billows of boiler smoke, which were soon joined by clouds of chemical smoke from the chemical generators aft. Shrouds of smoke drifted slowly across the lagoon, masking the moon and leaving the ships in choking darkness as their radars pierced the gloom in search of unwelcome intruders.

The raiders were detected on radar and were tracked inward until 0253, when the range began opening. SOPA ordered the cessation of smoke generation, but soon thereafter another group of bogies appeared west-northwest and the vigil continued. But these contacts too failed to press the attack, and the weary sailors could only watch and wait in case the enemy pilots changed their minds.

Finally, at 0333, the ship secured from general quarters. Those who had not been on watch prior to the alert returned to their bunks to salvage what was left of the night to catch some shuteye. Lieutenant Welch resumed his watch on the bridge, and with the adrenaline surge of GQ subsiding, he resumed his battle with drowsiness, resorting to a cup of coffee, grateful that this one was freshly brewed.

Five hours later, Evans called away the sea and anchor detail, and *Johnston* made her way across the lagoon to come alongside the oiler *Suamico* for another drink of black oil. Topped off, she returned to her previous anchorage, "dropped the hook," and awaited further orders.

Those orders were not long coming, and soon the crew was making preparations for the next major operation, the capture of Eniwetok, an atoll some four hundred miles northwest of Kwajalein. *Johnston* was ordered to provide fire support for the new operation, just as she had done at Kwajalein.

At last Evans got his ammunition, from a sister ship, USS *Ringgold* (DD 500): Working parties from both ships transferred 150 rounds of both projectiles and powder. Several boatloads of provisions arrived soon after, and again a working party was called away to receive and stow the much-needed supplies. Seaman Harley Chronister was willing to do his share but was glad when his next load did not include a case of large cans; by the time he got them down the ladder leading to the storeroom, he "thought my arms were going to fall off."

At 1845, on orders from the Commodore, *Johnston* got underway to head out of the lagoon to Patrol Station 2 where she would conduct antisubmarine patrols for the rest of the night. The night passed uneventfully except that a passing squall caught some of the men trying to sleep out on the weather decks to avoid the heat in the berthing compartments, causing a chorus of profanity that Ed Digardi could hear inside the pilot house.

Returning to Kwajalein Atoll midway through the morning watch, *Johnston* again topped off her fuel tanks from *Suamico*, took on more stores from the battleship *New Mexico*, and then departed the lagoon to join up with Task Group 51.11, assuming patrol station 13 in cruising disposition 91 as the American forces converged on Eniwetok to carry out Operation Catchpole.

In many ways, Eniwetok was a rerun of Kwajalein. On the night of 17–18 February, *Johnston* joined Fire Support Unit 1 and screened the bombardment group as they shelled Engebi Island during the forenoon watch. At the north tip of Eniwetok Atoll, Engebi is a triangle-shaped island where the Japanese had built an airfield. Navy aircraft quickly neutralized the airfield, and by the end of the day, Marines were ashore on the small island.

The next day, *Johnston* responded to a call from the commander of Task Group 51.11 and, entering the lagoon via the deepwater entrance to Eniwetok Atoll, took up station five hundred yards south of Parry Island. At 0853, Bob Hagen closed the firing key of his 5-inch battery, opening fire on a series of pillboxes and knocking them out before shifting fire to the wreckage of a Japanese plane, reasoning that the "wreckage was on the beach at the water's edge and was ideally situated to conceal machine gun nests," as reported in the ship's war diary.

For the next several days, the ship alternated between shelling Parry Island and conducting antisubmarine patrols outside the wide passage to the south of Eniwetok. The shelling was nearly continuous except when they had to cease firing to allow air strikes on the island, and once when the battleship *Pennsylvania* complained that *Johnston* was in her line of fire. Captain Evans concluded his action report on the 21st by noting "All ordnance material performed satisfactorily, and it is again desired to emphasize that this type of ship with its 5" battery can hit any target which it can see."

The night of 22 February was quiet as the ship lay at anchor. There was no breeze, and the water was glassy in the faint starlight as Seamen Bobby Chastain and Harley Chronister sat on the fantail near the depth charge racks staring across the lagoon at the shadow-like outline of Parry Island. Chronister was only half-listening as Chastain related a rather long story about a neighbor's dog that barked too much, when they heard the sound of small-arms fire coming from the island and could see the hyphenated streaks of tracer rounds briefly pierce the darkness. Then the cruiser *Indianapolis*, several thousand yards off their port side, fired two rounds. The two men stared at the island waiting for the shots to land but were surprised when, instead, two illumination rounds burst over the island. It looked as though two stars had suddenly come down from the heavens, bathing the island and the sea around it in a brilliant white light that sputtered and flared, held aloft by the parachutes that slowed their descent. It was a hauntingly beautiful sight that belied their purpose of illuminating the battlefield below, as U.S. Marines battled the Japanese defenders of this otherwise insignificant lump of coral somewhere in the vast Pacific Ocean.

As the two seamen listened to the rattle of gunfire emanating from the island and watched the two flares snuffed out as they dropped into the sea, Chastain said, "Kinda glad I'm here and not there." Chronister stared across the obsidian-like water at the now barely discernable silhouette of the island and merely said, "Yeah."

For the next week, *Johnston* routinely screened other elements of the task group around Eniwetok until 29 February when she received orders to proceed with Task Group 51.6 for a return visit to Majuro. Arriving on 1 March, the ship spent the next six days anchored in berth D-8, refueling, reprovisioning, taking on ammunition, performing much-needed maintenance, and making repairs.

Six days later, *Johnston* stood out through Majuro's northern pass and proceeded to take station 3 screening the escort carrier *Manila Bay*. In accordance with established doctrine, the ships in the formation began zigzagging together to complicate Japanese targeting calculations in case any enemy submarines were lurking in the area.

The ship was buzzing with scuttlebutt as to their destination—something that had not yet been revealed by the commander of the task group. *Johnston*'s war diary recorded, "Our destination still secret from us. Can either be Funa Futi or Espiritu Santo in the New Hebrides." The next night, the deck log provided a clue when it recorded a change in time zone. The diary concluded, "Must be Espiritu Santo because of the changing date and continued south heading."

Whatever their destination, it was somewhere south of Majuro, and before long the heretofore elusive equator loomed ahead, causing the shellbacks to again make preparations for initiating the pollywogs into Neptune's realm. At 1400 on 9 March, the ship passed over that invisible line that bifurcates Earth and officially entered the Southern Hemisphere, while a minority of the crew inflicted much humiliation and discomfort on the majority. The war diary entry for that day laconically recorded, "Neptunus Rex and his Royal Party came aboard and initiation ceremonies for all slimy pollywogs were held in accordance with ancient tradition." The ship's log for that day reported that two crewmembers, Electrician's Mate Third Class James Sorenson and Seaman Second Class Robert Beckstrom, had received cuts on their heads; the latter's cut was deep enough that Doc Hadfield administered four stitches.

The now familiar night sky of the Northern Hemisphere was left behind, and the navigator and his quartermasters now relied on the Southern Cross and other new (and fewer) constellations of stars for their dawn and dusk sightings. They cracked open new publications, changed their star-identification templates, and adjusted to southern latitudes as they plotted their fixes and laid out their tracks. At first quartermaster-striker Bob Billie had some difficulty getting used to the latitudes getting larger instead of smaller when the XO—Lieutenant Commander Howard Baker—let him lay the track as they headed southward. "It just seemed upside down at first," he later mused.

The voyage south was uneventful, except that at 1438 on 11 March, the port lookout reported an object in the water nearly dead ahead. As Lieutenant Bob Hagen cautiously maneuvered the ship for a closer look, the object was clearly identified as a mine. Bill Mercer remembered seeing "that ugly thing with the horns of the devil" projecting threateningly outward and was "very happy when we blew it to kingdom come with our 20-mms."

By now it was clear that they were indeed headed for Espiritu Santo, and the next morning lookouts reported several islands looming out of the heavy mist as the ship passed through several rain squalls. As *Johnston* snaked her way among the New Hebrides, the weather cleared, and *Manila Bay* launched one of her aircraft towing a target sleeve. *Johnston*'s 20- and 40-mm guns practiced antiair gunnery for several minutes as the sleeve fluttered by. "Just remember," Hagen grumbled over the sound-powered net, "the Japs won't be such easy targets and will be shooting back."

Less than three hours later, *Johnston* entered Pallikulo Bay, Espiritu Santo, through Diamond Pass, where she replenished from a fuel barge and then anchored for two days before exiting the bay and heading through Segond Channel to her assigned spot, berth 27.

Situated well to the southeast of the Solomon Islands, Espiritu Santo had been a vital strategic point early in the war, providing a base of operations that helped keep the lifeline open between the United States and Australia. In the spring of 1942, Navy Seabees began carving out an advance base. Removing large swaths of coconut plantations and wild jungle, the SeaBees laid down four six-thousand-foot runways. Channels were dredged leading to webs of piers and wharves, cranes pierced the skyline, and warehouses and countless Quonset huts dotted the landscape. By 1944 Espiritu Santo had become the largest American advance base in the Pacific outside of Pearl Harbor.

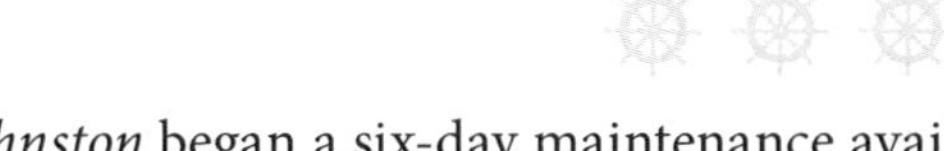

Johnston began a six-day maintenance availability at Espiritu Santo that included her going high and dry resting on keel blocks in a floating drydock for much-needed work on her corroded sonar dome. By now this well-equipped base provided a relatively safe haven where such important work could be done unmolested by enemy forces and where a weary crew could get a respite from the daily grind of wartime operations. In addition to the enhanced maintenance capabilities, there were opportunities for recreation that included softball diamonds and movie theaters.

Despite this respite from the demands of combat readiness, the crew remained at war with that ever-present enemy of the modern sailor: rust! Underway, the metal surfaces of the ship were under constant assault from the salt spray and the immersive waves that swept across the weather decks whenever the sea decided to resist this man-made intruder. Now moored at this peaceful sanctuary in the South Pacific, the sound of chipping hammers and the pungent smell of red lead preservative and fresh gray paint were frequent irritants. This was not the prewar cosmetic competition of Navy ships trying to outdo each other in their pristine appearance—the so-called spit-and-polish Navy. This was an existential battle with natural corrosion that, if not effectively countered, could have deleterious effects on the strength of a ship's hull and could render vital equipment useless.

And it was not just rust that had to be controlled. Machines needed lubrication; gunsights required calibration; vacuum seals had to be maintained; electronics needed testing and adjustment; failing vacuum tubes had to be replaced; chronometers must be wound; pots, pans, and utensils needed scrubbing; and clothes required frequent laundering. These things and more demanded much attention and could make the difference between success and failure, victory and defeat, life and death. Here, in this temporary haven, there was time to devote to such things, but when underway—as they were most of the time—these vital tasks had to be relegated to second place behind combat readiness, which required nearly everyone to devote significant blocks of time to manning their battle stations, sometimes to fight, mostly to endure the tedium of being ready just in case. And all of this was done without a discernible end in sight—these sailors were in it for the duration. And no one knew how long that would be. With survival not guaranteed, they could only look forward to that day when one side could declare victory and the other acknowledge defeat.

And so it was that the men of GQ Johnny could draw exaggerated pleasure from a softball game ashore, or a "swim call" in the warm waters of a lagoon while armed shipmates manned the motor whaleboat and patrolled nearby in case sharks decided to join the festivities, or two cans of beer (which had to be consumed on an alongside barge because the consumption of alcohol on U.S. Navy ships had been banned by a teetotaling secretary of the Navy thirty years before).

But there was another pleasure—more like a compensation—that was rarely mentioned but was felt by most. There was the knowledge that every day that passed—whether marked by taps or reveille or some other milestone—they were fortunate to be alive. With countless numbers of people dying in a world war, with periodic calls to battle stations a part of their daily existence, and with someone they knew—or knew of—joining the list of casualties, these men were acutely aware that survival was not a given and that death lurked uncomfortably close.

For many, faith was an antidote to this discomfiture, offering divine protection or the promise of an afterlife. Whenever possible, the church pennant was hoisted on Sunday mornings, and those believers not on watch would gather together to draw solace from communal worship and hope from the words of the Sailor's Prayer: "Preserve us from the dangers of the sea and the violence of the enemy, that we may return in safety to enjoy the blessings of the land."

Humor was a frequent remedy to that lurking specter as well. The tension that accompanied such things as incoming radar blips or amplifying sonar echoes could often be dispelled—or at least reduced—by a well-timed wisecrack. Sarcasm was the most frequent form of humor, but off-color jokes often served the dual purpose of injecting levity while reminding the men of pleasures—past or hoped for—as they struggled to deal with the challenges of their current existence.

No matter how they coped, the men of GQ Johnny were by this time functioning well together. Although they complained plenty, they kept their frustrations and longings in check, exhibiting teamwork and ever-increasing efficiency. There could be little doubt that continuous practice and repetitive drills were a significant part of their improvement, but there was also a growing maturity—the byproduct of working so closely together under arduous circumstances, of a growing realization that they owed one another a commitment to survival. They were learning that the term "shipmate" was not just another archaic term in the strange lingo of the sailor's lexicon. It was an unspoken oath of allegiance to one another that went beyond "friend," or "colleague," or "team member." It was a special bond that required both commitment and trust and would serve them well in the tribulations that lay ahead. For those who survived, that bond would remain unbreakable long after the war ended: Many of them would organize and attend reunions time and again for decades, until the day came when they would at last reunite in a different way with their fallen shipmates.

CHAPTER 8

ODYSSEY

Many histories of the Pacific War use phrases such as "the march across the Pacific"—a legitimate description, since the U.S. campaign against Japan began at Pearl Harbor and proceeded westward until it ended in Tokyo Bay nearly four years later. But if we consider the travels and experiences of USS *Johnston* as typical of the many ships that made their way across the Pacific, we see a pattern that is nothing like a straight-line march. Tracking the ship's movements on a nautical chart is a bewildering exercise that becomes a tangle of courses with stops all over a large area of the Pacific Ocean. It is a journey that rivals the seagoing odyssey of Ulysses, taking the ship and her crew to many exotically named places, some of them multiple times.

On the morning of 20 March, *Johnston* departed the New Hebrides and headed northwest to the Solomon Islands, a voyage of nearly nine hundred nautical miles, to conduct gunnery exercises before mooring at Purvis Bay on the southern side of Florida Island. Three days later, she departed with the destroyer *Trathen* (DD 530) to rendezvous with other units of Destroyer Squadron 27 in waters northeast of New Ireland in the Bismarck Archipelago. She remained in that area until the 27th, when she was ordered to proceed north in company with destroyers *Hailey*, *Haggard*, and *Franks* to the Caroline Islands "to carry out destruction of any surface or shore targets on Kapingamarangi Atoll." There *Johnston* bombarded Nanakitsu Island, destroying a radio station, a concrete blockhouse, and a barracks. Evans continued to be pleased with his crew's shooting, recording that "ninety percent of the ammunition fired [165 rounds of 5-inch and 190 rounds of 40-mm] was observed to hit the target area." He considered that "excellent when the small area of the target, the flat trajectory of the battery, and the lack of suitable vertical targets in the target area are taken into account."

In company with several other destroyers, *Johnston* next headed south for Bougainville, a sizable island east of New Guinea, and made landfall at 0545 on 30 March. The destroyers were ordered to engage Japanese barges that were attempting to move troops and supplies in support of a Japanese counteroffensive in the long campaign in that area and to provide shore bombardment against various targets in the area. For the next several days, *Johnston* moved about the area, patrolling the waters around the Treasury and Shortland Islands and bombarding shore installations in Empress Augusta Bay, receiving a "well done" from an Army spotter.

After more patrolling and several more periods of shore bombardment, the ship returned to Purvis Bay on the morning of 4 April, where she remained until the 8th. At 0645 on 9 April, she got underway as part of a column with the destroyer *Haggard* leading, followed by *Hazelwood*, then *Hailey*, and finally *Johnston*. Two days later, the group rendezvoused with the oiler *Millicoma* and her escort.

Refueling at sea was a relatively new practice when the Pacific War began, its origins more or less coinciding with the development of destroyers, which had "shorter legs" than the larger combatants and thus needed more frequent refueling. This requirement was exacerbated by the long distances encountered in the vast Pacific, making in-port refueling stops less practical.

Early attempts at underway replenishment several decades before began with the oiler trailing hoses behind on floatation devices that could be retrieved by the receiving ship. Alongside methods eventually proved more efficient—though more challenging and potentially more dangerous—and both the British and the Americans led the way in perfecting this practice during World War I and the interwar years. By 1944, mobile logistics support was being supplied by service squadrons that moved westward with the advancing combatant forces, and underway replenishments had become commonplace for the U.S. Navy.

But commonplace did not mean easy. Bringing large vessels close enough together to pass hoses across was dangerous. Because so many of the officers in the burgeoning fleet were not professional mariners and were the products of accelerated training programs, some captains always chose to conduct these maneuvers themselves. The better ones, however, had the confidence to allow their junior officers to learn under their supervision. For this refueling, Captain Evans allowed Lieutenant (jg) Ellsworth Welch to make the approach on the oiler when it was *Johnston*'s turn to come alongside for fuel.

As indicated by the signal flags fluttering on her halyards, *Millicoma* was plodding along at twelve knots on a replenishment course of 277 degrees heading into a light wind. Welch successfully brought the destroyer around in a sweeping arc to fall in astern of the oiler, steadying up on 277 degrees and slowing to twelve knots. Bob Hagen, the officer of the deck, peered through a handheld stadimeter and reported that they were about nine hundred yards astern of the oiler. As all three men moved to the port wing of the bridge, Welch was pleased to see the oiler's wake streaming down *Johnston*'s port side, since they were slated to come alongside *Millicoma*'s starboard side. Evans told him to increase speed to close the distance to a waiting station six hundred yards astern of the oiler. Welch complied, ordering seventeen knots to close the distance, then resuming the oiler's speed of twelve. When he had settled in, now matching the oiler's speed, Evans told him to shoot a bearing to the side of the oiler, explaining that to be properly positioned for the approach to the oiler, the bearing should be 3 degrees to the left of the base course. Evans further explained that when it was time to make their approach, he should steer the ship so that when he was three hundred yards from the oiler the bearing would be 6 degrees. This "3–6/6–3 rule" would aid in bringing the destroyer into her station about ninety to one hundred feet off the oiler's side, close enough to get lines across and then rig hoses for refueling.

After about twenty minutes of waiting—during which Welch frequently adjusted the rpm of his ship's screws to keep the distance steady based on the ranges supplied by Hagen—*Millicoma* signaled *Johnston* to come alongside.

Evans instructed Welch to increase speed to seventeen knots. As *Johnston* surged forward, Evans reminded Welch to keep shooting bearings to measure his position relative to the oiler and told him to slow to twelve knots when they were about 180 yards from the oiler's stern.

Welch was reassured by the oiler's straight and steady wake, indicating that she had a good man on the helm. The trick was for the oiler to maintain a very steady heading and speed, allowing the destroyer to make small adjustments to come alongside at the optimal distance and to keep her there, such that the two ships—though both making way at twelve knots—would be virtually standing still relative to one another.

Evans seemed relaxed and allowed Welch to make the approach on his own, only once telling him to come left a bit when the destroyer's bow was nearly even with the oiler's stern, explaining that the hydrodynamic pressure wave generated by the oiler's motion would force *Johnston*'s bow away from the base course a bit, requiring compensation. Welch could sense that Hagen seemed less comfortable, apparently biting his tongue on several occasions when he seemed to disagree with Welch's actions.

As Hagen called out the range to the oiler at 180 yards, Welch glanced at Evans, who nodded, and Welch ordered twelve knots. As they continued forward, the pungent smell of the oiler's stack gas caused Welch to cough and his eyes to momentarily burn. *Millicoma* looked huge as *Johnston* moved up alongside. They were close enough now that Welch could make out the faces of the sailors stationed along the oiler's starboard side. The destroyer's momentum continued to move her forward, but Welch could sense her slowing, which was confirmed when the quartermaster called out the readings of the actual speed from the ship's pitometer log. He was relieved when the destroyer stopped her forward motion relative to the oiler and the two ships began moving in unison. Minor adjustments to *Johnston*'s heading and speed kept the destroyer in position as someone on the oiler blew a whistle and men on the forecastle and fantail hurled lines with weighted "monkey fists" across the narrow expanse of water between the two vessels. Soon heavier lines were passed across, and a line of sailors on *Johnston*'s deck heaved them in. Hoses followed, and soon fuel was flowing from the oiler to the destroyer. Welch continued the necessary small adjustments—as little as 0.5 degree and

2 rpms at a time—to maintain the precarious balance as the two ships moved along as one. He suddenly realized that he had been gripping the railing in front of him so tightly that his right hand was cramped.

With his confidence growing, Welch allowed himself to take his eyes off the oiler long enough to scan ahead and felt comforted by the destroyers that were screening *Millicoma* and her "customers" in case enemy submarines or aircraft made an unwanted appearance.

Once *Johnston* had topped off, the lines between the two ships were extracted and Welch ordered the helmsman to come right to 380 and the lee helm to increase speed to fifteen knots. With the oiler now clear off *Johnston*'s port quarter, Welch ordered, "All engines ahead flank, right standard rudder." He could feel the rumble of the ship's engines as *Johnston* surged ahead. With the relative wind in his face and the slight bucking motion beneath his feet as *Johnston* raced ahead to take up her assigned screening station, Welch basked in the moment, feeling like a true professional ship handler. His elation was compounded when Evans said, loud enough for the watch team to hear, "Well done, Mister Welch." He would later recall it as "one of those special moments you never forget."

With her fuel tanks full, *Johnston* continued to move among the various island groups, first returning to the Bismarcks, then making a foray west to the Admiralties, and again returning to the Bismarcks, where she operated near Emirau and Mussau Islands. Nothing extraordinary occurred during this period, except that on the late afternoon of 14 April, sonar reported a sound contact. After nearly a half hour of prosecuting the contact, they concluded it was a large school of fish that was providing the return echoes and not an enemy submarine. Such occurrences were a source of both relief and frustration. Encountering a Japanese submarine could be "a quick ticket to the bottom," as Chief Burnett warned, but it was nonetheless disappointing to find that a sound contact was nothing more than a natural form of sea life, or a false reading caused by the right combination of temperature and pressure in the sea.

After several days of continued patrolling in the vicinity of Emirau Island, on 18 April *Johnston* rendezvoused with Task Unit 34.9.1 to escort the cargo ship *Mintaka* (AK-94) and two merchant ships bound for Seeadler Harbor at Manus, the largest island in the Admiralties. Having seen these ships safely to Manus, *Johnston* returned to patrol operations in the vicinity of Emirau in the Bismarcks. From there she proceeded to the Treasury Islands south of Bougainville, mooring at Blanche Harbor on 23 April. On the 26th, she got underway to escort the transport *President Monroe* all the way to New Caledonia, then returned once again to Purvis Bay in the Solomons, arriving on the morning of 28 April.

By now Ed Digardi sensed a change in Evans. More than once, he observed the captain settling heavily into his chair on the bridge, exhaling loudly as one does when something is amiss. Evans did not say what was bothering him, but Digardi believed that the captain was growing dissatisfied with the mundanity of their operations. There was little doubt that potential harm was present in their operations, and it seemed they must be contributing to the war effort, but the crew had so far not encountered the kind of naval combat that Evans had experienced in the Java Sea or that Bob Hagen described on those occasions when he spoke of his time in *Aaron Ward* in the Solomons. Most of the crew seemed content with this state of affairs, but lately Evans often gave off an aura of impatience without actually saying anything.

If Digardi was right about Evans, the skipper's disappointment would not be relieved anytime soon. The ship remained in the Solomons, effecting some repairs at Purvis Bay and then pinballing her way around the various islands, patrolling and escorting in the vicinity for the next several weeks. Participating in mine-laying operations in the waters of Buka Pass at the northern end of Bougainville offered a change of routine, but it was hard work, and many of the crew did not care for dealing with these "ship killers."

At last, during the morning watch on 16 May while the ship was on patrol northeast of Buka Island, Digardi handed Evans a promising message reporting that an enemy submarine had departed Truk several days before and was believed to be headed their way. *Johnston* was soon joined by seven other destroyers of Destroyer Division 93. The eight destroyers searched all day and into the night until about 2130, when *Haggard* made contact and moved in with *Franks* to attack. Both ships sowed depth charges, but the explosions rendered *Haggard*'s gyrocompass inoperable, so she stood off and coached *Johnston* to the point of last contact.

With *Hailey* patrolling to the northwest, *Franks* to the northeast, and *Haggard* to the south, *Johnston* commenced her attack run. Sonarman Second Class Walter Wiegand operated the sonar; the XO, Lieutenant Commander Baker, maintained the sub's track. On Evans' command, *Johnston* rolled four 600-pound depth charges down the rack on her stern and into the frothing wake, two set to explode at two hundred feet and the other two at three hundred. With the resulting detonations felt in the ship's hull, Evans instructed the conning officer, Ensign Henry Wilson, to put his rudder hard over. Circling back, Evans continued to coach Wilson as he maneuvered the ship to keep the submarine out of the ship's baffles (the zone where the noise of the destroyer's churning propellors could mask the echoes coming off the submarine) and then commenced a second attack run. This time Sonarman Second Class Arleigh Cody was at the sonar set, watching the pale green oscillations on the cathode ray tube while listening to the vacillating tones and harmonics collected by the hydrophones as the telltale echoes off the submarine's hull competed with the natural sounds of the sea and those of man-made machinery. When Cody reported to the bridge that he was sure the ship was passing directly over the target, Evans ordered five 600-pound charges dropped, three set for 200 feet and two for 250. White blooms roiled up in the green water off the ship's starboard quarter as the destroyer heeled over in a tight right turn, and this time the explosions could be felt more strongly, raising hopes that the charges had found their prey. Sonar contact was lost—another hopeful sign—and soon an extensive oil slick cluttered with much debris confirmed that the Japanese navy now had one less submarine.

Haggard, *Franks*, and *Johnston* officially shared in the kill, but it was clear to GQ Johnny's crew that it was their depth charges that had delivered the fatal wound. Cheering could be heard in various parts of the ship as *Johnston* resumed her patrol within sight of Buka Island.

Although Evans and his crew would not be aware until nearly two months later, intelligence analysts would identify the submarine as the I-176 and would conclude that the sinking caused the Japanese naval command to shift the position of its cordon of submarines in the New Guinea–Carolines area, which had been established to intercept the movements of U.S. carriers. The intercepted radio traffic accompanying the move proved crucial in the subsequent destruction of that cordon. It was clear that GQ Johnny had made a difference beyond the routine, and Evans was awarded a Bronze Star.

Even without that knowledge, the crew's morale was high on the morning after the sinking of the submarine. Ed Digardi had the bridge watch when Evans emerged from his sea cabin and climbed into the captain's chair in the pilot house without the usual audible exhalation. Digardi was sure he detected the hint of a smile.

It is a reasonable assumption that Ernest Evans wanted to fight. He said so very directly at *Johnston*'s commissioning ceremony, warning his crew of his intentions to never again retreat from the enemy as he had been forced to do at the Battle of the Java Sea in early 1942. The men in his crew generally agreed that their captain was determined to make good on his commissioning day promise to go "in harm's way." Some shared his determination; others were worried by it. One confided that he was "scared stiff that the skipper was going to get us killed."

The other bridge watch standers agreed with Ed Digardi that Evans seemed frustrated when his assigned missions were mundane in nature—that he seemed happiest when using GQ Johnny's weapons. He seemed obsessed with obtaining (and expending) ammunition, often making a nuisance of himself in his quest for more. And it was rare that another ship was in closer to the beaches during fire support missions.

But Evans rarely voiced these things, and no one ever described him as blustering or bragging. He would occasionally express his satisfaction or his disappointment in the ship's performance but never dwelled on either, keeping his assessments succinct and subdued. Bob Hagen—who had more than once referred to his previous skipper in the *Aaron Ward* as a "screamer"—envied Evans' cool demeanor and recalled that "the Skipper never raised his voice in anger." Ed Digardi accepted Hagen's assessment and shared his gratitude, but he described his captain's voice as "resonating" and "leaving no doubt that he was in command" when he was giving orders.

Lieutenant Jack Bechdel and Digardi were good friends, and Bechdel confided to Digardi that he found Evans to be "a little scary," but "someone you just had to look up to." Els Welch echoed other officers' assessments when he described Evans as "kind of mysterious." Several recalled the half-smile that Evans often wore, but there was disagreement as to what it meant; some described it as "self-confident," while others thought he just enjoyed being captain. Chief Burnett thought it reflected his sense of humor.

Evans' relationship with the officers was good. None complained in general about his leadership, and most were quick to acknowledge that they were lucky to have him as their captain. Two men served as his executive officer in the year of his command. His relationship with each of them was not typical of many commanding officers of the time. The rapid expansion of the fleet with the onset of war had caused the Navy to award commands to men with less experience than had been the practice in the peacetime navy, and it was not uncommon for these relative neophytes to rely on their XOs for advice and reassurance. Evans did not seem to need those things from anyone, relying on his own judgment and often discussing plans and options with his officers more as mentor than as collaborator.

He treated Howard Baker, his first XO, well and assessed him favorably in his fitness reports, as evidenced by the Navy rewarding Baker with his own command of a *Fletcher*-class destroyer—USS *Charles F. Ausburne* (DD 570)—in May 1944. Evans never seemed to warm to Baker, even though they both were Naval Academy graduates, but no one observed any overt hostility or any serious disagreements between the two men. (Baker was subsequently awarded the Silver Star while in command of his destroyer for "action against enemy Japanese forces during the invasion of Lingayen, Luzon, Philippine Islands, on 7 January 1945. When an enemy destroyer attempted to attack the disposition of which his ship was a member, Commander Baker boldly closed the hostile vessel and directed his gun batteries in delivering accurate fire which contributed to its destruction.")

When Baker left the ship, Bob Hagen filled in as temporary XO until Lieutenant Elton B. Stirling "fleeted up" when he returned to the ship on 3

June after attending radar school in San Diego. Like Baker, "Silver" Stirling was an Academy graduate. He was described in his class *Lucky Bag* as having a "pleasing, even-natured personality, characteristic of his Scandinavian blood." Pictures of him show a boyish, handsome face topped with blond hair. Although Evans treated Stirling the same as he had Baker—relying on him to carry out his duties as XO but not often depending on him for counsel—most of the wardroom felt that Evans seemed to like Stirling more than he had Baker.

By the summer of 1944, there were twenty officers listed in *Johnston*'s official deck log. As gunnery officer, Lieutenant Bob Hagen was third in the chain of command. He and Evans got along well, although Evans would occasionally chide Hagen good-naturedly for his intensity. While Hagen's title was "gunnery officer" in 1944 terminology, today he would be called the "weapons officer" or "combat systems officer," reflecting the fact that he was in charge of all the ship's weapons—guns, torpedoes, and depth charges—as well as the ship's CIC (Combat Information Center). As such, he had seventy men in his gunnery department and had five officers working for him: three assistant gunnery officers (Lieutenant [jg] Henry M. Wilson and Ensigns Alex Himchak and Gordon W. Fox); the torpedo officer, Lieutenant (jg) John K. Bechdel; and a plotting room officer, Ensign Stanley B. Sandberg.

While serving as temporary executive officer, Hagen had also temporarily assumed the duties of navigator. Describing himself as a "rookie," he was less than confident when the ship entered the harbor at Bougainville at night. Evans had the conn, and Hagen was having trouble keeping up with the captain's maneuvers. In a burst of excited agitation, Hagen yelled, "Slow down, you are ahead of me! How can I make recommendations?" Evans calmly replied, "Don't worry about it, Hagen. I know where I'm going." Evans did indeed and soon had the ship safely at anchor. Hagen was embarrassed and a bit miffed at Evans' "showing up my ignorance." Trying to make light of his inability to keep up, Hagen said, "Well, I am only about a thousand yards back." He was relieved when Evans leaned over the chart table, and he could see his captain smiling in the red light reflecting off the chart.

Lieutenant (jg) Donald A. Bowman was the first lieutenant. In charge of deck operations—anchoring, handling mooring lines, operating the ship's boats, and maintaining the weather decks—he was also the damage control officer in charge of the ship's repair parties and was assisted by Lieutenant (jg) Arthur C. Secrest.

There was also a medical officer, Lieutenant (jg) (Doctor) Dale Hadfield, and a supply officer, Lieutenant (jg) William B. Stallings, who handled pay and other supply functions.

Although their titles might be different, all these officers would be recognized by sailors as far back as the age of sail; but now, in the 1940s, advancing technology required new officer billets.

The engineer officer (also known as the "chief engineer"), Lieutenant Joseph L. Worling, was tasked with the operation and maintenance of the ship's boilers, turbines, generators, and other engineering equipment. He had three assistants—Lieutenant (jg) Walter Deutsch, Ensign Jesse D. Cochran, and an enlisted machinist, John A. Merritt, who was included among the officers in the ship's official deck log and would subsequently be promoted to ensign.

With signal flags and semaphore enhanced by radio, there was a need for a communications officer, and Lieutenant (jg) Ed Digardi had fleeted up from assistant to take over that role. He was now assisted by Lieutenant (jg) Ellsworth Welch and Ensign John F. Sterling (not to be confused with XO Elton B. Stirling).

The advent of radar required a radar officer billet, which was filled by Ensign Don B. Rentschler, who was later replaced by fleeting up Sandberg.

Of the twenty men listed as officers in the 31 June deck log, four claimed the state of Washington as their home of record, and four others claimed California. Two each were from Pennsylvania, Illinois, and Ohio. The rest claimed Florida, New York, Rhode Island, Indiana, New Jersey, and Oklahoma.

Eleven had wives, and the other nine listed their parents (five fathers and four mothers) as their next of kin.

Seven of the officers, as Naval Academy graduates, were considered "regular Navy" and appended "USN" (for United States Navy) when signing their names and ranks. Wartime requirements caused the more junior officers to spend only three years at Annapolis instead of the usual four. The other officers had earned their commissions through accelerated naval training at the Naval Officer Candidate School in Newport, Rhode Island, or at a number of civilian colleges and universities that were part of the Navy's V-7 United States Naval Reserve Midshipmen's School program. They were considered "reservists" rather than regulars and appended their names and ranks with "D-V (G), USNR," indicating that they were "Officers of the Volunteer Reserve to the line for general service in deck duties."

Four of the twenty would leave the ship before the ship's final battle (Secrest, Sterling, Rentschler, and Hadfield), and two new officers would join the ship in the months remaining: Ensign Charles H. Kilpatrick would relieve Sterling, and Lieutenant (jg) Robert T. Browne would relieve Hadfield as ship's doctor.

These officers and the men they led had been brought together by the Fates to serve in USS *Johnston* under the command of Ernest Evans. All had exhibited a degree of courage by joining the Navy in the midst of a world war. In such an eclectic group there were significant differences in how they felt about serving under a captain who seemed determined to fight, but one of the exceptional characteristics of command at sea is that individual attitudes are subservient to those of their captain. If he chose to go in harm's way, they would all go in harm's way. His courage was their courage, and whether a member of the crew was the gunnery officer or worked in the ship's laundry, his and every other man's fate would be determined by what Ernest Evans chose to do in the face of the great adversity that waited for them over the horizon in a place called Leyte Gulf.

Leyte Gulf was nearly four months and many, many steaming miles away. Although the ship would participate in more shore bombardments as the Pacific Fleet continued to take more islands and atolls in its slow but relentless westward march, most of the time was spent in transits, patrols, replenishments, repair availabilities, and escort duties. Deck logs and war diaries provide a mind-numbing account of long, often monotonous days at sea, punctuated by anchorages in places they had been before. Letters home more often reflected hopes for a postwar future than descriptions of shipboard life. Repairs and preventive maintenance—such as lubrication and rust removal—were a part of nearly every day and were essential to the ship's ability to perform with proficiency but were devoid of any excitement or color. Drills and exercises that included firing weapons, employing exotic equipment such as radar and sonar, and learning military procedures and argot were once deemed fun to the novice crew but had long since been reevaluated as too frequent, too repetitive, and too tiring. Watch stations were maintained twenty-four hours a day, varying only by whether the ship was underway or moored, and were often preceded or followed by routine tasks of cooking, laundering, sweeping, and swabbing. There never was enough time, yet it often seemed to crawl.

Comfort was a scarce commodity. Heat was prevalent, with insulation rare and air-conditioning nonexistent. The interior of the ship often felt like a furnace, and the heat radiating from decks could be felt through the soles of shoes. Running through a squall could sometimes bring relief as small clouds of steam rose from the griddle-like weather decks. When the "greyhound" was running at full or flank speed, a merciful relative wind could provide a healing tonic, but when the ship ran downwind, that respite was canceled, and the stifling heat was often joined by swirling stack gases that burned the lungs as well.

Because the boilers drank prodigious amounts of fresh water and took precedence, "water hours" could be mandated if the ship ran low on water, restricting even drinking water to limited periods of consumption. One fireman who before the war had preferred other beverages swore that after the war he would never look at a glass of water the same. Except on those rare occasions when the ship had the luxury of topping off her tanks with fresh water from pipelines ashore, the destroyer made her own fresh water by taking in seawater through intakes on the underside of her hull and processing it through the onboard evaporators. Once, during an underway replenishment, the ship followed an oiler whose wake left a sheen at the edges, presumably caused by her leaking of some kind of fuel. Soon thereafter, *Johnston*'s drinking water smelled and tasted vaguely like fuel oil. Doc Hadfield assured the crew that the water had been tested and was safe to drink, but the resulting scuttlebutt claimed that someone had actually gotten the water to ignite using a Zippo lighter.

Limited water meant that the crew lived with frustrating brief "Navy showers." Woe betide the sailor caught indulging himself by taking more than his share of the precious water! One seaman second class who was new to the ship had committed this cardinal sin and was saved from several forms of threatened retribution by Chief Burnett, who extracted from the young offender a very sincere apology and an earnest promise not to repeat.

After another visit to Kwajalein in early June, a change in venue was presented when *Johnston* was ordered to head west for the Marianas to take part in an impending invasion of Guam and Saipan, code named Operation Forager. *Johnston*'s war diary entry for 15 June recorded, "Proceeding toward Guam. Most of the day was spent listening to the progress of operations at Saipan by monitoring various circuits, particularly the Task Force Gunfire Support Common, which we received particularly well, in spite of the fact that units operating on the circuit in close proximity to each other were having considerable trouble and requiring a great deal of repetition."

If Evans' perceived frustration was real, it is likely that having this "ringside seat" for the landings taking place on Saipan but being unable to participate caused his frustration to fester during this transit. The invasion of Saipan was of great strategic importance, since its occupation would put the Japanese home islands within range of Army Air Force bombers. Consequently, considerably more ships and troops were committed than had been for previous assaults.

Evans' frustration was probably also fueled by the momentous events taking place in the days that followed, while *Johnston* languished in a kind of limbo. For five days (16–20 June), *Johnston* was ordered to proceed westward during the day only to retire eastward at night, keeping her in a "box" 150–300 miles east of Guam, waiting to take part in the assault on Guam. Meanwhile, on 19 and 20 June, Japanese and American carrier forces engaged in a huge aerial battle that became known as the "Great Marianas Turkey Shoot" because of the lopsided American victory. Twenty-four carriers and over thirteen hundred aircraft took part, and the Japanese lost roughly half of their aircraft as well as two of their fleet carriers and a light carrier. Nearly 3,000 Japanese personnel were killed in action, compared to 109 Americans. *Johnston*'s war diary (signed and possibly written by Evans) reported that "it was a period of great anxiety and we watched with interest the progress of operations against Saipan and the Japanese Fleet."

The subsequent invasion of Guam had been scheduled for 18 June but was postponed, and for the next nine days *Johnston* continued steaming "back and forth awaiting further orders." Then, on the midwatch of 27 June, she and the destroyer *Franks* were ordered to screen the attack cargo ship *Centaurus* (AKA 17), the attack transport *Harry Lee* (APA 10), and the coastal minesweeper *Vigor* (AMc 110) as they steamed south to rendezvous with an eastbound convoy. After delivering those three auxiliaries to the convoy, the two destroyers were ordered to return to their previous task group.

Making no further progress toward Guam, *Johnston* was ordered to return once again to the Marshalls on 30 June. The 3 July war diary recorded, "Arrived at Eniwetok Atoll after a very uneventful passage."

After undergoing voyage repairs and conducting several offshore patrols while at Eniwetok, *Johnston* received orders to return to the Marianas. She escorted the transports and carriers of Task Unit 53.7.4 as they sortied from Eniwetok, heading through "Deep Passage" at the north end of the lagoon. She then took up station in the antisubmarine screen for the uneventful voyage to the Marianas. At 0430 on 21 July, she detached from the screen to proceed independently to Fire Support Area 6-1 in Agat Bay on the west side of Guam. There she reported to the commander of Task Force 53.5.6, who was embarked in USS *Pennsylvania* to "fire counterbattery and neutralizing fire" and then to provide close supporting fire for the landing of the First Provisional Marine Brigade.

Coordinating with the battleships *Colorado* and *Pennsylvania*, *Johnston* carried out multiple firing missions, as recorded in her official Action Report:

> From 0530 until 0840, 21 July 1944, this ship shelled Agat town, beaches, pill boxes and strong points, fired counter battery fire, and, in general, cleared the territory of our landing beach of the enemy and his guns; from 0856 until 1520, same date, the ship was on call fires, but during periods when services were not needed by shore fire control party, fired

> counter battery, anti-personnel fire, and at targets of opportunity along the beaches north of Agat.

Johnston moved in very close to the beach as the Marines landed on the beach, providing close fire support as well as clearing vegetation with her secondary battery, earning a shore fire control party's praise: "beautiful shooting." She continued more of the same the following day before heading out to sea to take up an antisubmarine patrol. Returning to Agat Bay on 23 July, she anchored to stand by for call fire duty. At 1110, small-arms fire from the beach produced a loud rattling sound as several rounds struck the plating just below the bridge. No one was injured, but Bob Billie decided "that was as close as I ever wanted to get to flying bullets."

Evans often deliberately maneuvered his destroyer in close to the beach as landing craft were approaching, deliberately drawing fire from Japanese defenders because "we have a lot more protection on this ship than the Marines in those landing craft," he told Bob Hagen. In his after-action report, he recorded that although the Japanese frequently straddled the ship with their fire, "small amounts of maneuvering prevented any hits."

On two occasions, when ammunition was running low, Evans had his gig lowered into the water and asked his coxswain to take him over to the task group's flagship to ask for more ammo. On both occasions, he got it.

Several times during the bombardment, *Johnston*'s firing was so intense that her gun barrels glowed red, forcing Lieutenant Hagen to call a ceasefire to allow the guns time to cool down. During one of those cool-down periods, Bob Hollenbaugh left his perch in Mount 54 to check on conditions in the upper handling room, when he encountered a number of Marines who had been wounded while in an LVT and brought on board to be cared for by *Johnston*'s medical team. As Hollenbaugh passed, a young Marine managed a weak smile—despite having had his arm shot off. Hollenbaugh stopped and asked how he was doing, and the Marine said, "I'm fine, sir." The two men talked for a minute, and the Marine told Hollenbaugh that he had joined the Marines just nine weeks earlier. Hollenbaugh thought he looked like he was just fourteen years old and remembered thinking, "My God, what is this world coming to?" That evening, he told fellow gun captain Clint Carter, "I'll never forget the expression on that kid's face. And he still had the presence of mind to look up at me and call me sir!"

Doc Hadfield did what he could for the wounded men, and a day later they were transferred to the attack transport *Harry Lee*.

In his war diary, Evans included an enthusiastic evaluation of the ships' 40-mm guns, noting that the weapon "is really a Jap killer." He also called the performance of his crew "marvelous," noting that "days and nights we were either shooting, standing by to shoot, loading ammunition, or fueling ship. Their only fear was that we would run out of ammunition and have some other destroyer ordered to replace us. It was an inspiring performance." Whether this reflects the actual feelings of the crew or his own is unknown, but the question is intriguing.

He also focused on his executive officer and his gunnery officer: "Lieutenant Stirling, with practically no rest or sleep, and often without meals, manned his station in CIC as evaluator and furnished target set up for all call fires, illumination, and night harassing fire. During the entire eight days and nights, in spite of his fatigue, there was not a single miscue in his performance." His description of Bob Hagen's performance was equally glowing, writing that he "took under fire every enemy battery which could be located and quickly silenced same. His fast and accurate fire prevented damage to this ship by enemy fire, saved lives and loss in the beach area, and contributed immeasurably to the success of the operation and to the small loss of life in the beachhead area."

Johnston remained at Guam performing numerous fire missions and other duties until 9 August, when she was ordered to—once again—return to Eniwetok. After effecting some repairs while in the atoll, GQ Johnny got underway for a return to Espiritu Santo in the New Hebrides for more upkeep, remaining there until 27 August, when she and seven other destroyers got underway and escorted a task unit of battleships and cruisers bound for the Solomons.

Arriving at Purvis Bay on the south side of Florida Island just before the forenoon watch on the 29th, she refueled and was soon underway again, but not before receiving forty-two bags of second-class mail (newspapers and magazines) that had at last caught up with her. While this bonanza of reading material was happily received by the crew, most would have preferred first-class letters.

For the maintenance of crew morale, only food and sleep mattered as much as letters from home. When "mail call" was sounded over the 1MC, the ship reverberated with the sound of boondockers on steel as men not on watch rushed to get their paper treasures. Once they had their precious missives, many would share their newly acquired news (some of it months old) with shipmates, while others would seek some quiet place where they could deal with the emotions these often-weathered pages evoked. It was not unusual to see men sniffing at the pages in hopes of garnering some traces of perfume. Some opened their letters with nervous trepidation, fearing bad news such as a death in the family or the dreaded "Dear John" letter telling them that a girlfriend had moved on.

Moving these prized pages from the farms and towns and cities of America through the fleet postal center in San Francisco and on to the distant corners of the Pacific to find their moving targets was a gargantuan task. Letters often arrived out of sequence or never arrived at all. Most postal clerks treated them as the treasures they were, but some letters arrived barely legible, having been subjected to rough handling or to natural forces such as rainstorms or intense heat and humidity.

Sailors could send letters back home for free. They only had to write "Free" in the upper right corner of the envelope and include their name, rank or rating, and military branch with their return address in the upper left corner. The standard postage rate for civilians was three cents.

Letters were subject to censorship to avoid revealing information that might be useful to an intercepting enemy. Sailors could not tell their loved ones where they were and could say little about what they were doing. A carelessly written letter could arrive with large blocks of text blacked out.

As the war progressed, to reduce the volume of letters that took up valuable cargo space needed for other wartime essentials, the postal service introduced "V-Mail" (short for Victory Mail). V-Mail letters were photographed using Recordak machines, which had been developed by Eastman Kodak. They were then sent as negatives on microfilm and were reprinted on paper at specially equipped stations overseas. Sixteen hundred letters could be stored on one roll of film, reducing them to approximately 3 percent of their original weight and volume, a great space saver on crowded transports. To encourage its use, V-Mail received preferential sorting and transportation. More than a billion V-Mail letters were delivered during the war.

There were drawbacks to V-Mail, however. A combination letter and envelope on distinctive stationery was required, and letters were limited to seven hundred words. In order for the reprints to be legible, the originals had to be written using a typewriter or a dark pen or pencil. Because the received letter was reduced in size, it could be rendered illegible if the original print was too small. Perhaps worst of all, any perfume on the original was lost, and lipstick imprints affixed by the sender could gum up the Recordak machines, hence postal workers dubbed them the "scarlet scourge."

At the end of August, *Johnston* began screening escort carriers (CVEs) as they practiced for the upcoming amphibious assault on Peleliu in the Palau island group by bombing target ranges on Guadalcanal. This was a harbinger: *Johnston* would face her greatest challenge, screening CVEs at Leyte Gulf, in less than two months.

CVEs were relative newcomers to naval aviation. Known as "baby flattops," "jeep carriers," and more sardonically "combustible, vulnerable, and expendable," they were mostly built on merchant ship hulls and generally were about half as long as the fleet carriers, with only a third of the displacement. They could carry twenty-four to thirty aircraft, compared to over a hundred carried by the fleet carriers. A prime advantage was their relatively low cost, which allowed the United States to commission over a hundred of them. (Of the 122 CVEs built, exactly none of them exist today. They were a World War II phenomenon, operating in both the Atlantic and Pacific theaters, and were discarded after the war.) Too slow to keep up with the fast-moving forces built around fleet aircraft carriers, battleships, cruisers, and destroyers, the CVEs provided convoy air cover and ground support to troops during amphibious landings and sometimes served as "ferries" transporting replacement aircraft and other heavy equipment to combat theaters.

On 4 September, with the bombing practice on Guadalcanal completed, Task Unit 32.7.2—the CVEs *Saginaw Bay*, *Petrof Bay*, and *Kalinan Bay*, with destroyers *Hailey*, *Wells*, and *Johnston* providing antisubmarine protection—headed for the Palau Islands on the western edge of the Carolines. Arriving in time for "Dog Day" (the beginning of the assault on Peleliu), the CVEs launched scheduled and on-call air strikes in support of the troops landing on the beaches, while the destroyers screened the carriers against possible submarine attacks.

The task unit operated offshore to provide maneuvering room for the carriers to run into the wind to launch and recover their aircraft and then run downwind until it was time for the next round of flight operations. *Johnston*'s war diary included a familiar refrain: "We listened intently to the progress of the landing over the air observer's circuit and enviously to the bombardments over the Fire Support Common [circuit]. This was the first operation we have been in since commissioning that this ship had not been assigned to a close-in fire support mission."

For the next two days, the task unit operated within visual range of the island by day, then retired to the southeast at night. The war diary chronicled, "The period was very quiet, and the only diversion was an occasional sound contact which always proved to be non-submarine upon investigation."

One can sense the disappointment and frustration in these entries, and Bob Hagen made clear how he felt about screening CVEs rather than bombarding enemy-held beaches: "Now we were sore-saddled with those pestiferous flat-tops! How were we ever going to keep our shooting hand in, playing nursemaid to plane-toting tubs?" And with hindsight one can venture that *Johnston*'s good shooting might have been an asset to the struggles ashore. The capture of Peleliu was a bloody affair that was later described as "the bitterest battle of the war for the Marines." Capturing the small coral island cost the Army and Marines nearly ten thousand men killed and wounded, a 35 percent casualty rate.

On 18 September, *Johnston* was transferred to Task Unit 32.7.3, a similar grouping of CVEs—*Kitkun Bay*, *White Plains*, and *Gambier Bay*—with the same mission of supporting the landings on Peleliu. Evans seemed pleased by the change, recording, "Screening was greatly facilitated and afforded greater protection to the carriers as this OTC [officer in tactical command—Rear

Admiral Ralph A. Ostie] did not require the screen to reorient on every change of course but only on changes of base course." Apparently Evans disagreed with the tactics of the commander of the previous task unit. In order to lessen the chances of an enemy getting a good targeting solution on the formation of ships, task unit commanders periodically altered the formation course (zigzagged), while making sure that those alterations were designed so that the formation maintained a base course overall. Ostie's decision to allow the screening destroyers to base their maneuvers on the base course rather than the additional zigzags enabled them to maneuver less, obviating "mad dashes" to maintain their assigned stations and therefore allowing them to make less noise and have a better chance of detecting submarines that might be lurking in the area.

On 21 September, Task Unit 32.7.3 was assigned a new task unit designation—TU 33.12.2—with a new mission of providing air cover for Task Group 33.19, whose mission was to capture Ulithi Atoll, about four hundred nautical miles northeast of Peleliu. By the beginning of the first dog watch, *Johnston* was headed for Ulithi.

Several hours passed without event, but with less than an hour left to the midwatch, Lieutenant (jg) Robert Browne, the ship's new medical officer, was wakened from a sound sleep by a summons to the after berthing compartment. "Hurry, sir," the messenger of the watch urged. Clad only in a pair of khaki trousers and a T-shirt, Doc Browne headed aft to find Engineman Second Class Oscar Blondin unresponsive in his rack, apparently in a coma. Browne administered artificial respiration for more than an hour but at 0642 declared him dead.

Blondin had enlisted in the Navy in November 1942 and was one of *Johnston*'s "plankowners" (a member of the commissioning crew). Bob Hollenbaugh had gotten to know him and remembered him as "a swell guy, even if he was a snipe."

At 1530 that afternoon, those members of the crew not on watch mustered on the fantail to carry out the time-honored but onerous tradition of burial at sea. Wartime necessity made this the only option. Because ships could not spare any room for coffins, Petty Officer Blondin's body had been sewn into a weighted cloth bag and then laid out on a platform that had been positioned at the rail. An American flag was placed over his body with the union placed at the head, over the left shoulder. Standard procedure for burials at sea dictated that the ship should stop for the ceremony if possible, but because the threat of enemy submarines could not be discounted, the ship maintained her course and speed.

Since chaplains were generally assigned to larger ships, Captain Evans conducted the ceremony with a short eulogy and a reading from the Army and Navy prayer book. At 1538 the platform was tilted to allow Petty Officer Blondin's remains to slide out from beneath the American flag and plunge into the deep. Chief Burnett signaled the seven-man firing squad to fire three volleys with their M-1 rifles. A somber mood prevailed as the crew resumed their normal duties.

Johnston and the other ships arrived at Ulithi during the midwatch on 23 September. A reconnaissance of the atoll revealed no enemy troops, and the natives appeared friendly, so the scheduled bombardment was called off, and the main elements of TG 33.19 entered the lagoon at dawn, *Johnston* and several other destroyers remaining outside the coral ring to patrol for submarines south of Ulithi.

The next day *Johnston* and *Haggard* screened the carriers *Kitkun Bay* and *Gambier Bay* as they entered the Ulithi lagoon. Once inside the lagoon, *Johnston* moored alongside the anchored attack transport (APA) *Barnstable* to refuel and remain until morning. The APA was more than a hundred feet longer than the destroyer, and with her large freeboard, she towered above them like some great castle wall. Bobby Chastain noted that "at least one side of our ship was safe from a Jap attack." The war diary for that evening happily recorded, "We enjoyed a movie on the fantail."

At 0601 the next morning, 25 September, *Johnston* took in her lines and eased away from the transport. Twisting about, she headed for Mugai Pass out of the Ulithi Atoll, screening the escort carrier *Gambier Bay*. On their way out, Ed Digardi noted that this was "a hell of a big lagoon." His assessment was correct. Less than a week after their departure, the Navy's 18th Special Battalion of Seabees arrived to start construction on what would become the largest naval base in the world at the time. Using five islands of the atoll, the Seabees built piers, airstrips, a supply depot, a naval hospital, multiple

IMAGE 13 • A huge American task force anchors at the vast Ulithi Atoll.

repair facilities, a 1,600-man mess hall, a fleet recreation center capable of serving up to 20,000 sailors and troops, and staging for 150 aircraft to replace losses on the carriers. When fully functional, the Ulithi base required nearly 10,000 men to run its many facilities.

After prosecuting a possible submarine contact, dropping twenty depth charges before concluding that the contact was "doubtful," *Johnston* joined TU 32.18.1 to screen three escort carriers as they headed for Manus Island in the Admiralties, via Hollandia, New Guinea.

Arriving at Manus on 1 October, *Johnston* received a tender availability in preparation for her next operation. It had been nearly a year since they had left Seattle. They had steamed thousands of miles, were underway more than not, had earned five battle stars, and taken part in more operations than anyone cared to count. Chief Burnett recalled, "She had been rode hard and put away wet." Yet GQ Johnny was in remarkably good shape, if not quite the "thing of absolute beauty" that Ed Digardi had described back in her early days after commissioning. A few streaks of running rust had eluded the chipping hammers of the "deck apes," and there were some minor dents where Japanese bullets had struck just below the bridge during the assault on Guam. A few of the valves in the engineering plant required more muscle to open or close, and some of her electronics occasionally balked at the humid conditions that prevailed in the South Pacific, behaving erratically at inopportune times. But overall, as Bob Hollenbaugh put it, "she had kept her girlish figure and was every bit the fighting ship she was supposed to be."

The eleven days they spent at Manus were spent performing what had become routine maintenance. Bill Mercer was glad to get some new parts for one of the washing machines that had been giving him some trouble, and Harley Chronister remembered swearing to himself that when the war was over, he was never again going to touch a paintbrush. Years later, Ed Digardi would recall,

> Of course we didn't know this would be our last time not underway. By this time, we had gotten used to our lot in life, and I think we kind of thought things would go on the way they had until the end of the war. I certainly *hoped* it would. We had done plenty of shooting and had even gotten shot at, and I felt like we could go home and say we did our part in the war, but there was also this realization that others had done a lot more. We knew a lot of ships had been through a lot more than we had—some had been sunk. We had not been attacked by air and never even seen an enemy torpedo. We had missed the really big battles, and by this time it was pretty clear we were going to win. The one thing we didn't know was *when*. Some of the fellas thought it would be soon, but I remember thinking the war could go on a lot longer. After the war, a couple of them would say that while at Manus they had a feeling that something big was coming our way, but I didn't. I had no idea what was coming and am glad I didn't.

CHAPTER 9

"IT'S BEEN AN UNEVENTFUL YEAR"

On 21 October 1944, an Army general stepped from a landing craft into shin-deep surf and strode purposefully up the gentle slope toward the sand of Leyte Island. Generals do not usually wade ashore during an amphibious landing, especially when the sounds of mortal combat can be heard not far away, but this was no ordinary general and no ordinary landing.

In the gathering darkness of the early days of the war, when defeat had followed defeat, the brave but futile stand that General Douglas MacArthur's forces had made on the fortified peninsula of Bataan and the island of Corregidor had been a welcome ray of light. The general had been elevated to heroic proportions in the eyes of many of the American people, and the possibility of allowing him to fall into the hands of an enemy whose propagandists predicted that they would see him publicly hanged in the Imperial Plaza in Tokyo was simply unthinkable. So President Franklin D. Roosevelt had ordered the general to leave the Philippines.

Escaping by PT boat, he arrived in Australia and immediately proclaimed his determination to avenge this ignominious retreat, capturing the imagination of those Americans and Filipinos who had placed their faith in him with three small but powerful words: "I shall return."

Now, two years, seven months, and three days since his departure, he had indeed returned. As he waded ashore, in front of him were photographers and a microphone that he would use to tell the Filipino people—and the world—of his momentous return; behind him in Leyte Gulf were so many ships that the horizon was nearly invisible behind the near-continuous gray wall of hulls and superstructures.

Two separate American fleets had come to the Philippine Sea for this promised return. The powerful Third Fleet under Admiral William F. Halsey—with its four task groups centered around 9 fleet carriers and 8 light carriers and supported by 6 battleships, 15 cruisers, and 58 destroyers—was there in case the Japanese showed up to contest the landing. The Seventh Fleet, commanded by Vice Admiral Thomas C. Kinkaid, consisted of the amphibious forces for the assault on Leyte—18 escort carriers, 6 battleships, 5 heavy cruisers, 4 light cruisers, 34 destroyers, 17 destroyer escorts, 280 landing and support ships, and more than a hundred auxiliaries.

The bulk of Kinkaid's Seventh Fleet was inside Leyte Gulf, the transports and amphibious vessels busily putting troops and supplies ashore while gun-toting battleships, cruisers, and destroyers provided gunfire support. Outside the gulf, where they had more room to conduct air operations, steamed the remainder of the Seventh Fleet, the tiny escort carriers and a small contingent of destroyers and destroyer escorts whose task it was to guard the carriers against submarine and air attack. These diminutive flattops and their escorts were designated as Task Force 77.4—the Central Philippines Attack Force—commanded by Rear Admiral Thomas L Sprague. The eighteen carriers in the force had been further divided into three task groups, each consisting of six CVEs and their escorts. These task groups were formally designated as TG 77.4.1, TG 77.4.2, and TG 77.4.3 but were more commonly referred to by their radio voice call signs, "Taffy 1, 2, and 3," respectively. Admiral Sprague retained command of Taffy 1 as a "second hat," but he had designated separate subordinate commanders of the other two task groups. Taffy 2 was commanded by Rear Admiral Felix B. Stump, and Taffy 3 was the responsibility of Rear Admiral Clifton A. F. Sprague, who, despite the last name, was not related to his boss Thomas L. (but they were Naval Academy classmates—class of 1917).

Among the thirteen ships making up Taffy 3 was USS *Johnston.* She and the destroyers and destroyer escorts *Heerman* (DD 532), *Hoel* (DD 533), John C. Butler (DE 339), *Raymond* (DE 341), *Dennis* (DE 405), and *Samuel B. Roberts* (DE 413) were tasked with protecting the carriers *Fanshaw Bay* (CVE 70), Saint Lo (CVE 63), *White Plains* (CVE 66), *Kalinan Bay* (CVE 68), *Kitkun Bay* (CVE 71), and *Gambier Bay* (CVE 73).

Taffy 3's mission was to provide air support for the troops ashore on Leyte and to conduct antisubmarine patrols to keep away any marauding Japanese submarines that might be tempted to steal into the gulf where there were hundreds of tempting targets.

In the days following MacArthur's history-making moment on the Leyte beach, the largest naval battle in history took place as the Japanese sent the bulk of their remaining fleet to challenge the landing. Halsey's Third Fleet mounted massive air attacks on Japanese forces as they made their way across the Sibuyan and Sulu Seas, and other Japanese forces that attempted to enter Leyte Gulf through Surigao Strait to the south were confronted by those battleships, cruisers, and destroyers of Kinkaid's fleet that were inside the gulf.

Once again, it appeared that GQ Johnny had been relegated to the periphery of operations, carrying out important but relatively mundane operations in the waters outside the gulf, east of Samar Island, while big battles were raging elsewhere.

But this time Fate had other ideas. Because Admiral Halsey had mistaken a Japanese decoy force for a powerful carrier force, he decided to engage, a decision that was understandable and might have been of relatively little consequence except that he took his entire fleet northward toward Cape Engano, effectively leaving the door north of Leyte wide open to a potent Japanese force of battleships, cruisers, and destroyers.

As Clint Carter sat at the mess table hovering over a cup of joe, he was thinking about what he would do after the war. He liked being a gunner's mate, and he was good at it. Although he was just a third-class petty officer, he had been selected to be gun captain for the 5-inch farthest aft, Mount 55. He was glad that he held one of the so-called right-arm rates. (In 1913, the Navy required sailors in the seaman branch [boatswain's mates, gunner's mates, torpedoman's mates, minemen, quartermasters, and signalmen] to wear their rating badges on their right sleeves, while all the other ratings [engineering, supply, etc.] would continue to wear theirs on their left sleeves. While the correct term was "right-arm ratings," the shorter word "rate" was in common usage. There was an unofficial but prevalent feeling in Navy culture that the right-arm rates were more important because they were more like traditional sailors who served in the earlier, "swashbuckling" age of sail.

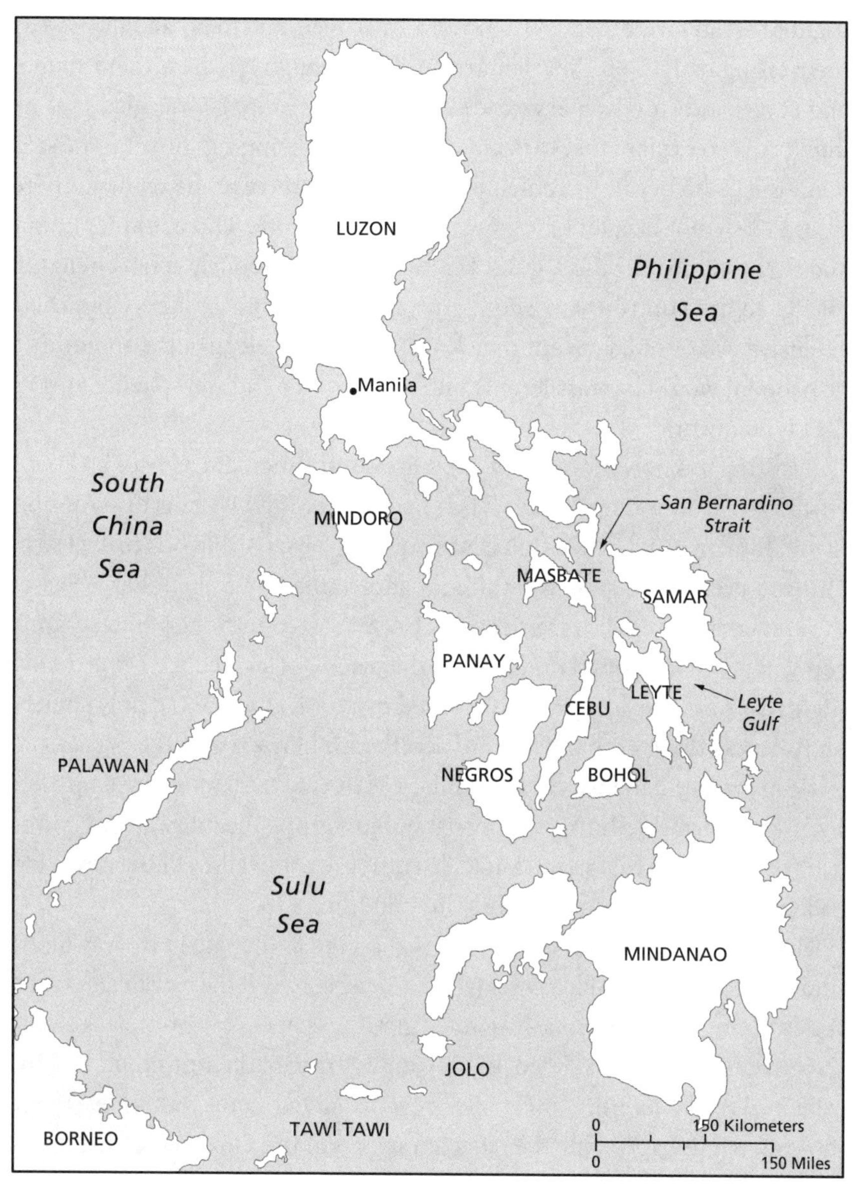

MAP 4 • Philippines

Right-arm rates were disestablished on 2 April 1949, and today all sailors wear their rating badges on their left arms.) Even though he knew that firemen and cooks and storekeepers were essential to the ship, he was glad that he didn't have to explain that to people back home—being a gunner's mate said it all. But as he began to contemplate the end of the war, he realized there would likely not be a lot of job openings for someone who could maintain and shoot 5-inch/38-caliber guns. He was thinking seriously about changing ratings to fire controlman. Those guys were also "right armers," but their extensive use of radar meant they knew a lot about electronics, something he believed would be transferable into some useful and well-paying jobs in the civilian world.

Wanting to know more about what fire controlmen did, Carter had convinced Fire Controlman Third Class Thomas (Tommy) Perkins to allow him to join him on watch when things were quiet to observe and hopefully learn. Things were indeed quiet as midnight approached on 25 October. Most of the crew not on watch was asleep. As Carter stared into the white ceramic cup with "USN" painted on its sides, the black circle of coffee rippled only slightly as *Johnston*'s engines thrummed rhythmically, and the only sounds on the mess deck were the hum of ventilation blowers and the occasional rattle of pans and utensils in the scullery as the mess cooks cleaned up after serving "midrats" to hungry sailors about to assume the midwatch. Perkins had the midwatch that night, and Carter took a last swallow of the now-cold coffee before heading up the ladder to join him.

Huddled over the cathode ray tube that served as the radar's display in the ship's combat information center (CIC), Carter stared at the blackened screen as a sweeping arm momentarily ignited glowing shapes of various sizes on the screen that then quickly faded, leaving only a trace of their position. Perkins explained that as *Johnston*'s SG radar antenna rotated on the mast above them, those glowing shapes were the reflected signals of the ships in the formation. He added that although *Johnston* was in sector F of the antisubmarine screen around the carriers in Formation 5R, the picture generated by her radar placed her at the center of the display, which meant that the other ships' positions were relative to her rather than true. Carter's head began to hurt.

For the next half hour, Perkins tried valiantly to explain what they were seeing on the radar scope and how, using parallel rulers, dividers, and a paper tablet with a "maneuvering board" printed on each sheet, he could employ polar coordinate geometry and vectors to graphically solve maneuvering problems. But Carter later admitted, "It was all Greek to me."

About the time that Carter was wondering if there might be a better rating for him to pursue, Perkins said, "Now that's interesting." He pointed the tips of his dividers at some fresh blips appearing intermittently on the outer edge of the scope. Several sweeps of the radar made the faint blips grow slightly brighter before fading.

"What *are* those?" Carter asked.

"Don't know," replied Perkins. "I've got the range cranked out so they are a long way off. They aren't part of our formation, that's for sure." Several more sweeps revealed that the blips were drawing closer to the middle of the display. "Better tell Mr. Digardi," Perkins concluded.

Lieutenant (jg) Ed Digardi had arrived on the bridge about fifteen minutes before midnight. After stumbling around the darkened bridge until his eyes had adjusted to night vision, he was ready to assume the watch. Standing behind the centerline binnacle, he saluted the current officer of the deck, Lieutenant Jack Bechdel, and uttered those traditional and legally binding words, "I relieve you, sir." Bechdel returned the salute and said, "I stand relieved." In a loud voice for all personnel on the bridge to hear, Digardi then said, "This is Mister Digardi, I have the deck." Out of the darkness came the replies of the watch team: "Helm aye, sir," "Lee helm aye, sir," and so on.

After a while, Bob Hagen emerged from the darkness and joined Digardi on the starboard side of the bridge. "Couldn't sleep," he explained. "I was down in the radio shack monitoring the radios and thought you might like to know that there is a big brawl going on down in Surigao Strait." He led Digardi to the chart table at the back of the bridge, and by the red light over the chart, they could see that Surigao Strait was a very narrow passage due south of Leyte Gulf.

"Apparently the Japs tried to come up through there," Hagen continued. "A lot of battleships, cruisers, and destroyers slugging it out, and it's pretty clear that the Japs are getting the worst of it."

Shielding the flame with his hands, Hagen lit a Lucky Strike and then said with apparent disgust, "And here we sit, miles away, mother-henning these floating airfields when we could be sinking some Japs."

Digardi marveled at how much Hagen sounded like their captain as he voiced his disappointment at not being "where the real action is." Digardi was just as glad to be quietly escorting CVEs rather than participating in the big surface engagement that was apparently taking place in Surigao Strait. He wondered if his friend would be as enthusiastic to join the fray if there were big Japanese guns firing at them. In the year since the ship's commissioning, they had earned five battle stars, but except for participating in the sinking of one Japanese submarine that had been unable to fight back, their combat experience had been limited to attacking Japanese islands that only occasionally responded with counter–battery fire. He guessed that was not the same as what they would encounter from an angry battleship. As far as he knew, no American ships had been sunk while providing fire support to amphibious landings, but there were many U.S. ships on the bottom of the Pacific that had encountered Japanese surface combatants. He was content to take his chances with screening these baby flattops, although he had to admit a tinge of excitement as he listened to the crackling radios narrating the big battle somewhere over the southwestern horizon.

Hagen interrupted Digardi's reverie by saying, "Funny thing earlier today. 'The Chief' pointed out that we are three days away from being one year old." Only occasionally would any of the officers refer to Evans by that nickname, and never in his presence. Hagen added, "He said it's been an uneventful year." Digardi pondered that, recalling the many rounds they had fired at Japanese-held islands and the sub they helped sink. "Not sure I agree with that, but I guess he has a different frame of reference." Hagen crushed out his cigarette, then said, "Yes, he does."

The two men fell silent, both of them pensively peering out at the sea, Digardi wondering what their next year would bring.

After a while, Hagen decided to go below and try to get some sleep. Without his friend to engage in conversation, it was a quiet watch as *Johnston* and the other destroyers continued to screen the escort carriers in case any Japanese submarines were in the area. Only the periodic zigzags of the formation broke the monotony of steady steaming.

Digardi was fighting the drowsiness that often accompanies such watches when Petty Officer First Class William Shaw relayed what Perkins had seen on his scope down in CIC. Digardi immediately called the captain. Evans emerged from his sea cabin in less than a minute, and he quickly descended the ladder to CIC before returning to the bridge and picking up the TBS radio handset (TBS stood for "talk between ships," the voice radio network that ships used to communicate with each other during World War II) to report the unidentified contacts to his superior.

Instead of an "attaboy," Evans received a dressing-down in reply, experiencing some of the hubris that American commanders had brought to Leyte Gulf. He was informed that those contacts Perkins had seen were American, and he was chastised for breaking radio silence to make the report.

Evans returned the handset to its cradle and wordlessly returned to his sea cabin. As Digardi watched the captain's door close, he felt a surge of anger. His captain deserved better. Evans was obviously trying to do what he believed was the right thing. With all that was going on around them, it was understandable that Evans might not know those ships were American. And what if those contacts were Japanese . . . ?

As darkness gave way to morning light, the wind barely whispered across the calm surface of the Philippine Sea. Intermittent rain squalls occasionally disturbed the otherwise tranquil scene and provided *Johnston* with a "freshwater washdown" that rinsed some of the glistening salt from her weather decks. In the growing light, Els Welch could see another *Fletcher*-class destroyer as he scanned the waters from the port bridge wing. Peering aft, he could see one of the six escort carriers they were screening, and through his binoculars he could barely make out figures scurrying about on her wooden flight deck as they made preparations for their morning launch.

Leaning over the rail, he could smell "delightful breakfast odors wafting up from the galley" and was looking forward to a hot breakfast once he was relieved as OOD on the 0400–0800 morning watch. But before he could indulge in such gastronomic pleasures, he had a duty to carry out. As was the routine most days at sea, the approach of daylight mandated "dawn alert," and it was time for the ship's crew to man their battle stations. Japanese air attacks often occurred at dawn or dusk, so it made sense to go to general quarters as a precaution during these times of extra vulnerability. Welch told the boatswain's mate of the watch to sound general quarters, and soon the sleeping ship came alive with men racing for their battle stations.

In all the many, many times that *Johnston*'s crew had carried out this disruptive but important routine, not one Japanese aircraft had attacked. Virtually no one dared tempt the fates by pointing this out, and complaints were rare, but this was indeed a somewhat onerous task: No matter what they were doing, every man had to pay homage to the god of war in case he should decide to make an unwanted appearance. Whether in the sack trying to squeeze out some elusive sleep or already standing a watch, they had to stop and run to their assigned battle station, don battle dress, and light off any equipment in their charge. They were of course glad when it turned out to be only a fruitless precaution, but human nature being what it is, it was sometimes difficult to suppress thoughts of "just once . . . " Usually this morning ritual was short-lived, and each man had to either resume his previous watch station or decide whether to return to his bunk for a few more winks before reveille.

And so it was that this morning began—as all the many others had—with a rush to battle stations followed by the somewhat frustrating but welcome words, "Now secure from general quarters," followed by further welcome words: "The smoking lamp is lighted in all authorized spaces." The familiar clink and rasp of Zippo lighters could be heard throughout the ship as men lit up Lucky Strikes, Chesterfields, Old Golds, and Camels that were sold in the ship's store or came with the C rations that were handed out during heavy weather.

With dawn alert behind them, some men were lining up for chow in the mess line in the age-old military tradition of "hurry up and wait," while the mess cooks in the galley wielded their oversized spoons, shoveling mounds of powdered eggs into large rectangular pans that were heavily dented from much use but were pristinely clean, as mandated by the chief cook and reinforced by the frequent inspections of the captain and the duty officers.

Down in the forward boiler room, snipes watched their gauges and adjusted valves to keep high-pressure steam flowing to the turbines as the roar of forced draft blowers precluded any conversation other than hand signals. Using swabs and brushes, several seamen under the supervision of a boatswain's mate striker took advantage of the recent rain to clean the deck near Mount 51 on the forecastle. Seaman Bill Mercer climbed to his top bunk to rest for a few minutes before tackling the bags of clothes waiting for him in the ship's laundry. On the bridge, keeping the ship on course 147, Gunner's Mate Second Class James Herring moved the helm 5 degrees without looking at the rudder angle indicator, relying on many months of experience steering GQ Johnny in all kinds of weather and sea state. With earphones clasped to his head, Sonarman Earl Edminster listened to alien sounds made by denizens of the deep. Clyde Burnett lay in his bunk waiting for breakfast to be brought down to the chief's mess. In the galley, Seaman First Class Harold ("Dusty") Rhodes waited impatiently for a fresh pot of coffee to finish brewing so that he could take breakfast down to the waiting chief petty officers.

Everywhere men carried out the routines now so familiar to them after nearly twelve months at sea. They were routines honed through practice and repetition, and their sameness and reliability brought a sense of comfort. But on this October morning these men had no way of knowing that within a very few minutes the reassuring tedium would yield to sheer terror, procedures would fall to chaos, and so many months of training and flood tides of adrenaline would have to suffice as they faced the unfamiliar and the inconceivable.

The names of Captain Ernest Evans and the crew of USS *Johnston* (DD 577) had heretofore been recorded in orders and logbooks. They were about to be added to the pages of history.

CHAPTER 10

CRUCIBLE

War is mankind's greatest folly. It is wasteful, tragic, and all too often unnecessary. But when it does occur, in an ironic twist, it can bring out what is best about mankind. What the men of USS *Johnston* did in just a few hours on the morning of 25 October 1944 defies vicarious description. The suffering they endured, the sacrifices they made, the fear that tried but failed to paralyze them, and the courage they found as their world collapsed into furious chaos can never be replicated with complete accuracy. Yet we cannot leave it to their memories alone because they are no longer with us and, as the beneficiaries of their deeds, we must not forget. So we must try to memorialize their thoughts and actions by trying to describe the indescribable, to use mere words to capture what can never be fully comprehended, in hopes of building a kind of monument to a moment in time when ordinary men did the extraordinary.

Ellsworth Welch's hopes for a hot breakfast were not to be fulfilled. As he scanned the waters around him for probably the hundredth time since assuming the watch as officer of the deck at a little before 0400, he knew something was wrong. The six escort carriers of Taffy 3 were all where they were supposed to be, scattered far enough apart to give them the sea room they needed for launching and recovering aircraft. Like *Johnston*, the destroyers *Heerman* and *Hoel* and the destroyer escorts *Raymond*, *Dennis*, *John C.*

Butler, and *Samuel B. Roberts* were all in their assigned screening stations ready to defend against air or submarine attack. So all was as it should be . . . except for those colored geysers!

At first, comprehension eluded him as he watched those tall columns of water climb up out of the otherwise calm sea and then collapse into a froth of boiling water below. Some—yellow in color—were erupting in the vicinity of the nearest carrier, but several of them were closer to *Johnston*, and those were red. After a few seconds he concluded that they must be the result of bombs falling from the sky, although he still did not understand the colors—but a quick scan of the sky above revealed no aircraft. Then he saw them—pagoda-like masts on the horizon off the port quarter—and now he understood that Japanese ships were shooting at them.

A speaker inside the pilot house crackled to life, confirming his deduction. A pilot on patrol to the north was excitedly reporting what he perceived to be "the whole damn Jap fleet" headed their way.

The door to the captain's sea cabin virtually exploded open, and Evans emerged barking orders. "All hands to general quarters!" he bellowed, followed by "Light off all boilers! Commence making smoke!"

Welch was momentarily paralyzed, not knowing what he should do. Hearing the captain's orders, he wondered, "Why didn't I think of that?" and, as he watched Evans issuing those commands, calmly but forcefully, he felt a great surge of relief that Evans was there taking charge.

Quartermaster Third Class Neil Dethlefs had just returned to the bridge from the mess decks. Someone had already sounded the GQ alarm, and its raucous bonging was reverberating throughout the ship. Without hesitation, Dethlefs flipped the switch on the 1MC and leaned toward the microphone: "General Quarters! General Quarters! All hands man your battle stations." Overhearing the captain, he repeated, "Stand by to repel surface attack." Then, seeing the confused look on Bob Billie's face as the young man stood clutching the edge of the chart table, Dethlefs added, "This is not a drill!" He had spoken on the 1MC many times before, but this time his voice sounded strange as he heard it echoing in the nearby compartments and across the open decks. Dethlefs grabbed the deck log and began recording the captain's orders, trying to control the shaking of his hand as he wrote.

Bob Hagen had been in CIC waiting for a breakfast sandwich to be brought up from the officer's mess when he began hearing unsettling reports coming in over the TBS. Not only were Japanese ships bearing down on them from the northwest, but they included battleships and cruisers. As gunnery officer, he knew that his 5-inch rounds would bounce off the thick hides of the battleships and that they were no match for the firepower of the cruisers. As he headed for his battle station in the gun director atop the pilot house, he muttered to himself, "I am David without a slingshot!"

Chief Burnett emerged from the ship's superstructure and stood dumbstruck on the main deck for a moment as he saw a "forest" of masts on the horizon and saw twinkling lights signaling the firing of their guns.

As Hagen stepped over the coaming onto the bridge on his way to the gun director, he heard Evans say, "All engines ahead flank. Left full rudder." Hagen saw that Evans' usual half-smile had changed into something more like a grin as he gave his orders.

As he headed for his battle station on the portside 40-mm gun tub just below the bridge, eighteen-year-old Bill Mercer had seen several of the Japanese ships emerge from the horizon and caught a glimpse of one of the cascading columns of water sparkling momentarily in the morning sunlight. He arrived in time to hear Evans' order for flank speed, which gave him comfort—running away from those nasty-looking Jap ships seemed to him like the best course of action. But his heart sank when he heard Evans order left full rudder and realized that they were turning *toward* the enemy ships. He began strapping on his life jacket.

Bob Billie left the chart table and headed for his battle station as the port after lookout, a position that gave him an unobstructed view of the oncoming Japanese ships. To his dismay he saw them swing around in an arc till they were ahead instead of behind, and they were growing larger. By now the rumble of distant gunfire was reaching the racing destroyer and the sound seemed to envelop Billie. He later recalled that this was "the only time I ever wanted to dig a trench."

As the ships of all three "Taffies" headed southeast as fast as they could go—a race they could not win, since the CVEs were limited to about eighteen knots and the maximum speed for the Japanese ships was nearly double that—Hagen was not surprised that, on his own initiative, Evans was turning his ship *toward* the enemy. In the past year of serving with this captain, Hagen knew that his commissioning day declaration to "never again run from the enemy" was not mere bravado. Everything he had observed while serving as Evans' gunnery officer convinced Hagen that Evans would fulfill his pledge to take his ship "in harm's way." As the bow stopped swinging around and centered on the leading enemy ships, Hagen muttered to himself, "He's not going to retreat—he doesn't know how!"

Ed Digardi arrived on the bridge to assume his battle station watch as officer of the deck. There was not much need for a briefing from Els Welch, since *his* battle station was junior officer of the deck and he wasn't going anywhere. The two men saluted and quickly assumed their respective duties. As a Japanese round passed overhead, probably headed for the CVEs, Digardi said, "Sounds like a freight train!"

Welch just nodded and watched as another geyser—this one green—erupted ahead of them, "Why are they different colors?" he asked.

Evans, standing nearby, said, "The Japs use colored dyes in their shells so that they can distinguish their own shots from other ships. Helps in their targeting."

For the second time that morning, Welch asked himself, "Why didn't I think of that?"

Without orders from above, Evans had ordered the making of smoke, apparently hoping to produce a screen that would make it more difficult for Japanese spotters to see their targets and the fall of their shots. "Making smoke" was accomplished in two different ways. By adjusting the fuel/air mixture to the boilers, the engineers could generate heavy black smoke from the ship's stacks, and on the fantail there were chemical smoke generators specifically designed for this purpose.

Normally the engineers were very sensitive to minimizing the smoke coming out of the stacks to maximize fuel efficiency and to prevent smoke from giving away the ship's position. In the last war, the famous Battle of Jutland—which Evans had studied in great detail—began when the belligerents located each other in the North Sea by sighting the telltale smoke from their coal-fired boilers. When Joe Woolf first passed Evans' order to "commence making smoke," the sound-powered phone talker on the engineering end of the JV circuit had misunderstood the captain's order, thinking he was chastising the snipes for erroneously making telltale smoke. A confused exchange followed that was resolved when, in exasperation, Evans grabbed the phone from Woolf and bellowed, "I want a smoke screen and I want it now!"

Back on the fantail, Seaman Second Class Bob Deal and the rest of the depth charge crew were struggling to open the valves controlling the chemical smoke generators, which had been corroded by salt spray and would not open by hand. Ensign Jesse Cochran called to the nearby torpedo shack for some hand tools, and a few seconds later Torpedoman First Class Jim O'Gorek came running aft, clutching a large wrench and a pair of vise grips. As he neared the group clustered around the port smoke generator, the ship careened sharply in one of her zigzags, and O'Gorek was thrown off his intended track. He would have gone over the side had it not been for the lifelines, which did their intended task and kept him on board.

After much effort and even more foul language, Deal was able to force the valves open, and billowing clouds of cottony white smoke joined the black stack-smoke to cast an eerie haze in the ship's wake.

"In the ship's wake" was the part that did not please Seaman John Mostowy. The smoky shroud that hung over the surface of the sea was *behind* the ship! With *Johnston* heading *toward* the enemy ships, her smoke was partially shielding the CVEs and the other destroyers, but the veil was doing nothing to hide GQ Johnny and her crew. Mostowy later recorded, "We were making smoke and zig-zagging and heading for the Jap fleet at flank speed and *alone*!"

As the clouds of smoke roiled in the ship's wake—to Bob Deal looking like "an upside-down chocolate layer cake with white icing"—the Japanese began firing illuminating "star shells," indicating the smoke screen was having some effect. Watching from his battle station, Ensign Jesse Cochran saw the "miniature suns" bursting above the haze, then slowly descending, first into the black layer and then the white before snuffing out in the sea.

Standing next to the depth charge racks, Deal marveled at the colors of the splashing shells, thinking they were "sorta pretty" in a bizarre kind of way. As the rounds passed overhead, he thought they sounded "like a trouser zipper opening and closing."

Hovering over his deck log on the bridge, wishing he could crawl into its pages, Neil Dethlefs was feeling that fate had dealt him a bad hand—literally. Less than a month ago he had been serving in the repair ship *Prometheus* at Tulagi when USS *Johnston* entered the harbor. She had not yet moored when her signal lamp began flashing a Morse code message calling for a quartermaster to replace one who was being put ashore because of a debilitating problem: acute seasickness. Dethlefs was one of two quartermasters on board, and it seemed inevitable that one of them would be sent to the destroyer. Neither was anxious to go, so they decided to cut a deck of cards, agreeing that the lower draw would volunteer to go. Leaning on the chart table in *Prometheus*' pilot house, Dethlefs drew an eight of spades and dropped it face up on the chart of Tulagi Harbor. When it was joined by a king of hearts, Dethlefs went below to pack his seabag. Now, with *Johnston* heeling over in a tight turn that sent the clinometer pointing to nearly 20 degrees, his feet tingling from the throbbing of the ship's engines as the greyhound raced along at top speed, and enemy shells passing overhead screaming like the banshees he had feared as a child, Neil Dethlefs thought, "I arrived just in time to get killed."

Standing near Dethlefs, not quite sure what to do with himself, was Lieutenant (jg) Joe Pliska. He was the squadron recognition officer and had been temporarily embarked in *Johnston* to teach the crew how to identify Japanese aircraft and ships. He had never actually seen an enemy ship, working exclusively through reconnaissance photos and diagrams. As he watched the derrick-like masts growing taller on the horizon and massive superstructures punctuated by the blinking lights of gunfire, he could only say, "Jesus Christ!" Evans, who normally discouraged profanity on the bridge, let it pass without comment.

Ed Digardi maintained his composure as the incredible scene unfolded around him. Thinking like the excellent officer of the deck that he was, he began calculating in his head. He knew that *Johnston*—scheduled to refuel later that day—was only marginally ready for a high-speed engagement. He knew she had only 12,000 gallons of fuel oil in her bunkers, and at normal cruising speed she burned 500 gallons an hour. But at flank speed she was gulping 5,000 gallons an hour and would run dry in less than two hours. He called up Lieutenant Joe Worling, the chief engineer, and told him to mix the remaining oil with the 10,000 gallons of diesel fuel stowed in separate tanks and normally used only by the ship's generators. Thinking like an engineer, Worling protested that mixing the two fuels would foul the ship's boiler tubes and require a subsequent painstaking cleaning by his men. When Digardi insisted, Worling charged up to the bridge to excitedly plead his case to the captain. Evans listened with one ear as he continued to monitor the increasingly hazardous situation, then calmly told Worling to do as Digardi had ordered. As Worling stormed off the bridge shaking his head in frustration, Evans smiled and said to Digardi, "He didn't seem to notice there's a battle in progress."

And indeed, there was a battle in progress! As the range between *Johnston* and her oncoming adversaries rapidly closed, the pagoda masts that had first pierced the horizon now sat atop what were clearly battleships and cruisers, whose firing was relentless, the thunder of their guns growing louder with each salvo. The big ships had been concentrating their fire on the fleeing carriers, but it did not take a master tactician to realize that soon they would be forced to engage this plucky little tin can who was charging at them as though she knew something they did not. Before long the Japanese gunners would have to lower their barrels and set their sights on GQ Johnny as she raced deeper and deeper into harm's way.

Many of the men who had a view of what was happening were confused. Among those who were aware that they were heading toward a number of Japanese ships, there were more than a few who did not understand *why*. It seemed that the logical thing was to head away as the rest of the American ships were doing. Others, including Bob Deal, wondered, "Why aren't we firing at the Japs?" What they did not understand was that there was a long way to go before they would be close enough to the enemy for their weapons to have a fighting chance of striking any enemy ships—a long way to go while they, in turn, would be within range of the bigger Japanese guns.

Up in the gun director, Bob Hagen understood the need to wait until the enemy was in range. But he also knew that when they could open fire, his

55-pound projectiles were no match for what the Japanese could throw back at them. The cruisers alone could retort with projectiles weighing five times more—never mind the battleships! Hagen felt powerless and vulnerable as they continued to close the distance. He had checked with all gunnery stations, and they were ready to fire but had no choice but to wait. Hagen felt "completely, sickeningly impotent."

When Clint Carter first climbed into Mount 55, he told the other members of the gun crew, "Admiral Halsey is shooting at us." He figured that had to be the case. Captain Evans, in his attempts to keep the crew informed of what was happening, had told the crew that the gargantuan Third Fleet was somewhere in the vicinity waiting to take on the Japanese if they showed up. It did not occur to Carter that the Japanese had gotten past Halsey's forces, so he surmised that it was a case of mistaken identity and that the Third Fleet was erroneously firing on them. What he and the rest of the crew—including Evans—did not know was that Halsey had taken his entire fleet northward in pursuit of what turned out to be a Japanese decoy force.

Ed Digardi, peering at the oncoming Japanese ships through his binoculars, was trying to identify them, but he was rapidly concluding that the task was all but impossible. Details were hard to discern at this distance, and the ships looked very different on the surface of the sea than they had on the pages of those enemy identification manuals Joe Pliska had recently brought on board. He was pretty sure that there was a column of destroyers a good way off on the starboard bow, and that the ships off their port bow that appeared closer and larger were probably cruisers. But he was not sure. The tactical situation was frustratingly opaque, made more so as *Johnston* careened about in her zigzags, frequently shifting the picture from one side to the other. Digardi thought of himself as a good officer of the deck—and Evans had verified this belief by making him the GQ OOD—but at this moment he felt much less confident than he did when enemy land targets were fixed in place and less formidable in appearance. He trusted that Evans had a clearer idea of what was happening than he did.

From his after lookout post, Bill Mercer had little idea what his captain was doing, and he felt a terrible loneliness as he watched the other ships of Taffy 3 growing smaller as they fled from the pursuing Japanese. Like *Johnston*,

IMAGE 14 • U.S. escort carriers laying smoke to confuse their Japanese pursuers

these tin cans were laying smoke, but it was only partially obscuring the retreating carriers, and he could still catch glimpses of unsuccessful Japanese shells making those colored splashes, grateful that none of them seemed intended for *Johnston*. It appeared to him that at least two of the carriers were launching aircraft, and he watched as the small dark forms climbed above the smoky haze and into the clear blue sky above, momentary flashes of sunlight glinting off their canopies. Seeing them gave Mercer some comfort. Some of the "airedales" he had met ashore at the Tulagi enlisted men's club bragged that it was airplanes that were winning the war. "Well, now is their chance to prove it," he thought as he watched several aircraft streaking north toward the Japanese behemoths.

Until this morning, the primary mission of the aircraft embarked in the CVEs was to provide support for the troops fighting ashore on Leyte;

consequently, they were armed mostly with antipersonnel bombs that produced a lot of shrapnel but were not potent enough to attack steel warships—especially those that were shrouded in armor. Although some of the aircraft were armed with aerial torpedoes—which *were* effective against the Japanese ships and actually sank three cruisers—others were armed with depth charges in case any Japanese submarines threatened the task unit, which were not going to have much effect on the Japanese surface units bearing down from the north.

Despite these limitations, the American pilots did not hesitate to attack the Japanese armada. Flying into curtains of antiaircraft fire with their limited payloads, these audacious flyers exhibited a kind of selfless courage that defies normal reason. With aerobatic skill they swarmed around the Japanese ships like angry hornets whose nest has been threatened, dropping what little ordnance they had and firing furiously with their machine guns. Astonishingly, when all their ammunition was expended, many of the pilots continued to feign attacks, doing no damage but confusing and complicating the work of enemy gunfire spotters and the officers on the bridges as they were forced to repeatedly duck for cover.

The actions of those American aviators was incredibly courageous and in some cases tragically sacrificial. But it was only the beginning. Before this day was over, it would mark a high tide of Navy courage, a day of valor that might someday be equaled but never excelled. As is nearly always the case, however, the toll for exceptional intrepidity would be extraordinary sacrifice.

By 0710, the range to the closest enemy cruiser had closed to 18,000 yards, the maximum range of *Johnston*'s 5-inch guns. Evans had given Hagen permission to fire on any Japanese ship that came within range of the 5-inch guns, so at Hagen's direction, Fire Controlmen George Himelright and James Buzbee fixed the heavy cruiser in the director's sights and Fire Controlman Tony Gringheri entered ranges using his stereoscopic range finder. This information was automatically fed into the ship's Mark 1A fire control computer, an analog device consisting of mechanical gears and cams. Within thirty seconds, the computer calculated the firing solution by accounting for a number of variables, including *Johnston*'s own motion (course, speed, pitch, and roll), bore wear within the guns' barrels, initial muzzle velocity of the round to be fired, the ship's current latitude and longitude, and the relation of her heading to magnetic north. When the dials indicated the target solution was ready, Hagen closed the firing key, and all five mounts of *Johnston*'s main battery simultaneously erupted. Five 5-inch/38 projectiles soared into the bright blue sky and followed a parabolic trajectory toward the lead Japanese heavy cruiser. In that instant, GQ Johnny crossed a threshold—almost exactly a year since she had broken her commissioning pennant alongside a pier in Seattle she was in her first surface-to-surface action, albeit fighting above her weight class.

In truth, destroyers were better designed to fight submarines and aircraft than other surface ships. Now *Johnston* was facing an enemy force of four battleships (including the world's largest and most powerful—super-battleship *Yamato*), six heavy cruisers, two light cruisers, and eleven destroyers.

On the bridge, the pungent smell of cordite blowing up from the two forward mounts made Ed Digardi's breathing difficult. As he scanned ahead, almost afraid to look, he could clearly see the massive cruisers ahead, their dull gray forms highlighted by the flashes of gunfire. Beyond them, he could make out the ominous forms of an echelon of battleships. This was sheer madness—one tiny destroyer charging an armada of some of the world's most formidable firepower!

Peering through his binoculars at the nearest cruiser, he saw hits registering on her superstructure and watched in fascination as pieces of twisted metal cascaded down her sides and fell onto the decks below or splashed into the water alongside. It seemed incongruous to watch such violence seemingly close through the lenses of his binoculars and yet hear no sound at the actual distance between the combatants. It was like a silent movie.

At first the Japanese ship seemed oblivious to the sting of *Johnston*'s shells, but then Digardi clearly saw a muzzle flash from one of the cruiser's guns that seemed pointed directly at him and was startled a few seconds later to see a large red geyser explode out of the sea close aboard. As the red-tinted water cascaded down over *Johnston*'s forecastle, Digardi reflexively ducked, then felt ashamed. He glanced over at Evans, who stood ramrod straight, that enigmatic smile still fixed in place in between his bellowed orders. There was something in Evans' demeanor that reassured Digardi that everything was going to be all right, even though his frightened but logical mind told him otherwise.

As the bantamweight contender continued to fire rapidly at the heavyweight cruiser, empty shell casings ejected through the bottoms of the mounts began cluttering the decks, making loud clanging noises as they rolled about in response to the destroyer's zigzagging. Ensign Jesse Cochran, as head of one of the repair parties aft of the torpedo tubes, was grateful that he had little to do at the moment and busied himself gathering up the rolling shell casings—taking care not to touch the recently fired ones that were still hot—and tossing them over the side into the rushing sea. Several other members of the repair party joined him in clearing the decks.

Back in Mount 55, Clint Carter's crew—like those in all the mounts—was feeding powder and shells into the breech of the gun at a very rapid rate, so fast in fact that Carter saw the paint on the gun's barrel beginning to blister and singe. Even though a blast of high-pressure air was shot through the barrel to clear the hot gases after each shot, it was clear that the temperature inside the barrel was getting dangerously high. As long as the gun kept firing, the time a projectile spent in the barrel was short enough to keep it from "cooking off," which would have had catastrophic effects on the gun and its crew. But when a sudden course change caused the gun to swing rapidly about in compensation, the gun entered a zone where cam stops prevented it from firing into the ship's own superstructure, and Carter realized that he had a live round in a very hot barrel with nowhere to go. Frantically, he called the gun boss on the sound-powered circuit, begging permission to take the gun out of director control so that he could swing it to a safe bearing and fire it manually. Before Hagen could reply, the ship swung rapidly again, taking the gun out of the safety stops, and the gun automatically fired, sending the heated round toward the enemy ship, to Carter's immense relief. There was danger enough in GQ Johnny's current situation without adding a self-inflicted wound to the list of problems.

Battleships and cruisers are formidable engines of war. Given battleships' belts of armor, cruisers' impressive speed for such large vessels, and the bristling high-caliber firepower wielded by both, they can strike justifiable fear into the hearts of those who earn their wrath. Once only vulnerable to each other, since late in the nineteenth century these goliaths have themselves had to suffer trepidation as technology found a way for them to be struck down by the seagoing version of a slingshot.

Ernest Evans understood that his guns were not capable of inflicting serious damage to his adversaries. He also knew, however, that the ten torpedoes carried by his *Fletcher*-class destroyer gave him a limited but potent punch that could not conquer but might seriously deter his much more powerful enemies. At the Battle of the Java Sea more than two years before, while serving as XO of USS *Alden*, he had participated in a torpedo attack that succeeded in causing a powerful Japanese force to turn away at a critical moment, allowing a group of Allied ships to escape from certain destruction. Now, in the Philippine Sea, Evans pressed the attack, even though *Johnston*'s chances of survival were poor and getting worse as she faced this formidable Japanese force. In a calm but matter-of-fact tone, the captain said to Lieutenant Digardi without looking at him, "We must not go down with torpedoes still in our tubes."

As *Johnston* closed the enemy at an alarming rate, Lieutenant Jack Bechdel, the torpedo officer, took the conn and steered the ship according to the firing solution provided by the torpedo directors analog computer, using the lead cruiser, which he had identified as *Kumano*, as his point of aim. Soon a strange language laced with mathematical and nautical terminology was echoing about Johnson's bridge: "Range 13,000 yards. Target speed two-five knots. Train Mount 1 to zero-five-zero relative; Mount 2 at three-two-five relative. Range 12,000 yards. Target angle zero-four-zero. Set running depth at six feet. Range 11,000 yards. One degree spread. Mount 1 three-five degrees right gyro angle. Mount 2, two-five degrees right gyro angle. Tube offset two-point-five degrees. Three-second interval. Range 10,000 yards." All the while, Japanese shells fell about *Johnston*, miraculously none finding their target, but the odds of such continued good fortune diminishing with each near miss.

While the ship charged headlong at the enemy, Digardi stood on the port wing of the bridge near the torpedo officer, the captain, a third-class signalman, and Lieutenant Pliska. Bechdel fired all ten of the ship's torpedoes and returned control to Digardi, who stepped into the pilot house to give orders to the helm. He gratefully steered *Johnston* into her own smoke screen to gain some respite from the cascading Japanese gunfire. Minutes later, the sound of distant underwater explosions indicated that some of the torpedoes had found their mark.

When *Johnston* emerged from the smoke screen, those crew members who could look were treated to the welcome sight of flames burning brightly on the Japanese cruiser. There was momentary elation as they realized they had not only survived this seemingly suicidal run but had succeeded in striking a blow on a Japanese cruiser. Bill Mercer heard one of the signalmen excitedly call down, "We blew off her whole damn bow!" Neil Dethlefs saw Lieutenant Digardi slap Lieutenant Bechdel on the back as the latter grinned broadly.

Then, at 0730, GQ Johnny's luck ran out.

It is notable that despite all the combat that took place between the Japanese and Americans during the war, the combatants only rarely saw each other. Carrier warfare confined sightings to the aviators, while the carriers and their escorts remained over the horizon during battles. Submariners saw their targets through periscopes, and much of the close-in surface combat took place at night.

As the Japanese surface force bore down on Taffy 3, it is not clear whether they realized that the carriers they were chasing were only diminutive escort carriers. There is strong evidence that they believed they had encountered Halsey's Third Fleet and were seeing his fleet carriers. In any case, the CVEs were the biggest targets and so attracted and maintained much of the enemy's attention. Only a few of the Japanese ships were firing at *Johnston*, and Evans used the technique he had once explained to his son when reading to him about the Battle of Jutland: Whenever a Japanese shell exploded nearby, Evans quickly adjusted course to head for that spot on the theory that the enemy was not likely to fire again at a spot that had missed the intended target and would adjust his fire. It appeared to be working, for *Johnston* was able to close within effective torpedo range without being hit.

But as *Johnston* emerged from the protective shroud of her smoke screen, spotters on the world's largest battleship—IJN *Yamato*—hurled a salvo of 18.1-inch projectiles at the hapless destroyer. Three of these shells—each weighing more than 1.5 tons—slammed into *Johnston* with unbelievable force. The ship rolled over so far that William Rogers, loading 5-inch shells onto a hoist under Mount 55 in the stern, thought the ship had been struck by a giant wave. At the depth charge rack on the main deck, Robert Deal thought the ship had run into some huge underwater obstruction.

With the ship still reeling from the big shells, three more rounds tore into her—6.1-inch shells fired from the big battleship's secondary battery—striking her around the after smokestack and the port bridge wing.

Bob Hagen was peering out of his gun director when the Japanese shells hit and described it as "like a puppy being smacked by a truck." The radar antenna on the mainmast, commonly referred to as the "whirling bedspring," was snapped off by the mere shock of the hits and "came tumbling down past my head." His helmet, telephone, and binoculars were blown off, and the metal pin, "which locked my stool in an elevated position so I could look through the telescope, snapped, causing me to drop downward and sustain a somewhat inglorious wound—a ¼-inch gash in my kneecap." Inglorious perhaps, but painful nonetheless. Yelling from the pain, he gathered himself together and looked out of the director at the ship below him. What he saw was enough to stop a strong man's heart.

Along the port side, steam poured out from two of three gaping holes in the main deck. There was twisted metal all around, most of it unidentifiable as to what it had been. But what momentarily arrested Hagen's attention was the men scattered about the decks in all sorts of postures, some motionless, others struggling to move, smears of crimson blood marking the paths of men crawling in random directions. *Johnston* had served in a war zone for nearly a year, sustaining only one death—and that one from natural causes—but now, in an instant, that enviable record had ended with many men dead and more dying.

What Hagen could not see was that belowdecks the damage was catastrophic. Both the after fire room and after engine room had been destroyed. Much of the after part of the ship's interior spaces was plunged into darkness.

Power to the three after mounts had been cut off, reducing them to manual operation. Escaping steam from the engine room killed or badly burned every man in the handling room for Mount 53 and forced the temporary abandonment of that compartment. The port screw was disabled, power to the remaining screw had been halved, controls to the rudder had been severed, and the after engine room was taking on water.

Ensign Jesse Cochran ran across the main deck to the steam stop valves above the after fire room. He grabbed the wheels and spun them, hoping to shut off the escaping steam. Nothing happened. The steam kept on jetting out of the jagged holes with a loud hissing sound. He deduced that the damage below included not just the steam lines but also the tubes in the boilers themselves. He could only imagine what it must look like down there. The damage must have been terrible, and the men who were down there would have been scalded to death if they survived the detonation of the shells. That escaping steam was well over 800 degrees and had been pressured to 600 psi.

On the bridge, the damage was extensive and the carnage horrific. As Els Welch had entered the pilothouse from the bridge wing, he was blown inward by the force of one of the exploding shells and found himself on top of a pile of wounded and dead men. For a moment, he was transfixed by the gore, unable to grasp the reality of what he was seeing. Limbs and fingers and pieces of unidentifiable flesh were strewn about the deck and sticking to the bulkheads. As Welch extricated himself from the grisly pile, he saw that Ensign Gordan Fox had been killed outright. Nearby, Coxswain Ed Block was missing a large chunk of his right shoulder, and small pieces of shrapnel were lodged between his eyes, under his chin, and in his right eye. But Welch saw that he was alive and shouted to no one in particular, "Block is alive." Doc Browne, who was trying to help several of the wounded men at once, handed Welch several syrettes of morphine. Remembering the training that had once bored him, Welch injected it into Block's wrist.

Getting to his feet, Welch turned and was glad to see the captain standing a few feet away. Evans' helmet and shirt had been blown away. The hair on his chest was singed and blackened, and shell fragments had slashed his neck and face. Blood was gushing from his left hand where two fingers had been shot away. Doc Browne rushed to his aid, but Evans waved him back with obvious irritation, saying, "Don't bother me now. Help some of those guys who are hurt." Welch watched with fascination as Evans calmly wrapped a handkerchief around the stumps of his fingers and carried on.

Lieutenant Jack Bechdel was propped in one corner of the mangled bridge complaining that his shoulder was hurting, unaware that he had lost a leg at the knee. Bechdel asked for a drink of water. Welch had none but pulled out another morphine syrette and stuck it in Bechdel's wrist. Thinking that seeing all that carnage was bad for morale, Welch then began gathering up body parts and tossing them over the side.

The ship was no longer responding to her helm, and the engine order telegraph had been blown off its deck mount. Miraculously, the 1MC still worked, and Evans—aware that the ship's antiaircraft machine guns were not likely going to be needed in this fight—had Dethlefs pass the word for the crews to report to emergency after steering to manhandle the rudder. Using the auxiliary sound-powered phone circuit, Evans began transmitting orders to the men now steering the ship manually. He then ordered the able-bodied on the bridge to assist in clearing the wounded.

Outside the pilot house, Bill Mercer heard someone above him call, "Stand by below" and watched as a pair of khaki clad legs dangled into view. Someone on the bridge was lowering one of the officers to the main deck. As the khaki shirt appeared, Mercer could see that it was sopping with blood. The lowering paused for a moment, and when it continued, Mercer saw to his dismay and horror that the officer's body had no head.

On the flying bridge, a piece of shrapnel struck the mouthpiece of Bob Billie's sound powered phone, shattering the instrument and filling the young sailor's mouth with blood and broken teeth. As he spat over the rail, he could see several dead and wounded men scattered about the deck below, and his wound seemed less important. A subsequent explosion lifted Billie into the air and slammed him down on the steel deck, knocking him unconscious. Upon reviving, he saw his shoes, still neatly tied, lying next to his head.

Orin Vadnais sat at his dormant 40-mm gun director amidships, glad that *Johnston* was not close enough to any Japanese ships for his guns to be useful. He felt a bit strange having nothing to do in the midst of such chaos but had no idea what to do other than wait for orders.

As he peered over the side of the gun tub, he saw chunks of solid explosives scattered about the deck below, apparently from a depth charge that had been hit during the recent barrage. Wondering what should be done about that, he was suddenly surprised to see the helmeted head of "Ski" (Harold Beresonsky) pop up from one of the gaping holes in the deck. Incongruously, he had a lit cigarette dangling from his mouth as he climbed up onto the deck and began gathering up pieces of the explosive and casually tossing them over the side.

Bill Mercer had no idea who the headless officer was but was relieved to see lieutenant's bars on what was left of the man's shirt collar. He felt terrible for the man but was glad he was not the captain—the idea of losing the skipper at this crucial time was particularly alarming.

On the flying bridge one deck up, Bob Billie discovered that he was bleeding from every limb and that the only one he could move was his left arm. In a state of shock, he again lost consciousness.

On the bridge, Ed Digardi turned his attention from the grisly carnage around him and lifted his binoculars to peer ahead. He noted that the image in the lenses was jiggling, and he could feel his right knee beating out a trembling cadence against the binnacle next to him. Despite the bouncing image, he could see the other Taffy 3 ships beginning to disappear. Miraculously, Mother Nature had taken pity on the outclassed Americans and provided a sizable rain squall to serve as temporary sanctuary. One historian has described it as a "seagoing foxhole," and the ships of Taffy 3 needed no encouragement to jump into it.

As Bob Hagen felt cool raindrops further soaking his sweat-soaked clothing, he felt it was "sheer Providence." He didn't mind that the pack of cigarettes in his shirt pocket was being ruined.

Back on the main deck aft, Jesse Cochran noted that steam was no longer pouring out of the holes in the deck. He and several of his repair party descended into the number 2 engine room. It was a shambles and pitch dark except for the narrow beams of light from the battle lanterns. There was a pall of smoke in the air, and they could hear the flow of water coming from somewhere below. Cochran carefully stepped over the body of Ensign Johhny Merritt lying face down on the grates where he had dropped at his station. In the stygian half-light, he could see the lifeless and mangled forms of others who were also near their posts, one with his hands still clamped onto a large valve wheel.

Struggling to maneuver in the jungle of twisted metal, Cochran and his team tried but failed to run some emergency cables to the after steering motor and fought valiantly to close the gate valve on the main injection to the condenser.

Deeming that it had cooled down sufficiently, they next moved into the number 2 fireroom. They were amazed to find several men emerge from the bilges below the grates, where they had sought refuge from the searing jets of steam. Although still alive, Cochrane doubted they would survive. They were badly burned, with steam still rising from their clothes, and could barely make it up the ladders with help from their shipmates. On the main deck above, Robert Sochor watched in horror as these men emerged from the hell below, "looking like ghosts." He too doubted they would survive.

Sochor helped several of the burned men move forward to the officers' wardroom, which was now serving as a first-aid station. Doc Browne and several pharmacist's mates were there doing their best to treat the wounded and ease the suffering of the dying. Sochor was deeply moved by what he saw there.

People who have experienced combat and its terrible aftermath know that no words in a book, no images on a screen, can ever come close to accurately depicting the sights, sounds, and smells they have experienced and are never able to forget. The inexperienced imagination cannot fully conjure the three-dimensional reality of carnage: the awful smell of burned flesh, blood, and other bodily fluids; the terrifying screams of pain; the weakening clutch of a comrade who is clinging to life; and the imploring looks in the eyes of those who realize they are not going to survive.

For those who do survive the actual combat, they know that despite the rush of gratitude that they have been spared, there is no compensation for witnessing the suffering and death of others in the aftermath; that there is an illogical but irrepressible sense of guilt at having survived when others did not. This is the price of admission to the senseless drama of war, the price that all must pay once they cross the threshold from which there is no return. This is what differentiates the neophyte eager to prove himself from the veteran who now truly understands why soldiers and sailors who have been tested in the crucible of war may accept the need to defend or to challenge evil but who have become devout pacifists when it comes to the ugly reality of killing.

Though he did not know it at that time, Robert Sochor would survive the ordeals ahead and would go on to live a good life with a long and happy marriage and six children. He was ever grateful for having survived, but as he turned and left the wardroom that morning, there were images burned into his brain that would haunt him for the rest of that good life. Whenever he reflected on his good fortune, there would nearly always be that quiet but persistent voice: "Why me?"

For a few beautiful moments as the ships of Taffy 3 were swaddled in the opaque clouds and sheets of rain, there had been no colored geysers, no deafening explosions. But the squall was moving faster than the ships hiding within it. As it moved on, taking its protective shroud with it, sunlight splashed across GQ Johnny's glistening decks, and it did not take long for the Japanese to resume their barrage of multicaliber gunfire.

As *Johnston* continued to head southwest, limping on only one screw, Hagen noted that the Japanese cruisers and battleships were loosely grouped on *Johnston*'s port quarter and a group of enemy destroyers were in pursuit from the starboard quarter. He estimated the ranges at 7,000 to 12,000 yards. It seemed to him that they were not adhering to any particular formation; they appeared to be disorganized and operating independently. The word "melee" popped into his head, and he wondered if that was because of *Johnston*'s aggressive charge and torpedo attack.

Lieutenant Digardi remained near the captain, amazed at how Evans seemed oblivious to his several wounds. The makeshift handkerchief-bandage was soaked with blood, and Digardi saw a red smear on the centerline binnacle where Evans had steadied himself as the ship careened in pursuit of one of the Japanese shells exploding off the port bow. As he looked about at the wrecked pilothouse, he marveled that he had escaped harm in the midst

IMAGE 15 • USS *Hoel* (DD 533), another of the *Fletcher*-class destroyers in the Battle off Samar

of the damage and carnage surrounding him. He had tried not to look when Lieutenant Pliska's headless body had been lowered to the deck below but could not help but stare for a brief moment. "Poor Joe," he thought. "On board only temporarily as the visiting recognition officer. Not even a member of the ship's company and here he ended his life." Digardi tried to gather some comfort in knowing that Pliska must not have suffered in his final moment.

By now Admiral Sprague, the officer in tactical command of Taffy 3, had ordered the screening ships to make a torpedo attack. Almost immediately, the destroyers *Heerman* and *Hoel* and the destroyer escorts *Raymond*, *Dennis*, *John C. Butler*, and *Samuel B. Roberts* all came about and headed northeast toward the Japanese armada.

Hagen watched as the ships sped by *Johnston*, bright white bow waves contrasting with the deep blue of the Philippine Sea, their red-white-and-blue ensigns stretched taught in the relative wind. Watching these comparatively tiny ships charging ahead at flank speed to engage their formidable opponents invoked a mix of emotions in Hagen. He felt a sense of pride at their pluckiness in the face of such odds. He also felt sympathy for their plight—knowing from very recent experience what they were facing. And he felt relieved that *Johnston*'s lack of torpedoes disqualified GQ Johnny from participating.

It did not occur to Hagen that Sprague's order applied to *Johnston*. Besides having expended their torpedoes, the ship was limping on one engine, so keeping up with the others was an impossibility. *Johnston* could have retired from the action with her honor intact. But Hagen had momentarily forgotten who his captain was. Evans' voice boomed from the bridge below, ordering "left full rudder" and adding, "We'll go in with the destroyers and provide fire support!" To himself, Hagen said, "Oh, dear Lord. I'm in for a swim."

On the bridge, Neil Dethlefs continued frantically trying to keep the log of what was happening. When he heard the captain's order to join the attack, he paused in his writing to inflate his life jacket.

As the American destroyers charged boldly at their Japanese adversaries, both sides were firing at one another at a furious rate. Tiny 5-inch shells bounced off the thick hides of the big Japanese ships, while heavy-caliber rounds roared through the air and peppered the water all around the Taffy 3 escorts, some of them slamming into the already wounded *Johnston*. As the escorts charged in to deliver their more potent weapons, smoke still billowing from their stacks, the hobbled *Johnston* valiantly struggled to keep up, firing her remaining guns with amazing persistence.

This display of tenacity and courage was not wasted. Just as had happened in the Java Sea, the Japanese were forced to turn away from their pursuit, mercifully opening the distance between them and the fleeing carriers. It was a momentary victory for the underdogs in this asymmetrical fight, one that would save many lives in the long run but would nonetheless exact a considerable toll among those whom fate had placed at the proverbial "tip of the spear."

The famed Prussian philosopher of war Carl von Clausewitz coined the phrase "fog of war" as a means of describing the confusion that inevitably clouds the thinking of both strategic planners and tactical warfighters. In the case

IMAGE 16 • American "tin cans" are shown laying smoke as they charge headlong at a far superior Japanese force of battleships and cruisers.

of this wild melee, that "fog" was literal as the American ships maneuvered about in the self-generated smoky haze, which had reduced visibility to a dangerous level.

As *Johnston* emerged from a particularly dense portion of the swirling smoke, the starboard lookout suddenly yelled in near panic. Digardi turned in the direction indicated by the lookout and saw that the destroyer *Heerman* was close aboard on the starboard bow and heading right for *Johnston* at full tilt. Before Digardi could react, Evans thundered, "All engines back full!" The command could only be partially fulfilled, since *Johnston* had only one functioning engine, but *Heerman* apparently did the same in a frantic attempt at avoiding collision. The two destroyers surged at each other as though drawn by some evil magnetic force, both vessels shuddering under the strain of propellers beating frantically in reverse. Then, by a margin of less than ten feet, the two ships managed to miss one another. With no time for even an exhalation of relief, the men of *Johnston* and *Heerman* immediately refocused their attention on the enemy.

Digardi turned his attention away from *Heerman* only to see a Japanese battleship looming out of the smoke at a range of seven thousand yards. For some reason, his recognition training kicked in, and he realized he was confronting the battleship *Kongo*. By now the only way *Johnston* could be steered was by sending the orders by sound-powered phone from the bridge to the after steering compartment, where exhausted sailors were laboring to operate the rudder's hydraulic system by hand. With such poor steering capability, *Johnston* was not able to effect her turn away until she was within five thousand yards of the giant adversary. The destroyer's 5-inch guns continued to hammer away at the huge battleship as the two ships closed on one another. Incredibly, *Johnston* got in so close to *Kongo* that the great vessel's guns were unable to depress their elevation enough to aim at the small gray ship so close aboard. For a brief moment, GQ Johnny was able to strike at will at an enemy who was unable to retaliate!

As *Johnston* emerged from the pall of smoke at about 0830, Evans saw the carrier *Gambier Bay* under heavy fire from a Japanese heavy cruiser. Informing Hagen that he intended to draw fire from the embattled escort carrier by attacking with his remaining guns, he ordered Digardi to head directly for the Japanese cruiser. Riddled with shell holes—many of them having passed completely through the carrier without detonation—*Gambier Bay* was clearly in danger of sinking. Hagen, once again having difficulty believing in his skipper's tenacious bellicosity, dutifully opened fire on the cruiser at six thousand yards, scoring five hits. Convinced that the Japanese commander could have sunk both the carrier and *Johnston*, Hagen later described his refusal to shift any of his fire to *Johnston* as "monumental stupidity." He began to wonder if they might somehow survive this impossible situation after all. Those thoughts were rapidly diminished as Evans ordered Digardi to come about and head for a group of enemy destroyers that were clearly closing in on the other CVEs.

IMAGE 17 • Escort carrier USS *Gambier Bay* (CVE 73) under fire from a Japanese cruiser (*circled, to the right*)

Closing to within 10,000 yards, Hagen opened fire on what appeared to be a lead destroyer followed by two three-ship destroyer divisions. He recognized them as "sleek, streamlined . . . our match in tonnage and weight of guns, but not our match in marksmanship, crippled as we were." *Johnston* landed twelve hits on the lead destroyer in rapid succession. The Japanese ships were returning fire, but with less effectiveness. Believing that "we should have been duck soup for the enemy," Hagen was happily surprised to see the lead Japanese destroyer cease firing and put his rudder over hard right, turning abruptly away.

Shifting his attention to the second destroyer, Hagen immediately scored five hits. To his astonishment, all six of the remaining destroyers ceased returning fire and followed their leader.

Waiting until they were well out of range of *Johnston*'s guns, the Japanese destroyers launched their torpedoes at the CVEs. None appeared to hit. From the starboard bridge wing, Evans looked up at Hagen grinning broadly and said, "Now I've seen everything!"

During *Johnston*'s engagement with the destroyers, the Taffy 3 commander ordered all of the escorts to interpose themselves between the carriers and a group of cruisers bearing down on them. With no helm on the wrecked bridge, Evans called down to the fantail using the auxiliary sound-powered circuit and ordered a hard turn to port. Moving as fast as her remaining screw would allow, *Johnston* headed toward the enemy cruisers off her port bow.

As Bill Mercer looked about his mangled ship, he saw that Mount 52 was firing at a furious rate, and the deck around the mount was filling up with expended shell casings that threatened to inhibit the mount's rotation. He and another 40-mm gunner, J. B. Strickland, ran forward and began jettisoning the empty casings as fast as they could. When they had cleared most of the brass from the deck, the two men returned to their guns. Almost immediately after their departure, Mount 52 took a direct hit.

Two of the gun crew were blown completely out of the mount. Mercer recognized one of them as his friend Glenn Heriford. He was lying on the deck just below the starboard bridge wing, unable to move. Mercer ran to him and helped him sit up enough to lean back against the bulkhead. As he did so, Heriford looked at him gratefully and said, "Merc, straighten my leg out." Mercer did not have the heart to tell him that there was nothing to straighten—his leg was completely blown off.

By now numerous fires were burning out of control belowdecks. The bridge was engulfed in smoke, and flames poured out of ventilators and several hatches that had been blown open. Controlling the ship from this ravaged bridge was no longer tenable, so, with Joe Woolf in tow, Evans headed aft. Getting to the fantail was a challenge in itself: The two men had to climb over twisted metal, dodge firehoses being whipped about by repair party personnel desperately trying to quell multiple fires, and avoid falling into gaping holes in the deck, some of them spewing flames.

When they arrived on the blackened fantail, Evans took up a position above the hatch leading down to the after steering compartment, where he could shout orders directly to the men below struggling to move the massive rudder manually.

In the compartment below, gunners whose guns had been destroyed and other displaced crewmembers took turns with the backbreaking work of turning the wheel that drove the rudder pump. Chief Clyde Burnett took turns with another big man, John Schindele, for a spell, until they could no longer find the strength needed and yielded the work to another pair of sailors, who continued cranking the rudder in response to the captain's orders coming down from above.

Before leaving the bridge, Evans told Lieutenant Digardi to destroy all the ship's code books and other classified material—a sure sign that Evans did not expect his command to survive. With three men in tow, Digardi headed for the radio shack. A Japanese shell had scored a direct hit, and Digardi and the others had to force open the door to enter the compartment. Inside they found it a mangled mess and everyone dead. Emptying the safe of its classified documents, they filled the weighted bags that were there for that purpose, then dumped the rest into a mattress cover that one of the men had retrieved from a berthing compartment, weighted it down with several empty 5-inch shell casings, and tossed all of it over the side, where it sank into many fathoms of water to safely reside away from unauthorized eyes. After clearing the other men from the compartment, Digardi attached a grenade to the coding machine—which was miraculously undamaged—and blew it up.

As Digardi and the three men left the radio shack, a seaman called to him from the deck below, telling him that Doc Browne needed him in the wardroom. He told the three sailors to head back to the bridge. As they followed his order and climbed up a nearby ladder, a Japanese shell slammed into the side of the ship, killing all three instantly. Digardi stood paralyzed for a moment, staring at the mangled ladder where the men had been an instant before, then headed for the wardroom.

Els Welch left the bridge shortly after Digardi, not sure where he was going or what he would do when got there. When he reached the main deck, he saw several men struggling to get a portable pump down a ladder. By the "crow" on his sleeve, he could see the man was a first-class petty officer, but his face was so blackened that Welch did not recognize him. Touching him on the shoulder, he asked, "Where is the captain?" The man said something that was drowned out by the detonation of a shell close aboard to port, but the petty officer jerked his head in the direction of the fantail, so Welch headed aft.

Ducking a large piece of metal still attached to the after deck house but swinging about wildly as the ship rolled from side to side, he stepped over what had been a pair of bitts that were now upended at an odd angle. He could feel through the soles of his shoes that the deck was hot and knew there must be a fire raging below. As he reached the fantail, kicking his way through the empty shell casings from Mount 55 that rolled back and forth, clattering together on one side of the ship before rolling back to the other, he suddenly had a clear view of the captain, standing over the open hatch to the after steering compartment, his head swiveling rapidly about as he surveyed the battle scene around him. As Mount 55 erupted, spewing smoke and flame with much concussive effect, Welch felt as though someone had violently smacked him on both ears at once, but Evans seemed oblivious.

At that moment, the destroyer escort *Samuel B. Roberts* steamed by close enough that Welch could see an officer on her bridge wing—presumably her captain—peering down at *Johnston*'s fantail. To Welch's astonishment, he saw Evans look up and casually wave at the other officer. It was as though the two men were yachtsmen, their boats passing on a Sunday cruise.

Poking his head out of the spotter's hatch on Mount 55, Gunner's Mate Jim Herring looked down from his perch and saw Evans near the after lifelines, seemingly oblivious to the thunderclaps of the gun's firing, Evans' voice thundering orders to the men in the after steering compartment below while he maneuvered the ship with only his seaman's eye to guide him. Herring was awestruck by the scene, later describing it as "something like you might see in a museum painting of John Paul Jones." Evans was smeared with blood, what was left of his uniform in tatters fluttering in the wind, one side of his face blackened from smoke, and his left hand spraying blood as he waved it about. "His guts and determination to whip the Japs single-handed kept me from being scared," Herring remembered. "It just made you want to whip the hell out of them too."

So far, a blend of incredible luck and tenacious skill had kept GQ Johnny not only afloat but able to fight despite the heavy damage she had suffered. But the jaws of a terrible vise began to close on her as she exchanged fire with the cruisers. More destroyers closed in, and by 0930 *Johnston* was battling two cruisers ahead of her, several destroyers on her starboard quarter, and two more cruisers on her port quarter, all within 6,000 to 10,000 yards as they hammered away.

A virtual avalanche of shells poured in on the already devastated ship. One of the 40-mm ammunition lockers was hit, and exploding shells began adding self-inflicted damage to the barrage. Her antennas and other radio equipment had been destroyed, severing her ability to communicate, and four of her five 5-inch guns had been heavily damaged or destroyed. Only Bob Hollenbaugh's Mount 54 was still able to fight back, and by now it was operating only manually, with no radar inputs and all electrical power lost. One of her smokestacks had been nearly severed and now hung over to one side, banging loudly with each roll of the ship. Several rounds crashed into the ship with devastating force, penetrating the remaining fire and engine rooms, obliterating the boilers and turbines. With the life punched out of her, GQ Johnny began to slow, her once-churning wake reduced to a diminishing froth, the gaping holes in her decks exhaling smoke and flames, those in her hull inhaling water.

Evans called down to the men in the after steering room to cease their efforts and to come topside. He paused for a brief moment, then uttered those words that have been anathema to all ship captains since man first ventured onto the great waters: "All hands, abandon ship."

Els Welch made his way forward from the fantail, repeating the captain's order to abandon ship. As he crawled over debris, he was doused by the spray of a shell detonating close aboard. Although *Johnston* was no longer able to fight, the Japanese continued the one-sided duel, continuing to hammer the hapless ship as she lay dead in the water.

Just outside the wardroom on the main deck Welch found Coxswain Ed Block lying on the deck, struggling to put on a life jacket. Somehow he had made it down from the bridge, but he was still somewhat detached from reality, presumably from the morphine that Welch had administered to him earlier. Welch helped him get his life jacket inflated and then helped him over the side into the water. He turned to help another sailor nearby but immediately realized that the young man was too severely wounded and beyond help. Welch had no more morphine, and with an aching heart he turned away from the sailor and headed into the wardroom to see if he could do any good there.

Inside the wardroom, Welch saw Doc Browne and his pharmacist's mates trying their best to help more men than Welch could count. As he looked about at the many wounds, he was surprised that he did not hear more moans and cries of pain. The scene was horrific, and Welch felt slightly dizzy. He saw one man trying to wrap a battle dressing around his mangled arm and stooped to help him. Just then he saw Evans enter the wardroom. The captain told Browne that it was time for him and the others to get off the ship, but the doctor replied that he needed to help these men get ready for the water and kept on working. Browne promised that he would leave as soon as he could, but for now he could do more here than in the water.

Evans left the wardroom and, with Lieutenant Stirling, helped several men launch the captain's gig. The XO climbed down into the gig, but Evans remained on deck. Stirling started the gig and began slowly motoring alongside the ship as Evans moved along the rail helping wounded men over the side and into the gig. To his very great disappointment, Stirling realized his feet were wet; looking down, he saw the deck was awash. The gig had apparently been holed and was slowly sinking.

So far, Bill Mercer had seen the headless body of Lieutenant Pliska dangling before him and had barely escaped death when Mount 52 was hit. Somewhat dazed, he joined a group of men who had gathered under the 40-mm gun tub on the port side. No one acknowledged his presence—several of them were staring blankly out at the sea, apparently seeing nothing—so he moved on, heading forward along the main deck. Behind him there was a loud explosion, and when he turned and looked back, he saw that all of the men in that group had been killed. As he turned to head forward again, another round exploded just ahead of him. He could feel a blast of heat on his face that was quickly dissipated by a cascade of red-dyed water that enveloped him.

Feeling exhausted and drained, Mercer leaned his back against the bulkhead just outside the galley and slid down until he was seated on the deck, not sure what to do next. Another friend, George Rinder, came out of the galley, gnawing on an unsliced loaf of bread. Rinder offered him some of the bread, but Mercer declined, saying he wasn't hungry. Several passersby told Mercer it was time to abandon ship, but he continued to sit where he was, unwilling to leave the ship, worrying that she might get underway again and leave him behind. It was not until he saw the captain telling others to abandon ship that he finally got up and went over the side.

Once in the water, Mercer remembered he had heard that it was important to get away from the ship "because it might suck you down with it as it sank." He joined up with Bob Marquard, and together they swam away from the ship, not stopping until about a hundred yards off the port quarter. As they bobbed there in the water staring back at their ship in her death throes, Marquard took a comb from his pocket and began combing his hair as though he was about to go on liberty. When he had finished, he flipped the comb away, saying, "I don't guess I'll ever need that again."

With twenty shrapnel wounds piercing his body and three limbs rendered useless, Bob Billie was still barely able to move. Dragging himself with his one good arm, he inched along the deck. Several men passed by him, but he was too weak to speak and the men must have presumed him dead, because they offered no help and continued on, disappearing over the ship's rail. Nearing that same rail, he was desperately trying to get over it and into the water when help arrived from an unexpected source. A Japanese shell exploded nearby, and for the third time that day, Billie was lifted up by the blast; this time he felt the sting of salt water as he plunged into the sea.

From his perch in the gun director, Bob Hagen had not yet heard the order to abandon ship. He could see several Japanese destroyers circling the ship "like a bunch of Indians attacking a prairie schooner." In his running gun battles with the Japanese over the last hour and a half, he had lost much respect for their tactics and their marksmanship, but now with *Johnston* dead in the water and the enemy closing in, he admitted to himself, "Even the Japs can't miss us." When the word to abandon ship was passed up from below, Hagen and the others in the director climbed down to the main deck and entered the water from the forecastle.

Ed Digardi saw his friend Jack Bechdel at the rail of the ship. The stump of his leg had been dressed, but he was too weak to get over the rail, so Digardi grabbed him by the back of his neck and the seat of his pants and hefted him over the side and into the water, which was much closer now as the ship was sinking.

Swimming a short distance, Hagen turned around and saw his friends Browne and Digardi still on board helping wounded sailors put their life jackets on. Hagen yelled, "Abandon ship. This is an order." But Browne chose his Hippocratic Oath over his military discipline and yelled back that they he had one more man to help and disappeared into the wardroom. Just then a round solidly hit *Johnston*. No colored dye this time, just a great eruption of debris into the air and a shockwave coming across the water and hitting Hagen in the face. To his horror, he saw that the round was a direct hit on the wardroom, and he was certain that Browne had perished there. Hagen recalled that he and the other officers had just celebrated the doctor's twenty-eighth birthday just a few weeks ago. Digardi was nowhere to be seen, and Hagen was sure that he also had been killed. He felt an overwhelming sadness that momentarily paralyzed him.

Hagen did not know that the round hitting the wardroom had not killed Digardi but had thrown him into the air. Digardi felt himself literally flying through the air and then felt the slap of the water as he landed about thirty yards from the ship. Catching his breath, he looked back at his sinking ship, noting how big she looked from this angle. As he swam backward, putting some distance between himself and the ship, he remembered how beautiful he thought *Johnston* was when he first saw her. Now she was a shambles of twisted wreckage barely recognizable as the ship she had been. Smoke and flames were pouring out of her in numerous places, she was listing to port, and her main deck was awash at the stern. He could see many of his shipmates scattered about in the water around him and thought of the captain. Knowing

Evans as he now did, he was sure he would not leave his ship until he knew every man of the crew still alive was off the ship. He wondered where Evans was now—he could not see him anywhere on the main deck or superstructure.

Seaman Second Class Leland Rawls had been knocked unconscious by a Japanese round that hit near him, just below the waterline. When he regained consciousness and struggled to his feet, he heard a voice say, "Abandon ship." He turned and saw the captain, bloodied and shirtless, his right arm hanging limp at his side. Evans repeated the order, and Rawls jumped overboard, but a wave washed him back onto the deck, which was awash by now. He moved farther aft, then jumped over again, this time able to remain in the water.

Chief Clyde Burnett had gone up one side of the ship to the forecastle and then down the other, telling the few men he encountered to get off the ship. He stopped to assist several men who were struggling to get a life raft untangled and into the water. As they labored, a Japanese round passed close overhead, and a young seaman threw himself to the deck and clutched his helmet to his head. Burnett took him by the arm and lifted him back to his feet: "If you can hear 'em, you're OK." The young man looked at Burnett, his eyes wide and seemingly uncomprehending, his face as white as paper. Making eye contact with Burnett, he seemed to understand, nodded vigorously, then joined the others in freeing the life raft.

Burnett moved farther aft and, seeing no one else, hefted himself over a lifeline and stepped into the water. He swam away from the ship, wishing he were younger as he pulled himself along. Pausing to rest for a moment, he was suddenly aware of a Japanese destroyer towering above him. The ship slid past him so close that he could see barnacles and seaweed clustered on the hull just below the waterline. He looked up and saw Japanese sailors standing along the rail hollering. Terrified at first that they were going to pick him up, then afraid they were going to shoot him in the water, and finally fearful that they might drop a depth charge, he felt a great surge of relief as the ship bore away, leaving him alone, adrenaline pounding in his ears. He realized he had never been so terrified in his entire life.

Els Welch removed his shoes, placing them neatly together on the deck, then dove into the sea. He swam away for some distance, then stopped to inflate his life belt. He watched as a cruiser fired at *Johnston*, noting when the guns would erupt and then trying to time it so that he could duck beneath the water when the shells hit. But he soon realized with some embarrassment that the life belt prevented him from getting his whole body underwater, leaving his behind exposed to the sky, so that to anyone watching, he "must have looked like a duck feeding on food below."

As Welch watched, *Johnston*—still upright though listing—serenely descended into the sea, heading for a resting spot deep in the Pacific where she would at last find peace and quiet. He was overcome by the sight, tears welling up in his eyes, already stinging from the salt water. But then he thought, "Welch, you might need that liquid," so he "ceased this un-seamanly display of emotion" and resumed swimming. With so many Japanese ships so close by and recalling the many stories he had heard of Japanese brutality, he worried that "the Japs might start strafing survivors," so for a time he stayed away from the clusters of men that were forming, figuring that they made tempting targets.

By this time, unlike Welch, men who had left the ship were beginning to join together in groups, many gathering around the floater nets that some of the crew had detached from their stowage racks and cast off from the ship. One group included Bob Billie, who miraculously was still alive; Neil Dethlefs, who shortly before leaving the ship had noticed some pies incongruously stacked up in the bakery waiting to be eaten; and Jim Herring, who naively thought about going home on survivor's leave as he climbed over the port rail. These three and several others had watched *Johnston*'s final demise and were trying to figure what they should do next when they saw a Japanese destroyer coming right toward them. Someone yelled, "They're gonna kill us," and several of the group began shedding their life jackets so they could hide beneath the water if the enemy chose to strafe them with machine-gun fire. Others feared the Japanese might drop depth charges and tried to float on their backs, hoping that would lessen the impact. Still others simply watched in fatalistic horror as the Japanese destroyer continued to bear down on them.

But the ship did not strafe and did not drop depth charges. Swerving slightly so that she did not pass directly through the cluster of men, the destroyer nonetheless passed close aboard the floundering group, close enough that some remembered the khaki uniforms and polished boots of the

Japanese sailors as they now peered down at their now-helpless adversaries. But what many of the Americans saw and would never forget was a Japanese officer staring at the sea where USS *Johnston* had been just moments before, a debris field temporarily marking the spot. As the ship passed by, her bow wave lifting the Americans up for a clearer view, they saw the Japanese officer slowly raising his right hand to the visor of his uniform cap, standing motionless at attention for a surreal moment . . . *saluting.*

CHAPTER 11

"FOR THOSE IN PERIL ON THE SEA"

USS *Johnston* was only one of many ships involved in the action off Samar. She was not alone in defending the escort carriers of Taffy 3 and was certainly not alone in making the ultimate sacrifice. The destroyer *Hoel* was the first to go down, the sea swallowing her whole after a valiant fight at about 0830. An hour and a half later, after displaying much courage and amazing effectiveness despite her small size, the destroyer escort *Samuel B. Roberts* followed *Hoel* to the bottom. *Johnston* had been the first into action and the last to succumb. Shortly after *Roberts* disappeared beneath the waves, *Johnston* ceased fighting and followed the others into the depths as her remaining crew leaped into the sea, unwilling to go with her.

As these displaced sailors adjusted to their new aqueous environment, they had no way of knowing that shortly after their demise, Takeo Kurita, the Japanese admiral in command of the marauding Japanese armada, had inexplicably broken off his attack and turned away, allowing the remaining Taffy ships to escape.

For the survivors of USS *Johnston* and the other ships lost off Samar, Kurita's retreat might have been a cause for celebration, but for them a new chapter was about to begin, one with new enemies and new priorities. It is an ordeal that is difficult to imagine and painful to recall, yet the story of GQ Johnny's crew is incomplete without acknowledging this final chapter when—yet again—ordinary men were called upon to do extraordinary things.

As night descended upon the waters surrounding the Philippine Islands, there was an air of peace on those tropical seas. With the final action off Samar ended, the great Battle of Leyte Gulf was over. Gone were the sounds of salvos fired in anger, the screams of diving aircraft, the cacophony and confusion of combat, the whispered prayers of men seeking deliverance from hell itself. A freshening breeze had erased the choking smoke, and the surface of the water was no longer cleaved by the sharp-edged prows of warships charging about in anger but was now shaped by the undulations of gentle swells.

But this seemingly tranquil scene belied the fact that for some, the struggle to survive was not yet over. In the darkening waters off Samar, sailors from GQ Johnny and the other sunken ships clung to life rafts, floating debris, and each other waiting to be rescued. But as daylight faded on this 25th of October, hope yielded to disbelief, as it was becoming clear that help was not soon to arrive.

And with the night came new dangers.

Ed Digardi was worried. The expected quick rescue had not come. They had seen U.S. aircraft several times in the afternoon, but no American ships had come to pluck them from the water. Only four of the ship's life rafts and two floater nets had survived the sinking, all of them damaged. There were many more men than there was room for. The fresh water that was stowed in the life rafts proved putrid. Some of the men were badly wounded, and Digardi feared that they might not last much longer under these adverse conditions.

Els Welch's morale was also declining. Earlier he had reasoned that with so many ships and aircraft committed to the landing at Leyte and participating in the various engagements in the area, there should be many opportunities for rescue. But as the day wore on and they remained alone in the vast seascape, his doubts grew, and he began to contemplate the possibility of spending the night in the water, a prospect that seemed more harrowing the more he thought about it.

Bob Hagen and Chief Burnett worked together, trying to boost morale by reassuring the men around them that help was surely on the way. Privately,

Hagen was not so sure. One of the pharmacist's mates asked him who among the crew should get the dwindling doses of morphine. Hagen replied, "The ones who cry the loudest."

Jack Bechdel had received several shots of morphine because of his severed leg, its dressing that Doc Browne had administered before his death now waterlogged. He was so out of it that he began singing. He actually had a good singing voice, and for a time the men welcomed the concert as an alternative to the "symphony of moans" that had been growing more audible as the hours crept by.

Bob Billie's many shrapnel wounds had taken their toll, and he was too weak to keep his head above the water, even with a life jacket on. Someone tied him to a stronger shipmate to keep him from drowning. He drifted in and out of consciousness and had no idea who the man he had been secured to was.

Some of the badly wounded had already succumbed to their wounds. Once it was certain a man was dead, he was slipped out of his life jacket and allowed to descend into the deep. Two men Bill Mercer knew as "Cooper" and "Walker" had been badly burned aboard *Johnston*, and both died shortly after dark. Mercer helped remove their life jackets and their dog tags, then watched his shipmates sink to their unmarked graves, their pallid faces ghostly in the eerie moonlight. He suddenly felt like "an eighteen-year-old boy going on forty."

An hour or so after sunset, a destroyer passed by, its silhouette discernible in the moonlight. Several men began waving and shouting, but Els Welch recognized it as Japanese and ordered them to desist. He caught them in the nick of time; one man had a flare ready to launch. The men fell utterly silent, holding their breaths as a searchlight suddenly switched on and began sweeping the water. The enemy ship, which was probably searching for Japanese survivors of the battle, shut off the searchlight after a few harrowing moments and slowly steamed by, fading into the darkness, apparently unaware of the Americans in the water. Welch began breathing again as he watched the glow of the ship's wake dissipate, then disappear.

The sharks arrived after the moon had gone.

Unbeknownst to the men in the water off Samar, Captain Charles Adair was hard at work aboard the flagship for the Northern Attack Force, Task Force 78, planning for the upcoming invasion of Luzon. As he shuffled piles of reconnaissance photos and scanned the many messages that the recent invasion of Leyte had generated, the words "many men in the water" jumped out at him. At first he just assumed that they had been rescued and went back to his plans. But then it began to nag him that he had seen nothing discussing rescue operations. He went back through the stack of messages and to his dismay could find reports of several ships having been sunk but no mention of recovery of the survivors.

Adair went to his boss, Admiral Daniel Barbey, and recommended the formation of a rescue task group using patrol and landing craft at their disposal. Work began to assemble a group of two patrol craft and five LCIs (landing craft, infantry) under the command of Lieutenant Commander J. A. Baxter to do what should have been done much sooner.

Stocked with fresh water and rations, and including a doctor and a pharmacist's mate, the tiny task group got underway and headed for the waters off Samar to search for any survivors of the recent battle.

Bill Mercer felt the shark brush up against him as it swam swiftly by. He kicked at it and used language his mother would not have appreciated. A faint trail of phosphorescence marked the predator's passage just below the surface. Out of the darkness came the curses and splashes of other men fighting off the intruders, and there were occasional screams of agony and terror as some of the sharks succeeded in their attacks. Ed Digardi could hear the dreadful thrashing sounds of sharks nearby as they tore apart the dead who had been cast adrift.

Spared some of the nightmare night by his periodic lapses into unconsciousness, Bob Billie was still tied to a man whose name he didn't know. Sometime during the night, Billie was aware enough of his surroundings to feel a sudden jolt. Before he could even realize what was happening, he and his companion were dragged beneath the surface, and salt water poured into his mouth and nostrils as they were whipped about like rag dolls. When Billie realized what was happening, he wanted to scream but could not. He was certain he was going to die, but suddenly his head broke the surface and he gasped for breath. Just as quickly as the attack had begun, it ended. Billie lay helpless, choking on the ingested water, trying to catch his breath. And then he realized with great horror that *he was alone*.

When morning came, those who had survived the hellish night with the sharks were grateful for the daylight. Even though the water temperature was in the 80s, that was still below body temperature, inviting hypothermia, and the men welcomed the sun's warmth. The predators had disappeared, and as a young second-class fireman exclaimed, "Things just look better when you can see them."

To Ed Digardi's sorrow, his friend Lieutenant Jack Bechdel had died sometime during the night. He tried not to dwell on it and to think of other things. As ship's navigator, he was pretty certain that the ship had gone down over the Mindanao Trench, one of the deepest in the world. It gave him an eerie feeling to know that there were so many fathoms of water beneath him and that his former "home" was now residing several miles down. He also knew that the wind and ocean currents were going in the right direction, so in order to keep spirits up, he supervised the rigging of a sail on one of the life rafts. It may have helped morale by keeping the men focused on something other than their misery, but it was a complete failure in terms of propulsion.

Bob Sochor's bleeding had mostly stopped. At first he was happy to see Otto Huebscher, "a good shipmate of mine who was the finest machinist I ever knew. Very skilled with his hands." But then Sochor realized that one of Huebscher's hands had been "blown nearly completely off at the wrist—only skin and gristle keeping it attached—and he was holding it on with his good hand." At Huebscher's request, Sochor tried to remove it completely using a pocketknife. The blade was too dull and he was having difficulty. Seeing Clayton Schmuff, a pharmacist's mate who had been moving among the wounded offering what care he could, Sochor called to him for help. Schmuff was able to finish the job with a sharper knife and tossed the severed hand into the sea. He was unable to stanch the bleeding, however, and Huebscher died less than an hour later.

In another part of the sea, Commander Baxter's search-and-rescue group arrived at the point they considered the most likely spot where survivors would be. All they found was floating debris and an occasional oil slick. For most of the day they faced mounting frustration as they broadened their search but found only open ocean occasionally marred by the detritus of war.

In the late afternoon, they at last spotted a man clinging to a wooden box but were disappointed to find that he was Japanese. They recovered him, searched him for weapons, then gave him food, water, and medical attention.

The would-be rescuers watched the sun descend into the sea with heavy hearts. The survivors—if there were any—would have to spend another night in the water.

The second night in the water was worse than the first for the *Johnston* sailors. More of the wounded died, and sharks continued to attack sporadically. But now the sailors had a new enemy: thirst. Some of the men had succumbed to the temptation to drink the seawater and were paying the price. Hallucinations and ravings became more common as the ingested salt water took its toll. Adding to their problems, some of the men realized they were keeping their waterlogged life jackets afloat, rather than the other way around. Slipping out of them, they would forlornly watch as the life jackets sank into the depths. Staying afloat had just become much harder.

The most seriously wounded were given what little space there was on the life rafts and floater nets. For those who were in the water, as many as possible had been tied to the nets using belts and what little line that could be found. But many had to cling using only their hands, and for them sleep became an enemy. As they nodded off, they would lose their grip and drift away. Digardi and Welch and some of the other men spent much of the night swimming out to recover these drifters. As the hours dragged by, their arms and legs become leaden with the frequent exertions.

Perched precariously on a large piece of wood, Bill Mercer and J. B. Strickland made a pact that called for one to sleep while the other stayed awake. Since both men feared going to sleep without the security of someone watching over them, this seemed like a workable arrangement. Strickland went to sleep first, his head on Mercer's shoulder. After a while—what seemed like hours to Mercer but, by his own admission, was probably more like five minutes—Mercer woke Strickland and said it was his turn to sleep. Strickland agreed, and Mercer laid his head on his companion's shoulder. But Strickland had immediately gone back to sleep, and both men rolled off the makeshift raft into the water. They decided not to try that again.

Sometime during the night, a passing squall rained on them. Some of the men pulled off their shirts and tried to catch the rain in the cloth and then wring it out into their mouths. Some who did not have to cling to something to stay afloat cupped their hands and captured a few precious drops. Some simply put their heads back and opened their mouths.

Clint Carter and Lloyd Campbell had just tied themselves together when someone yelled, "Shark!" An instant later, Carter felt a shark grab him in the back. He screamed in pain, then—placing his hands on Campbell's shoulders—he pushed himself upward, trying to get out of the water. In doing so, Carter pushed Campbell down into the water, nearly drowning him. Fortunately, after biting Carter twice, the shark lost interest and swam off. Realizing that Carter was bleeding, Campbell managed to get him out of the water and onto the raft. He was one of only a few who survived a shark attack that night.

One man had a major part of his stomach ripped away by a shark. He was in terrible pain and kept asking the men nearby to kill him to end his suffering. They declined, suffered their own agony as he kept pleading, and felt a mix of guilt and relief when he finally died.

Chief Burnett was in a whaleboat trying to get the engine started. Growing more and more frustrated at the recalcitrant engine, he suddenly realized he had been hallucinating. There was no whaleboat, only the edge of the floater net he was clinging to.

Later several men said they had seen the captain, and one of them told Burnett that the captain was on a ship and had come by telling them that he would be back to pick them up. Burnett knew that they too had been hallucinating.

Clinging to a life raft, Joe Check heard one of the men nearby say, "C'mon, let's go get a beer." He swam away, never to be seen again.

Johnston's survivors, dwindling in number with each passing hour, spent another long night in the dark Philippine waters. In those terrible hours, they fought the numbing cold of the water, battled with their own exhaustion, feared the carnivores lurking among them, witnessed the passing of many of their shipmates, and clung desperately to life when death seemed an easier alternative. For those who would live to remember, this would be the longest night of their lives, not only for the obvious reasons but because they would relive it again and again in their dreams for the rest of their lives.

With little hope of success in the darkness, Lieutenant Commander Baxter nonetheless persisted in combing the vast waters, hoping for a miracle. After several hours of fruitless searching the moonless waters, that miracle came to pass when a lookout reported several flares off to the west. Steering in that direction, Baxter's rescue force came upon a large group of men, and by 0400 they had rescued over two hundred men, ending their terrible ordeal. A muster of the recovered sailors revealed that they were all from *Gambier Bay*! Baxter was glad to have found them, but he knew that other ships had gone down in the battle, and so far, not one man of their crews had been recovered.

Seeing the poor condition of many of the rescued CVE sailors, Baxter wondered how long those other men could last. But he pressed on, haunted by the image of an hourglass with sand pouring inexorably downward as he scanned the empty sea.

Ed Digardi rejoiced when dawn arrived on 27 October. The sun's warmth was most welcome, and he knew that their chances of being rescued increased significantly with the arrival of daylight. But as he looked around, he realized that the sun that felt so good after the bone-chilling night was yet another enemy to contend with. Everywhere he looked he saw men with terrible sunburn. Faces, arms, and shoulders crimson red, swollen lips, bloodshot eyes. . . . Many of the men had removed their shoes and socks when abandoning ship, and their feet too were painfully red and blistered. It was a pitiful sight.

With Evans and Stirling nowhere to be found, Bob Hagen was the senior man among *Johnston*'s survivors, but during the night he had yielded to an apparent concussion, became delirious, and was now unconscious. The last thing he had said to Digardi the night before was that he had counted thirty-five men who had died since they had abandoned ship. With Hagen disabled, that left Digardi and Welch to exercise command, but by now that was nearly impossible. As a result of their exhaustion, injuries, lack of food and water, and mental depression, most of the men were unresponsive and nearly catatonic. It was apparent to Digardi that few would survive another hellish night like the previous two.

Welch was beginning to show signs of diminished mental capacity as well. Land could clearly be seen a few miles away, and some said they could hear surf. Welch said he wanted to try to swim there. Digardi dissuaded him, telling him that as officers they should remain with the men. He also reminded him that the island likely still belonged to the Japanese.

As the sun climbed into the sky, its rays beating down mercilessly on the surviving men of GQ Johnny, Digardi's tongue seemed glued to the roof of his mouth, and he was afraid to try to dislodge it for fear that it would tear. He looked at the motionless men around him, not sure which ones were alive and which might be dead. He peered down into the sea, watching the sun's rays dance about in the deep blue water beneath him. It was a beautiful sight despite this terrible situation; the water looked so cool and bright, it was difficult to remember it was unfit to drink. While he was staring into the mesmerizing water, he suddenly realized there was something else down there. Drifting slowly among the shadows cast by the cluster of floating men was a large group of sharks.

At that moment, his resilience collapsed, and he suddenly knew he was not going to survive. All of this suffering had been for nothing. He was never going to see his family again, never feel dry land beneath his feet, never know the future he had once hoped for.

As he closed his eyes and leaned back, about to open his aching fingers and let go, he heard someone shout, "There's a ship!"

CHAPTER 12

RECKONINGS

Exactly one year before, Ernest Evans had stood on the fantail of his newly commissioned ship, USS *Johnston* (DD 557), and told his crew that he intended to go in harm's way. Gesturing to the gangway, he had also told them that they did not have to go with him, that they were free to leave the ship and seek reassignment. No one took him up on that offer.

When the cluster of small craft was first spotted, there was general panic. "The Japs are comin' for us," yelled one of the men perched on a life raft. But J. B. Strickland was the first to claim they were American. He had caught a glimpse of red, white, and blue as the lead patrol craft veered slightly, exposing her ensign streaming in the wind.

Soon others could see the flags as the vessels drew closer. The sun's glare made it difficult, but Bobby Chastain stared in wonder at the oncoming seven vessels. He could not believe the ordeal was over.

Els Welch grinned at Ed Digardi, his white teeth contrasting with his sunburned face. "We made it," he said. "Son of a bitch! We made it!" Digardi smiled back, too weary to say anything.

The crews on the LCIs and the remaining PC (the other had detached and taken the *Gambier Bay* survivors back to Leyte) retrieved the men from the water. Most were too weak to get on board without help. Water was their first priority; it took much restraint to wait in line at the scuttlebutt. Some tried to eat. Milt Pehl was trying to consume the soup he was given, but he was "sure they had dumped a whole shaker full of pepper into it." Bob Hollenbaugh drank some soup, then rolled over and went instantly to sleep, as did many others. Bill Mercer, J. B Strickland, and Jim Herring shared a pot of coffee before sleeping.

Some of the men said prayers of thanks; others prayed for their shipmates left behind; a few stared out at the water, barely comprehending where they were. Most slept as the overcrowded vessels headed for Leyte Harbor with their precious cargoes. As a reminder that their ordeal was over but the war was not, the task unit was attacked along the way by a Japanese "Betty" aircraft. Many of the survivors slept through the exchange of gunfire.

Three of GQ Johnny's crew failed to muster among the survivors picked up by the rescue task unit. Neil Dethlefs, Orin Vadnais, and Bill Shaw had drifted away from the other survivors on the second night in the water and, enduring harrowing and challenging odysseys, washed up on the shore of a Philippine island, where they were cared for by friendly natives for a time. Carefully evading Japanese patrols with the help of their Filipino benefactors, they eventually made it to the jungle home of a Filipino guerrilla fighter, who was able to get them through Japanese lines to safely reunite them with American forces.

The total number of *Johnston* sailors recovered by the rescue group was 137. With the 3 who made it ashore, the total number of survivors was 140. Of the total crew of 328 that went into battle that final day, 188 died in the water or were killed or missing in action. Joe Pliska, the squadron recognition officer, was not a member of the crew, but his death brings the total losses to 189. That calculates to a 58 percent KIA rate. The number of wounded raises the total casualty rate much higher.

These are sobering numbers, to be sure. But their true significance cannot be measured without contemplating other probabilities. We can never know with certainty what Admiral Kurita might have done had he not been confronted by the Taffy escorts, but it is reasonable to imagine the deaths of many more Americans among the ships of Taffy 3 had he persisted in his attack. It is also quite possible that he might not have stopped there and continued on to attack the other two Taffy units. There was little to stop him. Halsey's Third Fleet had a long way to go before it could have been in striking range to prevent a further rampage.

And we must consider Kurita's original mission of attacking the landing forces at Leyte. Even though the U.S. Seventh Fleet had thwarted the Japanese plan of a pincer attack by defeating the other Japanese force that had tried to attack Leyte through Surigao Strait to the south, the surface units of the American fleet had been drawn away in pursuit of that force and were also far away enough to prevent them from arriving in time to prevent Kurita from doing serious damage to the vulnerable American ships.

Had those Seventh Fleet units arrived in time to engage Kurita's force, it would have been a battle of four Japanese battleships, eight cruisers, and eleven destroyers, facing an American force of six battleships, eight cruisers, and twenty-eight destroyers. But it is important to note that the U.S. battleships were old (all but one had been resurrected from the mud of Pearl Harbor), one of the Japanese battleships was the super-battleship *Yamato*, and the Americans had expended most of their surface-to-surface armor-piercing ammunition (having come to Leyte armed primarily with antipersonnel ammunition to provide shore bombardment). The outcome of such a battle cannot be assumed with any certainty.

But such musings are moot because Kurita broke off his attack and retreated even though he was clearly winning, an act that has perplexed observers and historians ever since. Many theories have been proffered, but two seem most likely. There is much evidence that he and his subordinates believed they were encountering portions of Halsey's powerful Third Fleet, a force that would have been more than a match for Kurita's armada. Supporting that theory, and with a veracity of its own, is that the audacious actions of the Taffy 3 escorts likely gave Kurita significant pause in his evaluation of the situation: that is, "What do they know that I do not?"

In any case, the Battle off Samar should not have happened at all; egregious miscalculations and miscommunications allowed Kurita to surprise and seriously threaten the U.S. Navy at Leyte Gulf. But because of the actions taken by those "tin can sailors" who charged rather than retreated, the battle is remembered less for the mistakes that allowed it to happen and much more for the courage and sacrifice of those American sailors who did their duty and more, turning a near-catastrophic disaster into an iconic moment that stands worthy of celebration and emulation.

It is also important to reflect on those sobering casualty numbers by considering the reactions and assessments of the men who made up GQ Johnny's crew. Among them were individual cases of permanent physical damage, post-traumatic stress syndrome (then more often known as "combat stress reaction" or "battle fatigue"), and many reports of survivor's guilt. And in the many written accounts and countless interviews left by these scarred men, there is much stoicism and no small amount of anger at having been forgotten by the Navy, forcing them to endure that nightmare in the water. But not one expressed the belief that Ernest Evans was to blame for what befell them. There was universal acceptance that Evans had done his duty, as had they.

Among the many testimonials to that effect was that of the ship's gunnery officer and senior surviving man of the crew, Lieutenant Bob Hagen, who recorded, "The Skipper was a fighting man from the soles of his broad feet to the ends of his straight black hair. . . . The *Johnston* was a fighting ship but he was the heart and soul of her."

Chief Petty Officer Clyde Burnett—who had earned the respect of the entire crew—concluded an interview by saying, "I just want to say that I am fully convinced if the captain hadn't made the torpedo run as he did on that 25th day of October, 1944, we would have lost six carriers instead of one, and it is entirely possible that we could have lost the beachhead on Leyte Island as well."

Gunner's Mate Third Class Joe Check wrote, "I am grateful that Captain Evans was a great leader and by his example in my early life has led me to believe in myself."

Seaman First Class Jim Correll's assessment: "Captain Evans was as good as any admiral or general . . . by using a severely crippled ship and for about two hours fought this ship in such a manner that the enemy thought we were several different ships. During this time, he either halted or slowed the progress of the enemy ships, which allowed many of our own ships to escape."

And Neil Dethlefs spoke for many when he wrote, "I wish with all my heart that we could have had a longer life together on the *Johnston* for the pride of being a 'tin can sailor.' . . . I am proud of the *Johnston*, I am proud to have sailed on her, and I am proud to have served under her captain, Commander Ernest E. Evans, and with the men that formed the crew of the 'GQ Johnny.'"

Days had passed since the survivors had been rescued. From the deck of a hospital ship, Ed Digardi, now wearing a fresh khaki uniform, looked around the harbor full of Navy ships, amazed at how many there were. It was nearly sunset, and the sound of a bugle drifted across the water, signaling "first call to colors." At first he thought of going inside the ship to avoid the coming ceremony, then thought better of it. There was a certain comfort in knowing that despite all he had been through, all that lay ahead as the war continued, the Navy's traditions remained intact, a reassuring sign to all sailors—from seamen to admirals—that they were part of something bigger than themselves, something that would endure and see this madness to a satisfactory conclusion.

He thought about Captain Evans and wondered if he was truly gone or might miraculously appear, having been rescued separately from the rest of them. He was pretty certain that the skipper had perished with his ship, and he wondered if, in his final moments, Evans was fully satisfied that he had fulfilled his promises to "go in harm's way" and "never again run from the enemy." One would certainly think so, but only if he or she had never served under "the Chief."

He knew armchair tacticians would scrutinize what they had done in that final battle, that some would question whether Evans was too aggressive and should have waited to make his torpedo run in unison with the other escorts. But he was sure that the Navy's failure to retrieve the survivors in a timely manner and Admiral Halsey's ill-fated run to the north, taking the entire Third Fleet with him, would garner most of the criticism, and that the final verdict would be favorable for Evans and the crew of USS *Johnston*. Bob Hagen had said there was talk of a Medal of Honor, and Digardi believed that there was no one more deserving than his captain.

Digardi thought of his friend Jack Bechdel and of that once-beautiful *Fletcher*-class destroyer, both now resting quietly on the bottom of this vast ocean. For them, the war was over, and they had no more duties to perform. He almost envied them. As senior survivors, he and Bob Hagen had orders to Washington, DC, where they would be debriefed, do the necessary paperwork regarding *Johnston*'s final battle, and write letters to the families of their lost shipmates. Digardi was not looking forward to any of it—except maybe having an opportunity to "tell the brass what I thought of Admiral Halsey!"

Five minutes later, at the exact moment that the sun plunged into the sea, the haunting notes of a bugle carried across the water as every ship—in unison—lowered their ensigns and their jacks, while all on deck stood at attention and saluted. Just ahead of him, nearer to the descending flag at the hospital ship's stern, he saw a very young sailor saluting with his left hand while his right sleeve hung empty at his side. And Lieutenant Digardi wept.

EPILOGUES

September 1945

The waters of the city of San Pedro, California, had housed the bulk of the U.S. Pacific Fleet until it was moved to Pearl Harbor in 1940. Five years later, the Navy chose the city as the place for a special ceremony on a sunny Friday. With the dignitaries all in place, Ernest Evans' widow Margaret, their sons Ernest Jr. and Jerry, and his sister were escorted to their seats flanking the podium. All rose until the family members were seated. After a chaplain had concluded his invocation, an admiral dressed in his full-dress white uniform stepped to the dais, his several medals clinking against the podium as he began his remarks. He briefly spoke about Commander Evans, the man they had come to posthumously honor that day, noting that only one other destroyer captain had been so honored in the recently ended war. Then he opened a dark blue folder and began reading the citation it contained:

> For conspicuous gallantry and intrepidity at the risk of his life above and beyond the call of duty as Commanding Officer of USS *Johnston*, in action against major units of the enemy Japanese Fleet during the Battle off Samar on 25 October 1944. The first to lay a smoke screen and

> to open fire as an enemy task force vastly superior in number, firepower and armor rapidly approached, Commander Evans gallantly diverted the powerful blasts of hostile guns from the lightly armed and armored carriers under his protection, launching the first torpedo attack when *Johnston* came under straddling Japanese shellfire. Undaunted by damage sustained under the terrific volume of fire, he unhesitatingly joined others of his group to provide fire support during subsequent torpedo attacks against the Japanese and, outstanding and outmaneuvering the enemy as he consistently interposed his vessel between the hostile Fleet units and our carriers despite the crippling loss of engine power and communication with steering aft, shifted command to the fantail, shouted steering orders through an open hatch to men turning the rudder by hand and battled furiously until the *Johnston*, burning and shuddering from a mortal blow, lay dead in the water after three hours of fierce combat. Seriously wounded early in the engagement, Commander Evans, by his indomitable courage and brilliant professional skill, aided materially in turning back the enemy during a critical phase of the action. His valiant fighting spirit throughout his historic battle will endure as an inspiration to all who served with him.

So few words to say so much. Official Navy terminology, resplendent with suitable nouns and adjectives that strived to convey the incomprehensible, could only begin to capture the enormity of the event, to provide a mere glimpse of the cataclysm that brought out the best in human nature while experiencing what is worst.

Following the reading of the citation, Margaret Evans was presented with a blue and gold box holding the nation's highest military decoration: the Medal of Honor. It was no doubt an inadequate compensation for what she and her children had lost, but for the Navy that her husband had so faithfully served, and the nation that is served by that Navy, the award would provide a source of inspiration and of aspiration to those who would follow in Ernest Evans' wake, donning the same uniform and assuming the same responsibilities that can sometimes demand so much.

March 2021

Beneath the choppy surface, the vessel entered a quieter world as it descended toward the faraway bottom of the Pacific Ocean in search of the final resting place. Gone were the engine noises, the cry of investigating gulls, even the sound of the wind and the waves. Here in the aqueous world where man and his inventions were intruders rather than inhabitants, steel and other man-made substances were tolerated but not welcomed, and new forces—pressure, oxidation, and so on—were already at work exacting the price of admission.

At three hundred feet the penetrating sunlight had already begun to fade, the sapphire glow gradually yielding to a translucent indigo. Another four hundred feet down, the remnants of natural light disappeared, and an impenetrable black curtain enveloped the interloper for the rest of the journey downward. The temperature dropped and the pressure rose as the descent continued through layers with scientific names—Bathyal, Abyssal, and Hadal—with environmental conditions becoming more formidable for all but the most adaptable forms of life.

Four and a half hours since beginning the descent, the titanium ball that was the deep submergence vehicle (DSV) *Limiting Factor* was near the bottom of the Philippine Trench. Six miles of ocean lay above the tiny submarine, exerting a pressure one thousand times that on the surface, and the temperature was barely above freezing. Retired Navy Commander Victor Vescovo and retired Lieutenant Commander Parks Stevenson, the only members of the crew, peered out at the cone of diffused light that the DSV provided. Piercing the absolute darkness, the two men saw what they had come for. Glowing as though it had been painted the day before was the number "557."

GQ Johnny had been found and clearly identified. At this depth, there was virtually no oxygen, so there was very little of the corrosion and rust that had enveloped *Titanic* when she had been discovered in water only two-thirds as deep. *Johnston* appeared to be much the same as when she fired her last rounds in battle, showing only the massive combat damage and the stresses she had suffered as she impacted the edge of the Philippine ridge and slid down its sloping side. Her main batteries were trained out to starboard as they had been when they were exchanging fire with the circling Japanese destroyers that had come in for the final kill. Live ammunition could be seen in one of her 40-mm guns, waiting for the pointer to hit the firing key. As evidence of the pounding she had taken from enemy destroyers, cruisers, and battleships, rounded holes of various sizes marked the entry points of those rounds that had passed through her thin skin without detonating. Gaping wounds marked those rounds that had exploded, wreaking terrible damage and sealing her fate.

At this depth, there was virtually no current and she seemed frozen in time, the eerie light cast by the DSV emphasizing her ghostlike appearance, a clear reminder that here was a cemetery as well as a wrecked ship.

Having surveyed the wreckage as close as they dared, Vescovo and Stevenson began the long climb back to the surface, where their support ship waited to take them back aboard. They had been careful not to disturb the

IMAGE 18 • Portside view of the bridge of the USS *Johnston* and Mk 37 gunfire control system. Photo taken from inside the submersible DSV *Limiting Factor* by pilot Victor Vescovo during a dive on 31 March 2021 to 6,425 meters. *Victor Vescovo*

ship and would reveal her position only to the Navy to protect her from falling victim to predators with less honorable intentions.

Those who survived that horrific battle have now all virtually joined their shipmates interred in GQ Johnny's resting hull. The last to go was 101 years old and is now resting in Arlington National Cemetery.

November 2023

It was a birth of sorts. An invited crowd had gathered in Memorial Hall at the U.S. Naval Academy. There was an air of expectation and excitement as the distinguished visitors waited for the ceremony to begin, surrounded by stirring paintings of great naval battles and likenesses of naval heroes. Facing the gathering crowd was a huge flag with the words "don't give up the ship," and below that was a glass case with the names of the many Naval Academy graduates who had made the ultimate sacrifice to their nation.

As with all important naval ceremonies, there was much pomp and circumstance as the event got underway. Sideboys lined the entryway for the distinguished guests, a color guard of sailors and Marines paraded the colors, and a uniformed chaplain gave the invocation. At last Secretary of the Navy Carlos Del Toro stepped to the microphone to make the announcement that was the centerpiece of this gathering—the naming of the next *Arleigh Burke*–class guided-missile destroyer. Although there had been no previous announcement revealing who would be the ship's namesake, by now it was evident: A large photograph of a Native American midshipman flanked the dais, as did a large rendition of a Medal of Honor citation. Nonetheless, an approving murmur rose from the rows of attendees that filled the great hall as the Secretary of the Navy announced that DDG 141 would be named USS *Ernest E. Evans.*

It was not the first time that a ship had been named for Evans. A *Dealey*-class destroyer escort commissioned on 14 June 1957 that had borne his name—USS *Evans* (DE 1023)—but she had been decommissioned and sold for scrap in 1974. This new namesake was a more fitting tribute: This ship bore his full name and was much more impressive.

At her commissioning, USS *Johnston* had been a state-of-the-art destroyer, one of the famed *Fletcher*-class ships that had played such an important role

IMAGE 19 • (LEFT) A 1978 vignette in the *Navy Times* commemorating the heroism of Commander Ernest E. Evans while commanding USS *Johnston* at the Battle off Samar *Naval History and Heritage Command*

IMAGE 20 • (RIGHT) Bust of Ernest Evans in the U.S. Naval Academy Museum *Author*

in the Pacific War victory. As an *Arleigh Burke*–class destroyer, DDG 141 would also be a state-of-the-art warship, tasked with the myriad new challenges of modern warfare and well equipped to meet those challenges. Like *Johnston*, she would mount 5-inch guns, but these would be a more modern version and would make up a secondary battery, excelled by vertical-launch missile systems fore and aft that could launch a variety of missiles to meet a vast array of combat scenarios. Replacing *Johnston*'s nascent radar systems would be a highly sophisticated electronic sensor array that would likely have been beyond Bob Hagen's or Ed Digardi's wildest dreams. DDG 141 would be well suited to carry on the fighting tradition established by her namesake.

The Navy's traditions are one of its strengths, and this occasion did not disappoint. The ship's bell from the destroyer escort that had borne Evans' name had been brought to the ceremony and was used to signal the entrance and departure of the official party. As the ceremony concluded and the ringing of the bell echoed in that sacred chamber, it served as a symbolic "passing of the torch" from USS *Johnston* (DD 557) to USS *Evans* (DE 1023) to USS *Ernest E. Evans* (DDG 141). And if one closed his or her eyes and listened intently, one might also hear the whispered words "Give me a fast ship, for I intend to go in harm's way."

BIBLIOGRAPHIC NOTES

As explained in the preface, I interviewed many of the men who served with Ernest Evans in USS *Johnston*. Much of this book is based on those interviews, and in many ways they are the most important contribution to it. Also, many of GQ Johnny's surviving crew collaborated on a self-published book, appropriately titled *The Fighting and the Sinking of the USS* Johnston *DD 557 as Told by Her Crew*. Most of their remembrances are about the final battle and the time they spent in (hell) the water, but there are additional glimpses into other times in USS *Johnston*'s short life. These interviews and remembrances were extensively used in chapters 1 and 5–12.

One of the most important sources was the account of USS *Johnston*'s year of service as included in the *Dictionary of Naval Fighting Ships* produced by the Naval History and Heritage Command. While I found occasional discrepancies between this comprehensive account and official documents such as the ship's deck logs and war diaries, overall it was an amazingly useful document.

The monthly war diaries and action reports of specific engagements submitted by Evans during the war are enlightening not only because of the recorded facts but also because one can glean important insights into Evans' thinking, including his assessments of his crew's performance, which show an upward trend as the year progresses.

The ship's deck logs posed a tedious slog but were useful in confirming facts from other sources. The logs helped with checking name spellings and watch station assignments and a few other miscellaneous points.

Like the interviews I conducted with members of the crew, the official war diaries, action reports, and deck logs were used in chapters 1 and 5–12.

Besides the official logs and diaries, I also relied on the after-action report that Robert Hagen was tasked with writing, as the senior surviving officer. It is an impressive piece of work, especially when considering the circumstances under which he wrote it. His article that appeared in the May 1945 *Saturday Evening Post*, "We Asked for the Jap Fleet—and Got It," was useful as well.

I also relied on my own experiences as a naval officer and as an enlisted sailor. The latter included serving in a destroyer that, even though it was not a *Fletcher* class, was an *Allen M. Sumner* class that closely followed the *Fletcher*s into service. I know what it is like to handle hot shell casings inside a 5-inch/38 gun mount, to sit on a trough of flowing seawater in the head, and to struggle to keep my lunch in place during the wild rides that only "tin cans" can provide.

I of course recalled my own writings about the epic Battle off Samar, and to fully appreciate the sources I have used in this book, one should review the bibliography of my first book on the Battle of Leyte Gulf, which in the interest of space I have not duplicated here.

I also particularly benefited from the excellent accounts provided by Jim Hornfischer's classic *Last Stand of the Tin Can Sailors* and Evan Thomas' *Sea of Thunder*, both of which are well worth the read for anyone wanting to understand this important part of history. Other works, such as *The Last Epic Naval Battle* by David Sears, *The World Wonder'd* by Robert Lundgren, *The Battle for Leyte* by Milan Vego, and *Tin Can Sailors Save the Day* by Kevin McDonald, shed additional light and provide food for thought.

Anyone researching and writing about the Navy in World War II will do well to rely on Samuel Eliot Morison's monumental work *History of United States Naval Operations in World War II*. For this work, I especially used volumes 12 (*Leyte*), 3 (*The Rising Sun in the Pacific*), 7 (*Aleutians, Gilberts, and Marshalls*), and 8 (*New Guinea and the Marianas*). I also cross-checked some of this information in Walter Karig's *Battle Reports*, an interesting compilation that was published just two years after the war ended.

McClary's piece on Puget Sound Naval Shipyard and Booth's article on wartime San Diego were very useful in chapter 1, along with books by Raven, Scutts, Friedman, and Hodges that deal with *Fletcher*-class destroyers.

Some of the most useful information regarding Ernest Evans' time at the Naval Academy recounted in chapter 2 was derived from the 1931 *Lucky Bag* (the U.S. Naval Academy's college yearbook). Also useful was Sweetman's history of the Academy and some of the documents I found in the Naval Academy archive relating to Evans (including his entrance exam and the letter from the superintendent warning Evans of his deficiency in physical training requirements).

Chapter 3 was admittedly the most challenging because I came to it with very little previous knowledge. I relied on quite a few sources, including Morison's volume 3 (*The Rising Sun in the Pacific*), the Office of Naval Intelligence's combat narrative, Winslow's *The Fleet the Gods Forgot*, Williams' *The Last Days of the United States Asiatic Fleet*, Stille's *Java Sea 1942*, Hornfischer's *Ship of Ghosts*, and Cox's *Rising Sun, Fallings Skies.* Particularly useful was Hattendorf's *To the Java Sea*, which compiles diaries, letters, and reports by Henry Eccles, commanding officer of USS *John D. Edwards*, another destroyer whose experiences were nearly identical to those of Evans' ship USS *Alden*. Similarly, I also relied on *Edwards*' gunnery officer William P. Mack, whose August 1943 article "The Battle of the Java Sea" provides an excellent account, which is supported and enhanced in his later novel *South to Java*; although a work of fiction, the novel is largely based on his personal experiences. Lardes' *US Flush Deck Destroyers 1916–45* provided useful information on USS *Alden* as well.

Chapter 4 was derived largely from the war diaries for that period submitted by Evans, the aforementioned ship's history in the *Dictionary of American Naval Fighting Ships*, and the recollections of Ed Digardi, who was sure he could "feel" Evans' mounting frustration as the ship experienced repetitive operations and seemed to be backtracking rather than making tangible progress.

Books about *Fletcher*-class destroyers were very helpful in chapter 5. The previously mentioned works by Raven, Scutts, Friedman, and Hodges were used, along with McComb's *U.S. Destroyers 1942–45* and a series of Naval Historical Foundation articles on *Fletcher*s by Captain George Stewart, USN (Ret.).

Morison's volumes 7 (*Aleutians, Gilberts, and Marshalls*) and 8 (*New Guinea and the Marianas*) were useful in chapters 6 and 7, as were Nasca's *The Emergence of American Amphibious Warfare* and Mitchener's *U.S. Naval Gunfire Support in the Pacific War.*

Worrell Carter's *Beans, Bullets, and Black Oil*, coupled with my own experiences at sea, helped shape chapter 8.

The remaining chapters (9–12) were derived largely from my crew interviews, the book created by the crew (see Mercer in the bibliography), official reports, and my previous research and writings for my earlier book on the big battle and its aftermath.

BIBLIOGRAPHY

Bates, Richard W. *The Battle for Leyte Gulf, October 1944: Strategical and Tactical Analysis.* Springfield, VA: National Technical Information Service, U.S. Dept. of Commerce, 1953–57.

Blackley, Andrew K. "An Object Lesson on Allied Interoperability." *Naval History,* April 2023.

Booth, Larry. "Wartime San Diego." *Journal of San Diego History* 24, no. 2 (Spring 1978): 197–220.

Carter, Worrall, R. *Beans, Bullets, and Black Oil: The Story of Fleet Logistics Afloat during World War II.* Newport, RI: Naval War College Press, 1998.

Como, Byron G. *The Defenders of Taffy 3.* N.p.: Byron G. Como, 2019.

Cox, Jeffrey R. *Rising Sun, Fallings Skies: The Disastrous Java Sea Campaign of World War II.* Oxford, UK: Osprey, 2014.

Cutler, Thomas J. *The Battle of Leyte Gulf, 23–26 October 1944.* New York: HarperCollins, 1994.

———. *The Battle of Leyte Gulf at 75: A Retrospective.* Annapolis: Naval Institute Press, 2019.

Friedman, Norman, and A. D. Baker III. *U.S. Destroyers: An Illustrated Design History.* Annapolis: Naval Institute Press, 2004.

Hagen, Robert C. "We Asked for the Jap Fleet—and Got It." *Saturday Evening Post,* 26 May 1945.

Hattendorf, John B. *To the Java Sea: Selections from the Diary, Reports, and Letters of Henry E. Eccles, 1940–1942.* Newport, RI: Naval War College Press, 2012.

Hodges, Peter, and Norman Friedman. *Destroyer Weapons of World War 2.* London: Conway Maritime Press, 1979.

Hornfischer, James D. *The Last Stand of the Tin Can Sailors.* New York: Bantam, 2004.

———. *Ship of Ghosts: The Story of the USS* Houston, *FDR's Legendary Lost Cruiser, and the Epic Saga of Her Survivors.* New York: Bantam, 2006.

———. "A Warrior's Destiny." *Naval History,* October 2009.

Hoyt, Edwin P. *The Lonely Ships: The Life and Death of the U.S. Asiatic Fleet.* New York: Pinnacle Books, 1977.

Johnson, Clint. *Tin Cans and Greyhounds: The Destroyers That Won Two World Wars.* Washington, DC: Regnery, 2019.

Karig, Walter, and Eric Purdon. *Battle Report: Pacific War—Middle Phase.* New York: Rinehart, 1947.

Lardas, Mark. *US Flush Deck Destroyers 1916–45.* Oxford, UK: Osprey, 2018.

Lundgren, Robert. *The World Wonder'd: What Really Happened off Samar.* Ann Arbor, MI: Nimble Books, 2014.

Mack, William P. "The Battle of the Java Sea." U.S. Naval Institute *Proceedings*, August 1943.

Mack, William P., and Willliam P. Mack Jr. *South to Java: A Novel.* Mount Pleasant, SC: Nautical & Aviation Publishing, 1987.

Marshall, S. L. A. *Island Victory: The Battle of Kwajalein Atoll.* Lincoln: University of Nebraska Press, 2001.

McClary, Daryl C. "Puget Sound Naval Shipyard." HistoryLink.org, Essay 5579, November 2003. https://www.historylink.org/File/5579.

McComb, David. *U.S. Destroyers 1942–45.* Oxford, UK: Osprey, 2010.

McDonald, Kevin. *Tin Can Sailors Save the Day: The USS* Johnston *and the Battle off Samar.* Ashland, OR: Paloma Books, 2015.

Mercer, Willliam E. *The Fighting and Sinking of the USS* Johnston *DD577 as Told by Her Crew.* Huntington Beach, CA: Johnston/Hoel Association, 1991.

Mitchener, Donald K. *U.S. Naval Gunfire Support in the Pacific War.* Lexington, KY: Andarta Books, 2021.

Morison, Samuel Eliot. *Aleutians, Gilberts, and Marshalls, June 1942–1944.* Boston: Little, Brown, 1951.

———. *Leyte, June 1944–January 1945.* Boston: Little, Brown, 1958.

———. *New Guinea and the Marianas, March 1944–August 1944.* Boston: Little, Brown, 1953.

———. *The Rising Sun in the Pacific, 1931–April 1948.* Boston: Little, Brown, 1951.

———. *Strategy and Compromise: A Reappraisal of the Crucial Decisions Confronting the Allies in the Hazardous Years, 1940–1945.* Boston: Little, Brown, 1958.

Moulton, H. D., ed. *The Nineteen Thirty-One* Lucky Bag. Annapolis: U.S. Naval Academy, 1931.

Nasca, David S. *The Emergence of American Amphibious Warfare, 1898–1945.* Annapolis: Naval Institute Press, 2020.

Raven, Alan. *Fletcher-Class Destroyers.* Annapolis: Naval Institute Press, 1986.

Roscoe, Theodore. *United States Destroyer Operations in World War II.* Annapolis: Naval Institute Press, 1953.

Rottman, Gordon L. *The Marshall Islands 1944: Operation Flintlock, the Capture of Kwajalein and Eniwetok*. Oxford, UK: Osprey, 2004.

Scutts, Jerry. *Fletcher DDs in Action*. Carrollton, TX: Squadron/Signal, 1995.

Sears, David. *The Last Epic Naval Battle: Voices from Leyte Gulf*. New York: New American Library, 2005.

Stille, Mark. *Java Sea 1942: Japan's Conquest of the Netherlands East Indies*. Oxford, UK: Osprey, 2019.

Sweetman, Jack, and Thomas J. Cutler. *The U.S. Naval Academy: An Illustrated History*. 2nd ed. Annapolis: Naval Institute Press, 1979.

Thomas, Evan. *Sea of Thunder: Four Commanders and the Last Great Naval Campaign, 1941–1945*. New York: Simon & Schuster, 2006.

U.S. Navy Office of Naval Intelligence. *The Java Sea Campaign: Combat Narratives*, Washington, DC: Publications Branch, 1943.

Vego, Milan. *The Battle for Leyte, 1944*. Annapolis: Naval Institute Press, 2006.

Williams, Greg H. *The Last Days of the United States Asiatic Fleet*. Jefferson, NC: McFarland, 2018.

Winslow, W. G. *The Fleet the Gods Forgot: The U.S. Asiatic Fleet in World War II*. Annapolis: Naval Institute Press, 1982.

INDEX

Note: page numbers in *italics* refer to figures.

ABOUT THE AUTHOR

Thomas J. Cutler is a former petty officer second class and retired lieutenant commander who has served the U.S. Navy in various capacities for more than fifty years, including a combat tour in Vietnam and service in aircraft carriers, cruisers, destroyers, and patrol craft. The author of many articles and books, he is the Gordon England Chair of Professional Naval Literature at the U.S. Naval Institute and Distinguished Fleet Professor of Strategy and Policy with the Naval War College. He has received the William P. Clements Award for Excellence in Education as military teacher of the year at the U.S. Naval Academy, the Alfred Thayer Mahan Award for Naval Literature, the U.S. Maritime Literature Award, the Naval Institute Press Author of the Year Award, and the Commodore Dudley Knox Lifetime Achievement Award in Naval History.

The Naval Institute Press is the book-publishing arm of the U.S. Naval Institute, a private, nonprofit, membership society for sea service professionals and others who share an interest in naval and maritime affairs. Established in 1873 at the U.S. Naval Academy in Annapolis, Maryland, where its offices remain today, the Naval Institute has members worldwide.

Members of the Naval Institute support the education programs of the society and receive the influential monthly magazine *Proceedings* or the colorful bimonthly magazine *Naval History* and discounts on fine nautical prints and on ship and aircraft photos. They also have access to the transcripts of the Institute's Oral History Program and get discounted admission to any of the Institute-sponsored seminars offered around the country.

The Naval Institute's book-publishing program, begun in 1898 with basic guides to naval practices, has broadened its scope to include books of more general interest. Now the Naval Institute Press publishes about seventy titles each year, ranging from how-to books on boating and navigation to battle histories, biographies, ship and aircraft guides, and novels. Institute members receive significant discounts on the Press' more than eight hundred books in print.

Full-time students are eligible for special half-price membership rates. Life memberships are also available.

For more information about Naval Institute Press books that are currently available, visit www.usni.org/press/books. To learn about joining the U.S. Naval Institute, please write to:

Member Services
U.S. Naval Institute
291 Wood Road
Annapolis, MD 21402-5034
Telephone: (800) 233-8764
Fax: (410) 571-1703
Web address: www.usni.org